FROM RUMI TO THE WHIRLING DERVISHES

Music and Performance in Muslim Contexts

Published in Association with the Aga Khan University Institute for the Study of Muslim Civilisations and the Aga Khan Music Programme

Series Editors: Theodore Levin and Jonas Otterbeck

This series presents innovative scholarship in music, dance, theatre and other performative practices and varieties of expressive culture inspired or shaped by Muslim artistic, cultural, intellectual, religious and social heritage, including in new creative forms. Bringing together outstanding new work by leading scholars from a variety of disciplines across the humanities and social sciences, the series embraces contemporary and historical cultural spheres both within Muslim-majority societies and in diasporic subcultures and micro-cultures around the world.

Published and forthcoming titles

The Awakening of Islamic Pop Music
Jonas Otterbeck

From Rumi to the Whirling Dervishes: Music, Poetry, and Mysticism in the Ottoman Empire
Walter Feldman

edinburghuniversitypress.com/series/mpmc

FROM RUMI TO THE WHIRLING DERVISHES

Music, Poetry, and Mysticism in the Ottoman Empire

Walter Feldman

EDINBURGH
University Press

IN ASSOCIATION WITH

THE AGA KHAN UNIVERSITY
(International) in the United Kingdom
Institute for the Study of Muslim Civilisations

AGA KHAN MUSIC
PROGRAMME

Edinburgh University Press is one of the leading university presses in the UK. We publish academic books and journals in our selected subject areas across the humanities and social sciences, combining cutting-edge scholarship with high editorial and production values to produce academic works of lasting importance. For more information visit our website: edinburghuniversitypress.com

Edinburgh University Press Ltd
The Tun – Holyrood Road
12 (2f) Jackson's Entry
Edinburgh EH8 8PJ

Typeset in 11/15 Adobe Garamond by
IDSUK (DataConnection) Ltd, and
printed and bound by CPI Group (UK) Ltd,
Croydon, CR0 4YY

A CIP record for this book is available from the British Library

ISBN 978 1 4744 9185 3 (hardback)
ISBN 978 1 4744 9188 4 (webready PDF)
ISBN 978 1 4744 9187 7 (epub)

CONTENTS

MUSICAL EXAMPLES AND FIGURES

* indicates that example is on website (www.akdn.org/akmp/FromRumi)

Chapter 8

Chapter 9

IMAGES

A NOTE ON ORTHOGRAPHY AND TRANSLITERATION

The complex history of interaction among Turkish, Ottoman, Persian, and Arabic languages leads to unavoidable complexities of orthography and transliteration in any English-language work rooted in this linguistic nexus. *From Rumi to the Whirling Dervishes* includes transliterations from modern Turkish and Ottoman Turkish; from Persian in standard Latinisation and modern Turkish Latinisation; and from Arabic. The Latin alphabet replaced the Ottoman Arabic script for the language of the Republic of Turkey in 1928. Persian continues to be written in Iran and in Afghanistan in its variant of the Arabic script.

Persian in modern Turkish Latinisation appears in the selections from the Mevlevi *ayin*s, whose Persian lyrics have been printed in Turkish Latinisation beginning with the Darülelhan publications of the 1930s and continuing until today. Since this transliteration also reflects the manner in which Persian lyrics have been sung by the Mevlevis for many generations, readers are advised to become familiar with it. In addition, much of the relevant Turkish and Persian vocabulary originates in the Classical Arabic language. Most of these words appear in the Glossary of this book, together with their Arabic source word.

In modern Turkish orthography, several European languages – but not English – became models for writing consonants as well as for umlauted vowels. Five consonants show major differences from English orthography. These are:

C: pronounced like 'j' in 'joy'

Ç: 'ch' as in 'chair'

Ğ: soft 'g', used intervocalically or finally; it has no exact English equivalent. The soft g also varies between Istanbul and Anatolian dialects of Turkish. In various positions it is pronounced either as a glottal stop, or as 'y'.

J: 'zh' as in 'measure'

Ş: 'sh' as in 'ship'

In quasi-scholarly transliterations from Ottoman (adopted in this book), the apostrophe (') stands in for the Arabic glottal consonant *'ayn'*, as in *sema'* (Ar. *samā'*), or in *'ilm* (Ar. 'science'). Spoken and also modern written Turkish ignores distinctions among the glottal consonants. Thus initial 'kh' in Persian words becomes 'h'. A common example in this work is Persian *'khana'*, for 'house', which becomes *'hane'* (a section of composed melody), and is also used in compounds such as Mevlevihane (convent, 'house of the Mevlevis'). The letter *q* is absent in modern Turkish, and thus *k* stands in both for Persian and Arabic *k* and for *q*.

The vocalic usages in Persian and Turkish are also quite different. In the Turkish transliterations from the *ayin* texts, many of the Latin script vowels differ from the Persian. In the original Arabic scripts for both languages, this difference was invisible, since very few vowels had been indicated at all. The Turkish umlauted vowels *ö* and *ü* are pronounced as in German or Hungarian. These appear both in Turkic words and in the Turkish pronunciation of certain Persian words, i.e., Persian *gol* (flower) = Turkish *gül*.

Some frequently used Mevlevi terms and titles retain their Turkish spellings, e.g., 'Çelebi', while less commonly used Turkish terms are transliterated, e.g., 'Bektaşi' is rendered as 'Bektashi'. But the name of the founder of this Sufi Order remains Haci Bektaş Veli. An additional complication is the transliteration of Arabic or Persian words within a Persian or a Turkish context. Thus the Persian 'Masnavi' (from Arabic 'Mathnawi') becomes 'Mesnevi' in a Turkish Mevlevi cultural and historical context. As an example of Turkish orthography for Persian, we can take Rumi's poem from the First Selam section of the anonymous Ayin in *makam* Pençgah:

> The *sema* is the royal falcon at the side of the Lord of Glory.
> The *sema* cleans the heart for the people of ecstasy.

In standard Persian Latinisation (for English) this would appear as:

> *Shahbāz-e janāb-e Zoljalālast samā'*
> *Farrāsh-e qulūb-e ahl-e hālast samā'*

Within the *ayin*, and hence in chapter 8 of this book, it is transliterated as:

> *Şehbaz-ı cenab-ı Zülcelalest sema'*
> *Ferraş-ı kulub-ü ehl-i halest sema'*

TURKISH MUSICAL SYMBOLS AND THE INTONATION OF OTTOMAN MUSIC

Prince Cantemir's book and notations (c. 1700) describe a basic scale with 17 notes to the octave, which is akin to the scale still in use in Persian art music (see Feldman 1996: 207–13). But by the end of the eighteenth century, several new pitches were introduced, and these pitches only gradually acquired the names that rendered them 'expressible' within a theoretical and pedagogic system. By the beginning of the nineteenth century it appears that, while the nucleus of the older seventeen-note octave scale still existed, it had been supplemented by a larger and more differentiated general scale, which now could express differences of a single comma (T. *ırha*; 23 cents). As a modern theory of Ottoman music was created at the very beginning of the twentieth century and thereafter, it attempted to find mathematical ratios to explain its intervallic structure. This theoretical system, and the modified Western musical notation accompanying it, tended to ignore the older Persian general scale that still persisted in musicians' practice. By the nineteenth century, the older Persian intonation had been forgotten, although certain pitches continued to be used in cadential phrases. This Persian intonation forms part of the oral tradition of teaching on traditional instruments such as the *ney, tanbur* and others, as well as the voice. The result is an extremely complex intonational system, which is still not represented completely by the six distinct accidentals in Turkish music. In this book a very few examples from seventeenth-century notated sources include a symbol for the 'neutral' interval, called *koron* in Persian music, which is approximately 2.5 commas flat.

Fig. 0.1 Seventeenth-century Beyati scale with the note *segah* (*B*) (Feldman 1996: 226).

As this system gradually changed, allowing for several microtonal variations within 'secondary' pitches, all of the older compositions, whether Mevlevi or courtly, came to be performed with the modern intonation that developed in the nineteenth century.

When Western notation was adopted for official purposes after 1828, no provision was made for the intonation of Ottoman music. It wasn't until almost a century later that the Mevlevi musicologist Rauf Yekta Bey and his followers sought a way to express the intervals used in Ottoman music by modifying the standard sharp and flat signs of Western staff notation. By the middle of the twentieth century, this system was modified further by Subhi Ezgi, Sadettin Arel, and Salih Murad Uzdilek with the aim of making Turkish music appear less exotic from a Western perspective.[1] In the Ezgi-Arel system the whole tone consists of nine commas. Discrete signs are used according to the following scheme:

	Turkish name	accidental
1 comma flat	koma	↿
4 comma flat	bakiye	♭
5 comma flat	küçük mücennep	♭
1 comma sharp	koma	♯
4 comma sharp	bakiye	♯
5 comma sharp	küçük mücennep	♯

The above system has taken hold in Turkey and it is this system that has been adopted here, with the caveat that it is only an approximation of the actual intonational system of Ottoman music.

[1] For a fuller discussion of the issues involved in Western notation for Ottoman music, see Ruhi Ayangil, 'Western Notation in Turkish Music', *Journal of the Royal Asiatic Society*, 18 (2008: 403–47).

PREFACE

I wrote *From Rumi to the Whirling Dervishes* with the aim of illuminating the sophisticated interaction of music, poetry, and mystical praxis that underlies the characteristic ceremony of the Mevlevi dervishes known as *sema, mukabele,* or *ayin.* Primarily a work of historical ethnomusicology, *From Rumi to the Whirling Dervishes* traces the evolution of the Mevlevi ceremony, paying particular attention to its social history, musical and literary milieu, and religious context in pre-Ottoman Anatolia and Ottoman Istanbul. Indeed, while the title of the book mentions the Ottoman Empire, much of the historical treatment must perforce refer to pre-Ottoman Muslim Anatolia and its multiple links with Iran. Among its recurring themes is the high level of social coherence and cultural transmission within the Sufi order founded by the descendants of Mevlana Jalaluddin Rumi (d. 1273). A central part of this cultural transmission was an emphasis on musical creativity, both for the Mevlevis' own mystical praxis and as a formative influence on the art music of pre-Ottoman Anatolia and the Ottoman Empire at large. Unsurprisingly, the available source materials for a study ranging over five centuries and covering a broad cultural and geographical landscape, are diverse, and call for different approaches to understanding and analysing their content. The nature of this content, and of the sources themselves, determined the arrangement of the book into two parts. The first of these primarily addresses history and culture, while the second focuses on music, though the nature of the source materials resulted in considerable overlap between the two parts.

Part I, 'History and Culture of the Mevlevi Dervishes', begins with an Introduction that addresses the rupture in Mevlevi culture brought about by the prohibition of the Sufi orders in the Turkish Republic after 1925. It also discusses certain areas of continuity after 1925, especially in the domain of musical practice. Chapter 1, 'Defining the Mystical Music of the Mevlevi Dervishes', distinguishes the 'mystical' from the 'religious', and points to the utility of the 'mystical' as a conceptual basis for understanding the musical repertoires created by several Sufi and Gnostic groups in both Iranian and Anatolian Muslim societies.

Chapter 2, 'The Mevlevi Phenomenon', comprises a broad historical sweep extending from the lifetime of Mevlana Jalaluddin Rumi to the formation of the Mevleviye by his immediate descendants in Konya, and then to the later history of the Mevlevi order. It discusses the major Mevlevi centres in Anatolia and the Mevlevis' move to Istanbul, and includes a brief description of the training of dervishes. It also draws on some of the few remaining sources for the role of women dervishes within the Mevlevi order.

Chapter 3, 'Development and Cultural Affinities of the Mevlevi Ayin', brings together several kinds of evidence that document the history of kinetic movement in the Mevlevi ceremony as practised in its major centres during Ottoman times. This evidence includes Turkish and European paintings, and early Western descriptions of the *ayin/mukabele*. The chapter presents a broad overview of the formal development of the music of the *ayin* ceremony and hypothesises a substratum in the Mevlevi ritual that appears to be related to practices among rural Sufi and Gnostic groups in Anatolia and neighbouring regions of Iran. Chapter 3 concludes with a selection of theoretical and poetic statements from Mevlevi sources, in particular from Divane Mehmed Çelebi (d. 1529), which illustrate the concepts that determined much of the evolution of the *mukabele* ceremony over time.

Chapters 4 and 5 present a variety of sources delineating the role of the principal Mevlevi instrument – the reed-flute *ney* – and its practitioners. 'The Ney in Mevlevi Music' begins with a presentation of poetic texts, starting with Rumi and continuing through Mevlevi poets writing in Turkish. These verses relate a wide variety of myths and metaphors connected to the reed-flute. The second part of the chapter addresses the history of the instrument itself from Timurid through Ottoman times. It then treats the *taksim*, the form of flowing-rhythm improvisation in which the *ney* excels. Chapter 5, 'The *Neyzen* as an Ideal Representative of Ottoman Culture', portrays the unique role that the masters of the *ney* came to hold within Ottoman Turkey. After treating some of the classic figures of the seventeenth and eighteenth centuries, it focuses on three *neyzen*s in Istanbul who had formative roles in the transmission of the Mevlevi *ney* and its culture into the era of Republican Turkey.

Part II, 'The Music of the Mevleviye', includes detailed musical analysis of the Mevlevi *ayin* and examines the role of Mevlevi musicians in Turkish Muslim high culture from the pre-Ottoman Anatolian era into the Ottoman seventeenth and eighteenth centuries. Chapter 6, 'The Position of Music within the Mevleviye', serves as a bridge between the historical orientation of Part I and the musical analysis in Part II, and presents some of the poetic thought on music of the great Mevlevi polymath Kutb-i Nayi Osman Dede (d. 1730). It then focuses on the poetry of the Mevlevi follower Cevri (d. 1654), who was an active figure in the generation that witnessed the broader penetration of the Mevleviye into the musical life of Istanbul. Finally, chapter 6 offers some of the historical background for the decline of the Persianate art music repertoire in Istanbul during the sixteenth century that led to new opportunities and influence for Mevlevi and other dervish musicians in the music of the Ottoman court during the two centuries that followed.

Chapter 7, 'The Musical Structure of the Ayin', contrasts the music of the Mevlevi ceremony with the courtly concert suite *fasıl* as the latter developed during the later seventeenth and eighteenth centuries, and points to the greater antiquity and continuity of the Mevlevi *ayin* compared to the *fasıl*. This chapter also demonstrates basic musical techniques evident in Mevlevi compositions that were shared with Ottoman court music, along with some distinctive Mevlevi creations.

Chapter 8, 'Music, Poetry, and Composition in the Ayin', treats the longest and most central part of the ceremony, the opening First Selam, and offers evidence for the probable Persian Sufi origin of its rhythmic structure. This chapter also offers a detailed comparison between the First Selam of one of the early anonymous *ayin*s (Dügah) and the earliest *ayin* attributed to a known composer – the Beyati Ayin of Köçek Mustafa Dede (d. 1683), who lived in Edirne. Finally, it discusses musical innovation in the First Selam of the Saba Ayin composed by Ismail Dede Efendi (d. 1846). Rumi's verses in each *ayin* are discussed in connection with the musical analysis.

Chapter 9, 'The Sema'i in the Third Selam and the Son Yürük Sema'i': Nucleus of the Antecedent *Samā*'?', focuses on the genre known as *sema'i*, which is represented in the latter parts of the Mevlevi ceremony and may provide a link between the *ayin* and its musical antecedents in the traditions of other Turkic cultures. Early notation by the Polish convert Ali Ufuki Bey (c. 1650) as well as several parallels between the *sema'i* and Central Asian Turkic and Bektashi dervish music constitute major parts of the argument.

ACKNOWLEDGEMENTS

Most of the materials and conclusions presented *in From Rumi to the Whirling Dervishes* are the result of musicological, literary, and historical analysis. In several places, however, I include information acquired through a variety of artistic, spiritual, and personal endeavours that unfolded in Turkey and the United States, beginning over forty-five years ago. An even earlier personal background linked me to a Turco-Sephardi synagogue as well as to musicians among the Greek and Armenian communities in New York. These links resulted in my learning the Turkish language and elements of urban Turkish music. In 1975, following two earlier visits to Turkey, I was brought several times to the then secret *zikr* ceremony of the Halveti dervishes in Istanbul. During the late 1970s and early 1980s, the successful international outreach of Sheikh Muzaffer Ozak (d. 1984) of the Cerrahi (Jerrahi) Halvetiye allowed his dervishes to perform their *zikr* ceremony in North America and in Europe. I was invited to travel with the dervishes from New York to California and perform with them as a percussionist. While participating in these ceremonies I was also studying the vocal *ilahi* and *durak* repertoires with Halveti masters including Hafiz Kemal Tezergil, Sefer (Dal), and Kemal Baba. The American tours of the Halveti-Cerrahi also led to my introduction to the Mevlevi *neyzen*s Niyazi Sayın and Kudsi Erguner, the *kanun* virtuoso Erol Deran, and to the late *kemençe* virtuoso Ihsan Özgen (1942–2021), all of whom were invited at various times to participate in the Halveti public performances. I was briefly the interpreter for Süleyman Dede Loras (1904–85) during his 1976 visit to New York from Konya. I am grateful to my teachers for initiating me into the mystical music of the Halvetiye.

I began to lecture and write about these topics under the tutelage of Professor Harold Powers (1928–2007) while teaching at Princeton University from 1981–4. At the same time, I created several research projects in Istanbul, which also led to my studying secular classical repertoire with the vocalist Fatih Salgar (later Director of the State Classical Music Chorus) and classical *tanbur* with the preeminent virtuoso Necdet Yaşar (1930–2017). In 1984–6 I was the recipient of an NEH Translation Fellowship for the *Book of the Science of Music According to the Alphabetic Notation* by the Ottoman Moldavian Prince Demetrius Cantemir (1673–1723). This project necessitated several visits to Turkey, and further musical research with my teachers; I also commenced study of the *kudüm* with the master percussionist Hurşid Ungay. In Istanbul I was introduced to one of the most successful recent composers of the Mevlevi *ayin*, Cinuçen Tanrıkorur (1938–2000), who was also a leading performer on the oud. As our friendship developed, a window opened onto the current reality of the Mevlevi musical tradition within an essentially secular environment. I also had the privilege of accompanying Cinuçen's performances and interviewing him in the United States. I can only express my deepest gratitude to these superb masters and teachers of both the Ottoman secular and mystical traditions. Thus, by the time I published my first book on Ottoman music, in 1996, I was already somewhat aware of the situation of Mevlevi music within an Ottoman cultural context.

The years 2003–4 brought an unprecedented intervention when UNESCO approached the Turkish Ministry of Culture to suggest that Turkey nominate the Mevlevi ceremony for inclusion in UNESCO's Proclamation of the Masterpieces of the Oral and Intangible Heritage of Humanity (2001–5), which was subsequently folded into UNESCO's Convention for the Safeguarding of the Intangible Cultural Heritage. Through the association of the descendants of the Mevlevi sheikhs (the Mevlana Vakf) I was asked to co-direct Turkey's application to UNESCO. I did this together with my friend, the art historian Barihüda Tanrıkorur (the widow of Cinuçen). Although our Action Plan was never implemented, this experience allowed me to synthesise several kinds of information about the Mevlevi performance and its history.

Having been trained as a Turcologist, I was aided in my study of Persian poetry first by my colleague at Princeton, Jerome Clinton (1937–2003), and later by Iraj Anvar, then of New York University and now at Brown University. Iraj's translations of Rumi are outstanding, and he has contributed his insights to several poetic passages in this book. My appreciation of the Indo-Persian poetic tradition was aided by my former chairman at the University of Pennsylvania, the late William Hanaway (1929–2018), and then by our friend and mentor in India, the late scholar and poet Shams ur Rahman Faruqi (1935–2020), of Allahabad. For a deeper understanding of movements within Sufism in the Persian environment, I am indebted to William Chittick and Sachiko Murata, of the State University of New York at Stony Brook. Other scholars of Sufism – both known and unknown to me personally – are cited frequently in these pages.

I owe the impetus for the present book to the initiative of Theodore Levin, Senior Advisor to the Aga Khan Music Programme, and Arthur R. Virgin Professor of Music at Dartmouth College. He has also been an active and responsible editor of these pages. I would like to acknowledge the Aga Khan Music Programme, and its director, Fairouz Nishanova, for their support throughout the process of writing this book and its preparation for publication. My thanks to Charlotte Whiting, formerly Manager, Publications Department, at the Aga Khan University, Institute for the Study of Muslim Civilisations, for her enthusiastic support. And I thank Emma House, commissioning editor at Edinburgh University Press, for shepherding my book through the editorial and production process.

The impeccable musical digitisations are the work of the New York *tanbur* and oud player Adam Good. Most of the illustrations reached me with the help of my Istanbul friend and host, the noted graphic designer Ersu Pekin, aided also by Zeynep Atbaş, Curator of Manuscripts at the Turkish and Islamic Arts Museum, Istanbul. I also thank the outstanding traditional artist Gülbün Mesara, and the UNESCO Artist for Peace, Kudsi Erguner, for their help in securing other visual materials for this book.

Walter Feldman

PART I

HISTORY AND CULTURE OF THE MEVLEVI DERVISHES

INTRODUCTION: CONTINUITIES AND RUPTURES IN THE MEVLEVI TRADITION

Only a select few musical institutions of the Middle East have acquired a place in the Western cultural imagination sufficiently important to require Western names. Among these is the ceremony of the 'Whirling Dervishes' or 'Les Derviches Tourneurs' – virtually a household expression among people who may never have heard of the Mevleviye, or Mevlevi Order. The ceremony of the Mevlevi dervishes, known as *ayin* or *mukabele*, claims our attention because it is a ritual whose combination of choreographed movement and complex music achieves a result that is both transcendental and artistic.[1] That this ceremony is regarded as a major cultural phenomenon in our own time speaks to the enduring success of those who have maintained it, over a period of at least six centuries, as part of a mystical, rather than a purely religious institution.

The *ayin/mukabele* has elicited wonder since European travellers first viewed it in Istanbul in the early seventeenth century. In later Ottoman times a visit to one of the Mevlevi cloisters (*mevlevihane*) of Constantinople was a touristic must comparable to a visit to the Pyramids of Egypt or the Acropolis in Athens. Travellers' descriptions, from the seventeenth and eighteenth centuries, as well as European paintings of the ceremony, furnish some of its earliest documentation. Meanwhile, Mevlana Jalaluddin Rumi (Mevlana

---

[1] *Ayin*: Persian 'ritual' or 'ceremony'; *mukabele*: Arabic 'meeting'.

means 'Our Master'), who died in 1273, and whose lyrical Persian poetry has furnished the core 'libretto' for all classic *ayin* compositions since the later sixteenth century, is nowadays widely billed as 'the best-selling poet in the United States' and is known worldwide through translations into many European languages as well as Chinese and Japanese. In addition to its technical excellence, the *ayin* constitutes a vision of humans' role in the universe. The *ayin's* felicitous union of music, poetry, and philosophy is of major interest to humanity in general and represents possibly the most significant contribution of the Turkish nation to our shared civilisation.

Some early European writers appeared to be aware of the majesty of the Mevlevi ceremony and of the way of life supporting it. In the early seventeenth century the Venetian traveller Piero Della Vale described the Mevlevi ceremony in some detail. A century later the Moldavian Prince Demetrius Cantemir spoke of the Mevlevis with the highest respect and admiration. In the same generation, Lady Wortley Montagu – writer and wife of the English ambassador to the Sublime Porte – wrote effusively of the beauty of the music played by the Mevlevi flutes, the *ney*. These positive testimonies of the eighteenth century were also connected to European interest in Ottoman Turkish music as heir to the musical thought of ancient Greece as well as to Ottoman music in its own right. The notion of a link between Ottoman music and antiquity was of great importance especially to French musicians, such as the Porte interpreter Charles Fonton, whose *Essai sur la musique orientale comparée à la musique européenne* (1751) is the first serious study of Ottoman music in any Western language.

By the early nineteenth century, however, this situation had quickly changed. European art music had developed rapidly and become available to a broader social base at the same time that European colonialism was expanding in the Middle East and beyond, with the result that the music of the Ottomans was subsumed into a broader panorama of musical Orientalism and exoticism sweeping the continent. These 'exoticising' tendencies were not absent in the previous century, but then there had been actual points of contact with, and interest in, Ottoman music, expressed in somewhat different terms among both Eastern and Western Europeans.

While European intellectuals valued some aspects of the Persian literary tradition (less so the Arabic or Turkish), by the nineteenth century the

European imagination roamed over a broader realm, in which India and the Far East became more relevant and accessible. Travellers' accounts were replaced by serious textual studies written by researchers in the new science of Orientalism. However, little new information about Ottoman music was contributed by Western writers of that century, during which science and philosophy showed such prodigious development. With the emerging field of comparative musicology also laying claim to methodologies rooted in science, the experience of witnesses to the Mevlevi *ayin* no longer carried much musicological relevance. And, rather strangely, nineteenth-century European scholarship was completely unaware of the significant musicological writing, including several forms of indigenous notation, created by Ottoman Muslims and Christians during the eighteenth and nineteenth centuries.

A new attitude toward the music of the Mevlevis and the Ottomans in general is evident in the studies by the French Jesuit and musicologist P. J. Thibaut (1872–1938) – a friend and colleague of the great musicologist and Mevlevi musician Rauf Yekta Bey (1871–1935) – who was the author of the first serious research on the music of the Mevleviye, published between 1902 and 1911. The contemporary Turkish musicologist Bülent Aksoy sees Thibaut's work as the harbinger of a new era that signalled the 'closing of the nineteenth century, which had been an extremely unproductive period from the point of view of European publications on Turkish music' (Aksoy 1994: 250). Despite the Ottoman Empire's huge territorial losses, in the early twentieth century within Istanbul, Konya, and several other Anatolian cities, Mevlevihanes were still open and functioning. With access to performances of the *ayin*, and Thibaut's research as one very sound model of how to study it, one might think that linking up current practice, musical repertoire, and classic literary sources would have been a relatively easy and inviting task. But what might have been a burgeoning interest in the music of the Mevlevis was cut short not by any action of the European powers that had occupied Istanbul and Anatolia following World War I, but by the new Turkish Republic itself.

In the third year of the Turkish Republic, under Mustafa Kemal Atatürk, Law 677, promulgated on December 13, 1925 (1341 H), decreed the 'Closing of Tekkes (Dervish Lodges), Zaviyes (Central Dervish Lodges) and Tombs . . . All of the Orders using descriptions such as *şeyh*, *derviş*, *murid*, *dedelik*, *çelebilik* . . . and the wearing of dervish costume, are prohibited . . .'

This law remains in force today. In the following year, the Darülelhan Conservatory – under its founder, Rauf Yekta Bey – was no longer allowed to offer instruction in Turkish music. This prohibition was only gradually lifted almost twenty years later.

The Mevlevi tradition had been continuous from its inception, and its goal was to shape the inner life of human beings. It pursued this goal in various ways, determined by time and place, throughout Ottoman history, up until the final moments of the Empire. Sezai Küçük has aptly described the relationship linking the Empire and the Mevlevis as a 'common destiny' (Küçük 2007: 715). In the long history of this common destiny, the only event bearing any resemblance to the decree of 1925 was the prohibition of the Mevlevi ceremony from 1666 to 1684, under Sultan Mehmed IV, as a response to the anti-Sufi Kadizadeli movement. It is no small irony that in the seventeenth century the Mevlevis were the targets of a Sunni and 'populist' religious tendency, while in the early twentieth century they were regarded as a threat to a secularist national government. The seventeenth-century prohibition lasted for eighteen years, while its twentieth-century version has been in force, in various guises, for close to a century.

In relation to the Mevlevis, however, the 1925 prohibition was not carried out with the rigour of similar anti-religious policies in Stalin's USSR roughly a decade later, which had other targets, and were usually not announced officially as laws. In post-1925 Turkey, the strictures of Law 677 were not extended to the private homes or shops of individuals, and thus the processes of master–student pedagogy and transmission among musicians were usually able to continue, even though the full *mukabele* ceremony could not. But the training of Mevlevi dervishes, which had required long periods of seclusion as well as musical and poetic studies, was now impossible. Nevertheless, individuals who had already gone through all or some of the Mevlevi training prior to 1925, and who possessed high intellectual or artistic attainment, were sometimes able to segue into positions within Turkish academia or occasionally the world of art and museums. And even outside of this professional sphere, several well-respected musicians and teachers opened shops, especially bookstores, perfumeries, and sometimes, pharmacies – mostly in Istanbul – where older and younger generations could meet and discuss many issues freely. One of the best known of these was the circle surrounding the Mevlevi *neyzen* (*ney* player) and pharmacist Halil Can (1905–73). These meetings were by no means secret, and since the 1970s they have been the subject of published memoirs (such as Şehsuvaroğlu 1974; Özemre 1996).

Each generation, almost each decade, following the closure of 1925 presented the 'former' Mevlevis and their students and followers with new challenges, and, at times, new opportunities. A thorough study of the post-1925 situation would require access to a great deal of information, only a small amount of which is still available. Although this is not the focus of the present work, any attempt to penetrate into the Mevlevi reality must also deal with the post-1925 era to some extent. The Turkish writings of many Mevlevi sheikhs and poets of the past centuries are extant – and some of them are presented here. But the wider Mevlevi philosophy and many aspects of the musical tradition did not rely primarily on any written source, but rather on human transmission over time. The constellation of the public, the private, and the secret took a specific form in the Mevlevi culture that differed both from other mystical traditions and from the culture of the West in any period. However, the Mevlevi emphasis on learning and on a certain degree of public accessibility represent concepts that are shared with Western religious and fraternal orders.

Through their personal efforts, the Mevlevis were able to sustain some of their transmission and preserve its content for a time when better sociopolitical conditions might come into existence. Alongside the elaborate improvised *ney taksim* playing – which was an essential part of the Mevlevi musical aesthetic – the *mukabele* itself was based mainly upon extended metrical compositions. So long as the *mukabele*s were performed regularly, oral pedagogy had been effective, although even prior to 1925, some older compositions had been either lost or preserved only partially. Mevlevi musicians had shown an interest in notation since the illustrious Nayi Osman Dede (1652–1730) in the early eighteenth century, but notation had not been considered appropriate for the Mevlevi music; rather, it was considered the province of secular art music. The influential but erratic Üsküdar *neyzen* Aziz Dede (1835–1905) would even beat a student found with any musical notation. It would appear that by the following generation this prohibition was becoming looser. Thus, Rauf Yekta Bey, born in 1871, the last *neyzen* of Yenikapı Mevlevihane, who notated the *ayin*s for publication in the 1930s, was able to preserve the core repertoire so that later generations would have access to the music.

In the late 1940s, private meetings of a more literary nature, emphasising Rumi and his teachings and poetry, materialised in several Turkish cities. By 1953 the Mevlevis began to incorporate musical performances of the instrumental *peşrev* sections of the *ayin*s in the meeting on 17 December, held in Konya to commemorate the passing of Mevlana Jalaluddin Rumi in the Şeb-i Arus (Night of Union) celebrations. Three years later, in December 1956, they were allowed to perform a complete *mukabele* for the first time in a quarter of a century.

Western – mainly European – interest was not far behind, represented in the serious publication 'Die Mevlanafaier in Konya 11–17 December, 1960', by Helmut Ritter (Oriens 1962), and, in 1964, in the choice of the Mevlevi *ayin* to represent Turkey in UNESCO's *Musical Anthology of the Orient*, directed by Alain Daniélou and released in LP format on the Bärenreiter-Musicaphon label under the title *Turkey I: Music of the Mevlevi*. On this recording we can hear several of the heirs of the authentic Mevlevi tradition, including one who had been trained at Yenikapı prior to 1925: the *halilezen* (cymbals player) Osman Dede. All of the *neyzen*s came from the tradition – Halil Can, Ulvi Erguner – son of the *neyzen* Süleyman Erguner – and Niyazi Sayın, student of the *neyzen* and painter Halil Dikmen. The lead vocalist (*naathan*) was the extraordinary Hafız Kani Karaca, who would become perhaps the most significant singer of both mosque and Mevlevi music in Turkey. All of these musicians came from Istanbul, which had been the centre of Mevlevi musical life for the past three centuries.

Nevertheless, a crucial aspect that was absent was the traditional space for the *mukabele*. Mevlana's tomb in Konya was now a museum, and no Mevlevi space was made available for the commemorations. In order to accommodate the large numbers of visitors, theatre halls and sports gymnasiums had to be employed. By the early 1970s, invitations were received from various European countries, and Mevlevi tours were organised. Touring in the style of music ensembles or theatre troupes was completely alien to Mevlevi tradition, in which even the Sultan had to visit a Mevlevi space, for the *mukabele* was not performed in any Ottoman palace. What the Ottoman sultan had been unable to command was now presented on request to the European theatre-going public. But this new and diminished atmosphere alienated many of the Mevlevi performers from Istanbul, who withdrew their involvement.[2]

Nevertheless, in response to tours of Mevlevi ensembles organised by the Turkish government, Western interest has grown steadily. Nowadays, foreign tours by Mevlevi ensembles usually perform to packed concert halls, and the remembrance ceremony of Mevlana in Konya is a major destination for Western tourists to Turkey. These changes produced several results. First the Konya Tourism Association no longer wished to be dependent on Mevlevi musicians and *semazen*s (*sema* dancers) from Istanbul. This meant reaching out to local musicians and dancers with no Mevlevi background, with the ironic consequence that the Mevlevi performance in Konya, where Mevlana Rumi had lived and is buried, began to feature fewer and fewer people who could be described, however loosely, as 'Mevlevis'.

Amateur groups led by musicians with some Mevlevi education began to spring up in Istanbul in order to preserve and perform the music. A Turkish Sufi Music and Folklore Research and Preservation Foundation was organised, initially on the basis of the Halveti-Cerrahi Tarikat. By the end of the 1980s, this group was led by Ömer Tuğrul İnançer, a student of Emin Ongan, the head of the Üsküdar Music Society and a very active teacher of Ottoman music, along with the noted *kudümzen* (kettle-drummer) Hurşid Ungay. Later they would add Mevlevi performance as well. In 1990 the Turkish Ministry of Culture and Tourism in Konya founded the Konya Turkish Sufi Music Group, led by Mustafa Holat, with *neyzenbaşı* Yusuf Kayya and the local Konya *semazen* Bülent Ergene, a student of Ahmet Bican Kasapoğlu, from Istanbul. Two years later Tuğrul İnançer was able to form the Istanbul Historical Turkish Music Group as a Mevlevi performing organisation, supported by the Ministry of Culture and Tourism. Their *ayinhan* and artistic director was Ahmet Özhan, a respected younger classical singer and performer of *zikr ilahi* hymns from a Halveti background.

The form of the revival of the Mevlevi ceremony in the decades after 1956 – although drawing on human resources from within the Mevlevi tradition – was dictated by the perceived need to reinstate an important

---

[2] For an account of this period from the point of view of the Mevlevi musicians in Istanbul, see Kudsi Erguner, *Journeys of a Sufi Musician*, London: Saqi Books, 2005, 45–50.

aspect of Turkish culture to a wide audience quickly. Not long afterwards a commercial strategy developed that was linked to tourism as a major feature of the Turkish economy. Since the Mevlevi tradition itself had evolved from an ecstatic séance to an internalised and meditative performance that combined ecstasy with a degree of symbolic representation, as will be explained in the following chapters, it was relatively easy to create a stage performance that maintained the form of the *mukabele* while progressively losing its essence. A good example is the preparations in Turkey for UNESCO's 'Mevlana Year' (2007), described in the following excerpt from a Turkey Business Update in the *International Herald Tribune*:

> The tourism ministry published a comprehensive strategy plan last year that aims to strengthen infrastructure and training in the sector by 2023, the centenary of the republic, and make better use of Turkey's exceptional geographical and cultural diversity.
>
> The action plan designates several 'tourism corridors' as well as tourism cities that are earmarked for further development.
>
> Promotional activities have already borne fruit in such places as Konya, the final resting place of the mystic philosopher Mevlana, also known as Rumi. To celebrate the 800th anniversary of the Sufi philosopher's birth (which UNESCO recognised by declaring 2007 Mevlana Year), Konya sent advance delegations with whirling dervishes to 100 cities around the world. The events triggered a 30 percent increase in the number of tourists for Turkey, some coming from as far away as South Korea and Japan.
>
> – Turkey Business Update, *International Herald Tribune*, March 28, 2008.[3]

---

[3] In 2004 architectural historian Barihüda Tanrıkorur and I had co-authored the original Candidature File for UNESCO's proclamation of the Mevlevi Sema Ceremony as a Masterpiece of the Oral and Intangible Heritage of Humanity. This led to the UNESCO proclamation of 2007 – the eight-hundredth anniversary of Rumi's birth – as 'Mevlana Year', and then to the final inscription of the Mevlevi Sema Ceremony in 2008. 2007 saw a major international conference in Konya and Istanbul, whose proceedings were published in three volumes in 2010. Some major architectural restoration was undertaken, including the re-opening of the Yenikapı Mevlevihanesi in Istanbul. Yet, despite these positive developments, the broader thrust of the proposed 'Action Plan' of the Candidature File has still not been implemented.

The promotion of 'whirling dervishes' as cultural tourism notwithstanding, even in the early twenty-first century, key individuals within the public Mevlevi performing groups had been trained by persons who were part of an initiatic chain of transmission. And by the 1980s, and continuing today, a few talented composers, steeped in the Mevlevi repertoire and tradition, had composed new *ayin*s representing, in many cases, a natural development of the older repertoire. Consequently, any Mevlevi public performance contains two or more levels of reality to which most of the public, whether foreign or Turkish, will not have full access. In the absence of a Mevlevi establishment with its traditional training (discussed in Chapter 2), teachers of the *ney* and of the choreographic aspect of the *sema* now partly occupy the place of the former Mevlevi hierarchy of teachers (see Şenay 2014; 2017; 2020). And within any given audience, only a minority, whether Turkish or foreign, are likely to be fully aware of the background of all of the *semazen*s, singers, and musicians making an appearance – an inevitable result of staging state-sponsored public performances of a ceremony still officially proscribed by Turkish law.

1

DEFINING THE MYSTICAL MUSIC OF
THE MEVLEVI DERVISHES

From the outset of this exploration of the Mevlevi music and ceremony, we must acknowledge the gift bequeathed us by the great spirit and thinker Mevlana Jalaluddin Rumi (1207–73).[1] Mevlana's enormous significance within the Ottoman world, the Muslim world, and the world at large has naturally attracted attention to him and to his times. But the creation of his heirs within Turkey – the Mevleviye – is less known and understood, in part due to the simple fact that the Mevlevi Order was, and is, officially prohibited according to Turkish law. Yet all too many foreign observers and writers describe aspects of so-called Mevlevi performance since the 1960s and 1970s as though it represented a functioning Mevlevi culture. Naturally, much of the appeal of the 'Mevlana tourism' described in the Introduction hinges on the perpetuation of such myths.

In the chapters that follow, conclusions concerning the probable meaning of musical practices will be founded on detailed musical analysis. But from the outset I will need to define a few key words and terms. I will be speaking about 'mystical' music, and posing historical questions concerning the provenance of Mevlevi music and its relationship to Ottoman music in general.

---

[1] Rumi's name is also transliterated from Arabic script as Jalal al-Din; in Turkish, it is rendered as Celalüddin.

'Mystical Music' in the Anatolian Turkish Context

World languages and cultures, including those of Turkey, do not share complete equivalence in their use of concepts akin to English and French 'mystical' or 'mysticism'. For example, 'secular' is typically contrasted with 'religious', not with 'mystical'. Even such a major Turkish musicologist as Gültekin Oransay (1930–89) entitled his unpublished study 'Ali Ufki and Religious Turkish Music' (*Ali Ufki ve Dini Türk Musikisi*), although the mid-seventeenth century manuscript in question contains almost entirely pieces from the Sufi, which is to say, mystical, repertoires.[2] This coupling of liturgical music of the mosque with the music of the Sufi orders under the umbrella of 'religious' music is common in later twentieth- and early twenty-first-century Turkish musicology.

The binary contrast of 'religious' vs 'secular' is a legacy of medieval Western Europe, where the Latin Church and the Emperor spent centuries clarifying their respective spheres of society. Nevertheless, as far back as Roman times, there had been a distinction between the *religio* that connected all citizens of the state, and the *mysterium* that involved only a select group of adepts or devotees (*mystes*). The origin of the Latin term *religio* is surprisingly obscure. Nevertheless, Roman authors could agree more or less on the duties of a citizen toward the gods, and the emperor, when he was considered to be one. For both Greeks and Romans, public religion involved a cult, with its ritual service and sacrifices (*liturgia*) overseen by priests. Analogous systems existed throughout the ancient world, including the Jewish Temple in Jerusalem.

Mysterium took on a different meaning within Christianity, and the function of 'mysticism' differed somewhat among the Eastern and Western Churches. In particular, *hesychia* – the meditative quest for inner quietude – became part of mainstream Orthodoxy by the fourteenth century (Krstic 2011: 9). But the central *mysterium*, i.e., transubstantiation, was a fundamental part of the official *liturgia* for both Greek Orthodox and Latin Christianity.

---

[2] More recently Judith Haug, in her doctoral dissertation, has shown that the Muslim name of the Polish convert Bobowski (1616–75) was properly vocalised as 'Ali Ufuki Bey. I adopt Haug's spelling. See Haug 2019.

Judaism has developed Kabbalah as an overarching term for various forms of mystical thought. Jewish Kabbalah also inherited certain terms from earlier Gnosticism, which had its pagan, Christian, and Jewish manifestations, as a form of mystical knowledge (*gnosis*). The Mandaeans of modern Iraq – who claim to be of Jewish origin – employ the Aramaic translation of the Greek *gnosis* (Manda') as their group name.[3] Gnosis (Arab. *ma'rifa*/Turk. *ma'arifet*) is used by many Sufi groups as one of the highest stages of mystical attainment. An *'arif* may be defined in Sufi terms as a 'gnostic', a 'knower'.[4] As described by Marshall Hodgson:

> The sense of communion with God which some of the classical Sufis had spoken of, in which individual and cosmic meanings converged, thus led readily to a teaching of Gnostic type which combined old Hellenistic and Irano-Semitic elements with a new outlook appropriate to the Islamic setting. In this teaching were combined special notions of the place of mankind in the cosmos, and the place of the saint among mankind. (Hodgson 1974, vol. 2: 225)

Despite the obscurity of the name's etymology, in Islam *tasawwuf* ('Sufism') distinguished itself from the legal issues treated by the ulema through *sharia* law. Sufis were, of course, Muslims, and were bound, in theory, by the same legal structure as were other Muslims. But Sufis – in Turkey, at any rate – often stressed a hierarchy which led from *şeriat* (law), to *tarikat* (Sufi order), to *ma'arifet* (gnosis), and finally, in the best case, to *hakikat* – knowledge of the Ultimate Truth. This hierarchy even appears in a slightly variant form in a hymn of Yunus Emre (1238–1320) that holds a kind of canonical status among Bektashi and Halveti dervishes:

---

[3] Gnostic authority Kurt Rudolph accepts the probable historicity of this claim. See his *Gnosis: the Nature and History of Gnosticism*, New York: Harper One, [1977] 1987, 343–66 ('A Relic: The Mandeans').

[4] Annemarie Schimmel's *Mystical Dimensions of Islam* (1975) remains a lucid introduction to the subject; she also connects *ma'rifa* with gnosis. Ahmet T. Karamustafa's *Sufism: the Formative Period* problematises the broad use of the terms 'mysticism' and 'spirituality' outside of a historical and social context. See Karamustafa 2007, Preface and Chapter 1.

Şeriat tarikat yoldur varana
Hakikat maarifet anda içerü

To the seeker the Sharia and the Tariqa are on the Path
Ultimate Truth and Gnosis are within it.

Over the centuries there had been a wide variety of Sufi practices and phi-
losophies, some of them emphasising practice with little philosophical articulation. Others – especially the system of the Andalusian Muhyiddin Ibn al-Arabi
(1165–1240) – developed a mystical philosophical framework that was abstract
enough to show many points of similarity to mystical systems of thought that
had emerged completely independently of Islam.[5]

In the Islamic case, music had a very different status among Sufis than
it did among the ulema as a whole.[6] It is abundantly clear that most genres
of what could be termed 'music' were often held in disrepute by the ulema,
leading in several historical eras to the prohibition of many forms of music.
For example, in Turkey, from 1666 to 1684, elements of the ulema managed
to have the state prohibit Sufi ceremonies entirely, including the Mevlevi
ayin-i şerif. It is not surprising, then, that distinctions between 'religious' and
'mystical' are clearly parsed in Ottoman Turkish, as well as in Arabic, Persian,
and other languages spoken in Islamic and Islamicate lands.[7]

The knowledgeable twentieth-century Turkish writer Ahmet Hamdi
Tanpınar (1901–62) drew a clear distinction between religious music and

[5] A classic study of this type was undertaken by Toshihiko Izutsu in his *Sufism and Taoism:
a Comparative Study of Key Philosophical Concepts*, Oakland, CA: University of California
Press, 1983.

[6] For Kurds and Turks (and others) there was the added issue of shamanistic practices preserved within the tribal Sufi-like groups, such as Kurdish Yarsan and Turkish Alevis, which
are discussed in chapter 2.

[7] It is worth noting that with the rise of a world-music market for 'Sufi Music' in the early
twenty-first century, some Mevlevi practitioners turned against this term. This seems the background for the remark by master *neyzen* Niyazi Sayın (b. 1927) in a 2013 interview: 'There is
no such things as Sufi music. There is only religious music and non-religious music'. (Quoted
in Banu Şenay, 'Artists, Antagonisms and the Ney in the Popularization of "Sufi Music" in
Turkey', *European Journal of Cultural Studies* (2014), 1–18.

mystical music within a Mevlevi Sufi context. In his novel *Hüzur* from 1949, he presents a moving and convincing portrait of one of the last great traditionally trained Mevlevi musicians, Emin Dede Yazıcı (1883–1945), who was truly a bridge between the past and the present of the Mevleviye. Here Emin Dede is performing the Ayin in *makam* Ferahfeza, by Ismail Dede Efendi (d. 1846):

> [Ismail] Dede's Ferahfeza Ayin is not simply a prayer, a cry of the believing soul for Allah. Without losing the broad attack, which is the hallmark of the mystical [*mistik*] inspiration, its mystery or its great and ceaseless yearning [*hasret*], it is perhaps one of the most spectacular works of the old music. (Tanpınar 1949: 320)

We will return to Tanpınar, who penned one of the most subtle and accurate descriptions of the structure of Mevlevi music within modern Turkish fiction. Nevertheless, even he employed *mistik* (borrowed from French '*mystique*') as a somehow more universal term than the Ottoman *tasavvufi*, which has exclusively Islamic associations.

In societies that value mystical knowledge, such knowledge is imparted through a variety of means, which include forms of teaching and transmission as well as individual practices such as meditation. In order to be effective in the growth of the individual, mystical knowledge must not be divulged to those who are unprepared to receive it. Some societies prefer extreme secrecy in the transmission of mystical knowledge, including mystical art forms. As Jean During (1995) has observed, music and mysticism share many of the same structures of transmission. Artistic expression and creation formed a major part of the mystical materials used by the Mevlevis. They created a balance between aspects of the mystical tradition that were available to all, and aspects that had to be transmitted to the individual, or to certain individuals, over time. After 1925 this system of musical and mystical transmission could only function very partially (see Senay 2017 and 2020).

Within traditional arts in Japan, the secret aspect of transmission has been expressed in the following way:

> Secret transmission or secret teaching is significant in the traditional arts of Japan, and some scholars find a relationship between this concept of mystery and esoteric sects of Buddhism, which are very cautious about transmitting

their secrets. Most skills of traditional Japanese music have been transmitted orally from generation to generation. Pupils or descendants must learn by watching and imitating a master's performance. Even if there is written instruction or transmission, only specified people – mainly talented descendants – are allowed to read the texts. (Shimosako 2002: 549)

Comparison of *Sema* and *Zikr* (*Dhikr*)

The Mevlevi *sema* represents an expression of a mystical life-orientation whose basis is circular motion and music. It has taken on a complex philosophical meaning as part of the contrast between the 'rectilinear path' of sacred law and the 'circular path' of the true mystic. In the rectilinear path God is infinitely distant from the world, and believers spends their entire life on a journey to seek Him. In the circular path the mystic is in constant communication with God through His manifestations in the world. The *sema* is an expression of this continued contact between God and Humanity.[8]

The Mevlevi *sema* is distinct in many ways from the typical Sufi *tarikat* ceremony of *zikr* (*dhikr*) and the tribal Kurdo-Turkish *sema* and *ayn-i cem* ceremonies. Yet all of these ritualised practices in the broader Irano-Anatolian geographic sphere include forms of sacred song and instrumental performance that are highly differentiated both from secular genres and from the chanting in the mosque. Among them, the various Iranian groups, from Baluchis in the east to Kurds in the west, have been deeply studied by the French Iranologist and ethnomusicologist Jean During. In Turkey, the foundation for such work had been laid as early as 1943 by the Sufi sheikh and literary scholar Sadettin Nuzhet Ergun (1901–46) in his literary collection *Anthology of Turkish Music: Religious Works* (Feldman 1992: 187). This two-volume publication consists of an extensive collection of Sufi hymns, together with many observations on performance, but little about musical structure. Much of the music referred to by Ergun was finally published in several volumes during the early 1980s for the Kubbealtı Institute by Yusuf Ömürlü, who used the collections of Ali Riza Sengel and Abdülkadir Töre. These collections contain the hymns for the *zikr*, known as *ilahi* (Turkish: 'divine') as well as hymns – usually of Sufi origin – sung at the mosque on Islamic holidays and known as *tevşih*. There is yet another genre of vocal music, called *durak*, that is connected with the

---

[8] I thank Barihüda Tanrıkorur for this elegant formulation.

zikr but sung in rubato, apart from the rhythmic movement of the *zikr* itself. Examples of *durak* were published elsewhere by Dr Subhi Ezgi (1935), but generally as 'reconstructions', and not as they were actually performed.[9] All of these musical genres are highly differentiated from other forms of Turkish music, whether urban or rural in origin.

As an introduction to the topic, let us look at one *ilahi* of the Halveti dervishes, known as an *usul ilahisi* (basic hymn), as it introduces the *zikr* cycle (*devran*) in *makam*s Uşşak and Hüseyni. The *redif* (monorhyme) is the word 'Hū' ('It is He') – one of the names of God. The opening couplets are:

> *Safha-i sadrında daim aşıkın efkar-i Hū*
> *Şakirin şükrü Hū vallah zakirin ezkar-i Hū.*
> The page of the lover's breast forever
> Is inscribed with thoughts of Hū.
> The gratitude of the grateful is Hū,
> And by God, the remembrance of he who remembers is Hū.

> *Hū sadasından melekler gökte eylerler sema*
> *Hū safasından felekler eyledi ihbar-i Hū.*

> The angels in Heaven perform the *sema*
> To the sound of Hū;
> Through the joy of Hū the revolving spheres
> Conveyed the communication of Hū.

This poem by Sheikh Cemal (or Cemaleddin)-i Halveti (d. 1494) illuminates the significance of the link between the *zikr* from the heart of the dervish, the *sema* sacred 'dance' of the angels, and the heavenly spheres themselves. Sheikh Cemaleddin, coming from Eastern Anatolia, was the highly influential founder of the Halveti Dervish Order (Halvetiye) in Istanbul, and enjoyed the support of Sultan Beyazid II (Işın 1997). The composer of the

---

[9] See the discussion by Cem Behar, 'The Technical Modernization of Turkish Sufi Music: The Case of the Durak', in Anders Hammarlund, Tord Olssom, and Elizabeth Özdalga, eds, *Sufism, Music and Society in Turkey and the Middle East*, Istanbul: Swedish Research Institute 2009, 97–110.

music, a certain Cihangirli Ahmed, about whom little is known, flourished in Istanbul during the sixteenth century. A transcription of the music is reproduced on the website accompanying this book as Ex. 1.1.

Ex. 1.1 [website] Usul Ilahisi, 'Safha-yi Sadrında'.

As an *usul ilahisi*, the hymn is characterised by a stately and ponderous tempo. Incidentally, the rhythmic structure of the melody, while not contradicting the poetic metre, is certainly not determined by this metre, but rather works along purely musical principles. This fact is signalled by the many repetitions of syllables within the poem, which are determined only by musical, and not poetic or metrical, principles.

As an added feature, the melody must begin on a very low note. It concludes one tetrachord lower than the *makam* finalis, and then is pitched a note higher at each new stanza. And this whole is performed over the low droning of the *zakir* singers on the finalis, chanting the *redif* 'Hū' of the poem and of the *zikr*, calling to mind the droning *ison* of the Byzantine Church. This entire musical complex, while using techniques of urban Ottoman music, is unique. Though the hymn 'Safha-yi Sadrında' shows these distinctive features, analysis of a great many *ilahi*s of the Halvetiye demonstrates that they display a variety of compositional techniques, which, even within a small compass, represent a distinctive form of Sufi musical expression in Anatolian and Ottoman culture.

The main lesson to be learned from this piece, and from the larger *zikr* repertoire, is the degree to which Anatolian Turks belonging to various *tarikat*s or practising other forms of mysticism invested their energy in creating a differentiated musical form and repertoire to generate appropriately 'mystical' feelings, in conjunction with the poetry of the sheikhs. Yet, despite the beauty and spiritual distinctiveness of these Halveti hymns for the *zikr*, they do not form the musical basis for the Mevlevi *ayin*. The separate status, and the ritual music, of the Mevlevi dervishes – even at this early date – is confirmed by another couplet in the following poem by Sheikh Cemaleddin:

Naleden ney deldi bağrın Hū deyü nalan ider
Mevleviler Mesnevide eyledi iş'ar-i Hū.

The wailing of the *ney* pierces his breast;
He lets out a groan with a cry of 'Hū!'
In the Mesnevi the Mevlevis
Have communicated the meaning of Hū.

Sofi mest olup safadan devrider ya Hū deyü
Münkir inkarin bıraktı eyledi ikrar-i Hū.

Drunk within the circle of joy,
The Sufi cries 'Ya Hū!'
The denier abandoned his denial,
And confirmed the certainty of Hū.

There is no hint here of any competition between the charisma of the separate Sufi 'paths' of the Halvetiye and the Mevleviye. Rather, we see complementarity. Earlier in the poem, both the *zikr* and the *sema* are mentioned. In the two poetic lines translated above, both the poetry of Mevlana and the 'wailing' of the reed-flute *ney* are integrated into a dervish ritual, which is described only on the most abstract level. Sheikh Cemaleddin wrote his hymn in Turkish for a public that consisted mainly of speakers and readers of Turkish, but he evidently had only the greatest respect for the Sufi literary monument of Mevlana written in Persian. This very complementarity of the Sufi paths in medieval Anatolia raises the question of how Mevlevi music and ritual are linked to Ottoman culture, and to other possible sources within and beyond Anatolia. Before entering into a more detailed analysis, it may be helpful to pose this question more broadly.

Zikr (Arabic: *dhikr*) and *sema* (Arabic: *samā'*) have different origins and histories within Sufism as a whole. Both *zikr* and *sema* are broad terms for diverse customs and rituals, but certain distinctions are fairly clear, even allowing for separate developments within each category over time. *Zikr/dhikr* (from Arabic *dhakira*: 'to remember'; 'to mention') can refer to a meditative practice involving the repetition of Divine names, usually coupled with control of the breath. William Chittick explains:

> The Qur'an often attributes dhikr to God, as in the verse 'Remember Me and I will remember you' (2:152) . . . On the Human side, dhikr is both the awareness of God and the expression of this awareness through language

whether vocal or silent. . . . Being present to God is precisely *dhikr Allah*, 'the remembrance of God'. (Chittick 2002: 49–52)

The repetition of the Names frequently develops into a regular rhythm, and as such has become the basis for rhythmic movement, whether seated, standing in place, or rotating in a circle. As Chittick notes, the practice of *dhikr/zikr* is deeply Islamic, having both Sufi and non-Sufi forms. Forms of *dhikr* can be found among Muslims from China in the east to West Africa in the west.

In Turkish, the *zikr* in a seated posture is referred to as *ku'ud zikri*; the *zikr* standing in place is termed *kıyami*, while the circular motion is *devrani*. Naqshibandi dervishes often practice the seated *ku'ud zikri*; Kadiri [Qadiri] dervishes (in Turkey) often practice the standing *kıyami zikri*, while Halvetis perform the circular *devrani zikri*. There seems little doubt as to what form of *zikr* was performed among Cemaleddin's Halveti dervishes, as the first lines of his poem mention the *zakir* (performer of the *zikr*), and the last couplet given here describes the 'Sufi . . . drunk within the circle of joy', and mentions the technical term *devr ider* (circling), from *devran*.

The Musical Style of the *Zikr*

The musical semantics of the *zikr* may be seen as the opposite of the Qur'anic *tecvit* (Arabic: *tajwīd*), which represents the word of Allah descending to man. The *tecvit* employs a wide range of modality (*makam*), as in secular music, but it avoids any fixed metre (*usul*) and it must be improvised, without any pre-composed sections. The *tecvit* conveys timelessness, represented by a non-metrical flowing rhythm, and an emotion that müezzins characterise as *hüzn* (sadness), which represents Allah's compassion for Humanity. The *zikr*, by contrast, is Humankind's response to Allah: mankind seeks to imitate the worship of the angels by continually affirming the existence of Allah both through words and through circumambulation of His throne (*'ars*).

In the terrestrial *zikr*, time is continually marked by the dervishes' breathing and chanting, which establishes a sense of urgency not present in the *tecvit*. While the *tecvit* is a single unique voice addressing mankind, the *zikr*, as noted above, is humankind's collective response to Allah. Humanity must listen to the address of Allah through the recitation of the Qur'an, but one's duty in the *zikr* is to affirm the life of Allah by affirming the life that Allah has granted to humankind. In the *zikr*, the connection between life and time is continually emphasised by changes of tempo, both acceleration and deceleration. The *zikr* must always give the impression of organic life – moving, flowing, and even reversing itself. Although the *ilahi*s of some parts of the *zikr* may have certain fixed sequences, the ideal is never cyclical (as it is in the secular *fasıl* or the Mevlevi *ayin*). Rather, the *zakirbaşı* (*zikr* leader) and the sheikh continually alter the order and constitution of the particular hymns in accordance with their perception of the spiritual moment (*ān*).

The Turkish *zikr* represents a fusion of several disparate musical principles. The non-metrical, performance-generated – which is to say, improvised – *kaside* chant of the müezzin, essentially identical to styles used in the mosque, was integrated into a metrical context in which sound was divided into three timbral registers. The uppermost register was the müezzin's high-pitched solo voice. The middle register was occupied by the small group of specialists, the *zakir*s, who sang the metrical hymns (*ilahi*s). The lowest register was occupied by the mass of dervishes, who chanted and breathed the divine Names. The metrical basis of this chant might be reinforced by percussion, usually large frame drums (*daire*, *bendir*) but also kettledrums (*küdüm*) and cymbals (*halile*). The breathing and chanting of the Divine Names employ specific rhythms and tempos, which are essential to the structure of the *zikr*. Most of the *zikr* movements are done to the simplest rhythm of Turkish music. Its very name, *sofyan* (in the manner of the Sufis), reveals its long association with the *zikr*.

It would seem that the low pitch of the hymns used in the *zikr* reflects a Turkic concept of sacred and shamanistic musical expression. This impression is confirmed by the traditions of certain urban *tekke*s where the singing of the *kelime-i tevhid zikri* is dominated by the *shahada* singing of the *zakir*s rather than by the improvised singing of the müezzin. The *zakir*s in these traditions strive to emit a low growling tone that borders on the overtone singing of Turkic Central Asia and Mongolia.[10] This would seem to be a descendant of

[10] For a general historical thesis, see Fuad Köprülü, *Influences du shamanism turco-mongol sur les ordres mystiques musulmans*, Istanbul: Institute of Turcology, University of Istanbul, 1929. Also relevant are the timbral aspects of Turco-Mongolian vocalisations and bowed fiddle playing presented in Theodore Levin with Valentina Süzükei, *Where Rivers and Mountains Sing: Sound, Music, and Nomadism in Tuva and Beyond*, Bloomington: Indiana University Press, 2006, 48–58.

the 'rasping saw' *zikr* introduced in the twelfth century by the Central Asian Sufi saint and poet Ahmed-i Yasavi (Trimingham 1971: 197).

The term *ilahi* describes a genre, the hymn, that is both musical and literary – aspects that are not always coterminous. The divine nature of the *ilahi* sometimes refers to the text and sometimes to the music; this ambiguity has probably encouraged loose usage of the word *ilahi* both in the present and in the past. The *zikr-ilahi*s constitute one of the oldest and most distinctive functioning repertoires in Turkish music. Many current *tarikat*s in Turkey have initiatory chains (*silsile*) that began in the seventeenth or early eighteenth centuries, and many of the *ilahi*s sung in their *zikr*s evidently represent a continuous tradition dating from that period. Hymns ascribed to dervish composers such as Aziz Mahmud Hüdayi (1543–1628), Ali Şir-u Gani (1635–1714), Hafiz Post (1630–94), and Cihangirli Ahmed, as well as many anonymous compositions, use *makam* and compositional structure in archaic or idiosyncratic ways. All of these *ilahi*s contribute to the emic perception of the entire audible *zikr* complex in Turkey as a 'mystical' musical expression.

Terminology of the *Sema*

The Arabic noun *samā'* derives from the verb *sama'a*, 'to hear' or 'to listen'. By the tenth century of the common era it was used by Sufis for a variety of intimate sessions centred on listening to mystical singing or instrumental music, sometimes accompanied by spontaneous individual movement. While the preferred instrument was the reed-flute *nai* (Turkish: *ney*), there was often a percussive instrument, especially a frame drum. The identical Arabic term *samā'* remained in use for a variety of related Sufi practices in different areas of the Muslim world over many centuries. In general, I will use the modern Turkish spelling *sema* for the Ottoman Mevlevi choreographic movement, and retain the more direct transcription from Arabic (*samā'*) for earlier customs and for other regions of the Muslim world (including the *samā'* used in Mevlana's Persian verses).

Among the many medieval and later tracts that speak either for or against the practice of *samā'*, there are no clear descriptions of the actual conduct of such sessions. But both from the few terms used, and from the later practices where the term is still employed, it is clear that the movement of the *samā'* was individual. One of the clearest accounts is one of the earliest, by the influential scholar and Sufi Ahmed al-Ghazali (d. 1126). According to the description in his Bawariq al-Ilma, the *samā'* sessions took place after either morning or evening prayers, sometimes following a silent or seated *zikr* recitation. Under the guidance of a teacher, a singer with a fine voice sang various verses, which could be expounded by the teacher. The mood gradually became more intense as other singers performed different verses. Within this 'deep listening', individuals could enter into movement or even get up to move in various ways. Any kind of group movement or 'dance' was actively discouraged. Al-Ghazali describes the kind of movements that were current (Trimingham 1971: 196–7).

The *samā'* was essentially a practice of smaller groups, linked to a particular teacher. First described in the tenth century, it was generally urban, and usually connected with more learned and literate elements of Muslim society. Throughout the Muslim world, due to a variety of social and religious causes whose elaboration is beyond the scope of this book, the post-medieval era was characterised by the acceptance of various forms of musical *zikr* (*dhikr*) at the expense of the *samā'* practices. The major exception was rural and tribal groups, such as the Alevis, Gurans, and Yarsans, who were mainly speakers of Turkish, Kurdish, and Zaza, respectively, and who integrated the originally urban *samā'* practice into their own mixtures of Sufism, animism, and Gnosticism. Where the term *sema* (*samah*) is still used, as, for example, among the Alevis of Anatolia, movement, even coordinated within a group, is always individual. Thus, *zikr* and *sema* both manifest the 'circular path of the mystic', but in different forms and according to different concepts.

In the modern South Asian environment, gatherings at the tombs of saints accompanied by the singing of mystical poetry on the part of professional singers (*qawwals*), have led to a Sufi genre known as *qawwali*.[11] In some interpretations, notably that of Kenneth Avery (2004), an Australian scholar of Sufism, modern *qawwali* sessions may well have antecedents within the

---

[11] *Qawwali* has been studied notably by Regula Qureshi. See: Regula Qureshi, *Sufi Music of India and Pakistan: Sound, Context, and Meaning in Qawwali*, Cambridge: Cambridge University Press, 1986.

medieval Sufi *samā'*. But these modern events are often large gatherings that no longer partake of the 'mysterium' of the more private *samā'* sessions centred around living Sufi teachers, and hence they display a different etiquette.

In addition to *samā'/sema*, four different terms have been used to refer to the Mevlevi ceremony at least since the fifteenth century: *mukabele, devr, selam*, and *ayin* or *ayin-i şerif*. All are still in use, but no medieval or modern source defines them adequately. Their polysemy and overlapping meanings underscore the complex evolution of the mystical dance, its music, and the overall structure of the ceremony.

The term *samā'* was employed by Mevlana himself in many places, and in connection with him by Ahmed-i Sipahsalar (d. c. 1312) as well as in the writings of Mevlana's son Sultan Veled. In a general sense it represents a tradition that is highly differentiated from the *dhikr*. As the Mevlevi musical practice evolved over centuries, *sema* remained in use as a kind of default term that stressed the spiritual intention and historical affiliation of the Mevlevi ceremony, regardless of the choreographic structure, musical accompaniment, sequence, or cycles as they developed within historical time. Divane Mehmed Çelebi (d. 1529), one of the early Mevlevi 'theorists' writing about the significance of their ceremonial dance, in addition to using the pen-name Divane (The Mad One), also used the pen-name Sema'i, attesting to his deep commitment to the Sufi musical technique of *sema*.

Mukabele is another Arabic term, from the verb *qabala* 'to receive', in the third form, hence meaning a 'turning toward, receiving'. This is not a term with wide Sufi usage. *Mukabele* is quite suggestive, since it can mean an 'encounter' with the Divine, with the Angelic sphere, or simply with one's fellow dervishes in the ceremony. Divane Mehmed Çelebi (1529) had used the term *mukabele* to refer broadly to the Mevlevi ceremony. By the nineteenth century this term came to refer to the entire ceremony, including several musical genres (see below on *ayin*).

Devr, from *dawr*, Arabic for 'cycle' or 'revolution', is another highly suggestive term. In its highest mystical meaning it referred to the 'cycle of existence', whereby the Divine entered into the human, and then reached upward again toward its source in the form of the Perfect Man (Insan-i Kamil). In a more mundane sense it referred to any 'cycle', including a musical movement or section with a defined rhythmic structure that occurs within a sequence of such sections. It is used in this way by Mehmed Çelebi to signify the discrete sections within the larger *mukabele*. This term occurs in Divane Mehmed's text (discussed in chapter 3) in conjunction with the word *selam* (peace) as a greeting from Allah toward the individual dervish during the *mukabele*. Apparently it was through this semantic link that, since the nineteenth century, the word *devr* as a description of a discrete musical movement has been replaced by *selam* among the Mevlevis – a use that survives today.

Also since the nineteenth century, the term *ayin* or *ayin-i şerif* has been used by Mevlevis to refer to the entire ceremony – equivalent to the earlier usage of *mukabele* – including all the introductory musical genres that precede the discrete musical *selam*s. This use reflects the structural evolution of both the physical movement and the music of the *mukabele* in the course of the eighteenth and early nineteenth centuries (see discussion in chapter 3). However, *ayin* has a different etymology and separate cultural associations than the other terms. For one thing, it is of Persian origin, and in Persian, it means 'a ceremony'. In Ottoman it could refer to a variety of religious or secular ceremonies. *Ayin-i şerif* ('the noble ceremony') is often used to refer specifically to the musically composed part of the *mukabele*, with its four discrete sections. The choice of the term *ayin* to describe the Mevlevi ceremony probably also reflected the increasing 'ceremonialisation' of the ritual, removing it yet further from the kind of spontaneous and ecstatic ritual dance that early visual representations (several of which are reproduced in chapter 3) suggest occurred during the lifetime of Mevlana and the first three generations of his immediate descendants. Spontaneity would have tended to limit the role of pre-composed pieces in the ceremony, and figures such as Pir Adil Çelebi and Divane Mehmed Çelebi, in the mid and late fifteenth century, are credited with having shaped the development of the *mukabele* to include discrete sections (*devir*) that eventually would become the locus of musical composition.

Another layer of meaning connects the Mevlevi *ayin* with the other family of Sufi ceremonies employing similar terminology – the *ayin-i cem* of the Bektashi dervishes. This name translates as 'ceremony of unity', i.e. uniting with the Divine. Its pre-history probably goes back to the *jam'* (Turk. *cem*), the musical ceremony of the Ahl-e Haqq, or Yarsan, the Gnostic-Sufi sect of Iranian Kurdistan, researched extensively by During (1989). In a political sense the Mevleviye gradually came to occupy an opposing space from the

Bektashiye, who were allied with the Janissary Corps, especially following the assassination of the Mevlevi Sultan Selim III in 1808 at the hands of Janissary rebels. But some of the Mevlevihanes, even within Istanbul – such as Yenikapı – showed a confluence of Mevlevi and Bektashi tendencies. This link with the Bektashi and even Alevi, conjured up by the Mevlevi use of the term *ayin*, is thus not without relevance, since it illustrates older Anatolian connections of the Mevleviye that predate their establishment within Istanbul.

The *sema* of the Mevlevis seems to have evolved over several centuries into an elaborate ceremony. By comparing modern practice with earlier visual documents, it would appear that, at least since the seventeenth century, the individual rotation has evolved and become more disciplined. By the following century it involved a rapid spinning on the individual axis of each dervish, with the arms raised in a fixed position: the palm of the right hand raised toward the heavens, and the palm of the left hand facing downward toward the earth. This entire motion, and the spatial movement of the 'dancing' dervishes – known as *semazen* – acquired complex symbolic interpretations over time. Binbaş summarised the relationship of *sema* and *zikr* in the Ottoman environment:

> If we look from the perspective of music, unlike the situation in Central Asia, sama' and zikr never became the subject of a debate among different tarikats. Although some scholars such as Sakıp Dede, tried to combine the Nakşbandi zikr and the Mavlavi sama', not at the practical level but at least in definition, these views were absorbed in a flexible environment. In this way, we can understand that, while the practice of zikr was purging the sama practice from the tarikat rituals in other regions, in the Ottoman sphere these two practices found it possible to coexist. (Binbaş 2001: 79)

While this collegiality led to a high degree of mutual tolerance within later Ottoman society, the Mevlevis held themselves apart from the general practice. The Mevlevis never entered the *ta'ifa* (sect) phase – maintaining the unity of their order – and indeed strove to link their *tarikat* with the earlier classical *khanaqah* Sufism, characterised by a strong mystical teacher with a specific teaching. They became an order with a lineage of leaders, a sacred tomb, and most of the other characteristics of a *tariqah/tarikat*, but they endeavoured to preserve both freedom of thought – largely through the study of complex classical texts with wide-ranging discussions – and something of the ideals of the classical Sufi *samā'*. Whereas among almost all other Sufi groups, both in Turkey and abroad, the Sufi concert (*samā'*) ceased to be practised after the seventeenth century, it was precisely at this time that the Mevlevis began to develop their own, more elaborate musical ceremonies. By this period the elite systems of Sufi thought and practice could only continue to exist where the leading social classes of the state, with its bureaucracy, aristocracy, and higher clergy, granted them legitimacy and material support. While maintaining their institutional home base in Konya, by the early decades of the seventeenth century the Mevleviye became increasingly centred in Istanbul. The unique political and social conditions of the Ottoman state allowed the Mevleviye, a descendant of the culture of classical Sufism, and hence of Islam in its classical age, to flourish into modern times.

For these reasons the Mevlevis never accepted the musical *zikr* as their primary practice, nor would they permit their dervishes to participate in such a *zikr*, although, largely under Naqshibandi influence, the *zikr* acquired a role in their discipline. They used the term *esmacı* ('chanters of the Divine Names'), i.e., practitioner of the *zikr*, to refer to the members of other *tarikat*s. In the nineteenth and early twentieth centuries, several Sufi *tekke*s, including those of the Rufais and Naqshibandis, adopted the practice of inviting Mevlevi dervishes to perform the *sema* during their *zikr*. At times sizeable numbers of Mevlevis could be found there. And the no-longer functioning Gülşeni *tarikat* emerged as early as the sixteenth century as a synthesis of Halveti and Mevlevi traditions. The communality with regard to the Mevlevi *sema* is still practised by some *tarikat*s both in Istanbul and even in remote regions of Turkey. Nevertheless, the Mevlevi *mukabele*, with its complex composed musical tradition, including the use of musical instruments, is essentially the practice of the Mevlevis alone and not of other *tarikat*s.

The Mevleviye and Music

Part of the challenge in accounting for the Mevlevi *mukabele* as a musical phenomenon is its sui generis quality. It has no close known or surviving 'relatives', either in Turkey or elsewhere in the Muslim world, and the structural continuity of the Mevlevi Order could and did allow for a high level of technical development of the ceremony's musical elements. Hence the *ayin* was hardly a static survival from an earlier era. Moreover, the Mevlevi involvement with music was not confined exclusively to *ayin* compositions.

Mevlevis played a large role in the performance and composition of secular art music, as I explain in chapter 6. In particular, the performance-generated *taksim* form was held in great respect, both within and beyond the *ayin*, especially when it was performed on the most characteristically Mevlevi instrument, the reed-flute *ney*.

The earliest Mevlevi *ayin* by a known composer, the Beyati Ayin by Köçek Mustafa Dede, who lived in Edirne (d. 1683), displays a compositional structure that diverges fundamentally from the emerging courtly vocal repertoire as well as from the existing Halveti and Kadiri music for the *zikr*. The Beyati Ayin agrees in its structure with the fragmentary *ayin*s in the *makam*s Dügah, Hüseyni, and Pençgah. These anonymous *ayin*s were probably created earlier in the seventeenth century, or toward the latter part of the sixteenth century (see chapters 7 and 8).

The principle of cyclicity that characterises concert suites of the Muslim world – from the Moroccan *nauba* in the west to the On Ikki Muqam of Xinjiang and the Shashmaqom of Bukhara – features vocal pieces in which longer and slower rhythmic cycles occur toward the beginning while shorter and faster cycles occur toward the end. The Ottoman *fasıl* concert generally accords with this principle. The first vocal piece was usually a *beste* in the longest *usul – zincir*, a compound of five distinct *usul*s – leading into other *beste*s in long *usul*s, possibly a *kar* in a long *usul*, then a group of *ağır* (heavy) *semai*s in various forms of ten-beat *usul*s (*aksak semai* in 10/8 or *ağır aksak semai in 10/4*), finally culminating in a *yürük* (quick) *semai* in six beats.

By contrast, these early – and almost all later – Mevlevi *ayin*s commence with the first *selam* in a rather quick 14/8 *usul* (*devr-i revan*, or 'flowing' rhythm). The second *selam* is always in a stately nine quarter-beat *usul* (*evfer*), at a somewhat slower tempo. The third *selam* displays two contrasting rhythmic structures. The opening section uses *devr-i kebir* (of the seventeenth and mid-eighteenth century) in fourteen quarter notes (14/4). *Ayin*s from the earlier eighteenth century retain the older form of this *usul*, while those from the later part of the century and thereafter use the newer form, which is twice the length and considerably slower, better understood as 28/4 (Feldman 2001). With the entrance of the much shorter and faster *semai* rhythm in 6/8, the second part of this *selam* displays a marked contrast. This rhythm and some of the melodic structures seem to refer to an older body of Turkish-language Sufi hymns more Central Asian in inspiration, and were not part of the Halveti-Kadiri complex.

Some of the difference between the rhythmic structure of the *fasıl* and that of the *ayin* can easily be explained by the function of sacred *sema* 'dance' within the latter. But all of the extant *ayin*s demonstrate a mature aesthetic based on contrasting sections as well as a musical climax quite beyond what might have been needed for a sacred 'dance'.

The importance of music in the thinking of Mevlana Jalaluddin Rumi is evident in the frequent appearance of musical imagery in his poetic works. His participation in mystical seances and other musical performances was in keeping with the practice of the musical *samā'* among Sufis of the medieval period. This practice seems to have continued among the early generation of his successors, and no doubt aided in stabilising both musical practice and theory in the Seljuq and, later, Karaman territory. Sources agree that both Rumi and his son Sultan Veled played the *rabab*, and that the latter also composed a *mesnevi* entitled *Rababname*. In Rumi's time, the *rabab* appears to have been a skin-faced plucked lute, rather than a bowed instrument (Feldman 1996: 117–19; During 1991: 123).

Image 1.1 Player of *rabab* on Seljuq painted bowl (late 12th–early 13th century). Metropolitan Museum of Art, accession no. 57.61.16. Henry G. Leberthon Collection, Gift of Mr and Mrs A. Wallace Chauncey, 1957.

One of the most elegant testimonies to the *rabab* from Rumi is the following quatrain:

Dāni ke che miguyad ān bāng-e rabāb?
Andar pāy-e men beyā ve rehrā beyāb
Zirā be-khatā rāh beri suy-e savāb
Zirā be-suāl rāh beri suy-e javāb

Do you know what this lute music tells you?
It says: Follow me and you'll find the way.
Mistakes will make you stumble toward goodness.
Questions will put you on the answer pathway.

(Anvar and Twitty 2008)

The integration of mystical and secular music is most brilliantly expressed in several verses by the later fifteenth-century Karaman poet Ayni (Baki 1949). Little is known of the life of Ayni, who was a courtly and not a Mevlevi poet. Nevertheless, in his works, Ayni refers to the tomb of Mevlana, and the Mevleviye were then centred within the Karaman Beylik territory. Ayni's poetry exemplifies the early integration of Sufi and secular music in Anatolian Turkish culture. In the following poem, Ayni speaks not about the *rabab* but about the *tanbur*, an early version of the long-necked lute that would later come to dominate Ottoman courtly music.[12]

1. *Gel ey mıtrıb alıp ağuşa tanbûr*
   Fürûğ-u nağmeden kıl bezmi nûr
   Come, oh minstrel, and take to your lap the *tanbur*,
   Through pleasure and melody, fill the party with light.

2. *Getürsün zühreyi raksa sadâsı*
   Sipihre velvele versin nevâsı
   Let its tones set Venus to dancing,
   Let its sounds put the spheres in commotion.

[12] This poem and its interpretation are taken from Feldman *Music of the Ottoman Court: Makam, Composition and the Early Ottoman Instrumental Repertoire*, Berlin: VWB 1996: 87–9. See also pp. 143–8: 'The Origin of the Ottoman Tanbur'.

3. *Nevâ-i kilk ile minâ-i tanbûr*
   Olur neşvefşân rind-i mahmûr
   The sound of the plectrum and gourd of the *tanbur*,
   Spreads intoxication over the wine-besotted *rind*.

4. *Dü 'âlem sırrı var zîr-ü beminde*
   Elestü keyfi târ-i mülheminde
   In its treble and bass are the mysteries of the Two Worlds!
   In its inspired string is the pleasure of 'Am I not your Lord?'

5. *Makam-i Evç'den kılsa terâne*
   Çıkar perde be perde lâmekâne
   When it makes music in the *makam* of the apex,
   Note by note it ascends to the sphere Beyond Space.

6. *Kulağı bursa bir sâzende nâgâh*
   Eder bin gâfili bir anda âgâh
   When the player suddenly twists its ear,
   A thousand dullards of the Truth are aware.

7. *Hümâ-î nağmeye mizrabı perdir*
   Sa'âdet lânesi şeklinde zâhir
   Its plectrum is a feather of the Bird of Paradise,
   Which becomes manifest as the nest of felicity.

8. *Şarâb-i nağmesinden ey kadeh nûş*
   Muhit-i neşve-i 'irfân eder cûş
   Drink a cup of melody's wine, and
   The intoxicating ocean of gnosis will overflow!

   (Levend 1943: 243; English translation: W. Feldman)

In the opening couplet the poet locates the poem in the party or feast (*bezm*), a multivalent term which is both secular and mystical. *Mıtrib* is the term both for a secular musician and for the members of the Mevlevi ensemble. The rhyme word *nûr* (light), however, adds a mystical element to this apparently worldly feast. The second couplet refers to a standard topos of medieval Persian poetry, in which Venus (Zuhra) dances to the music of the harp (*çeng*), replaced here by the *tanbur*. In the third and fourth couplets the absence of any apology for the use of the stringed instrument (not the dervish *ney*) is noteworthy; on the contrary, these couplets emphasise the physical concreteness of the musical instrument as a manifestation of the divine mysteries. '*Keyf*' is a multivalent term meaning 'quality' but here 'pleasure,' usually derived from some form of intoxicant. '*Elestü*' is a Sufi hypogram, which conjures up the myth of the time prior to the Creation, when Allah confronted the souls of humankind with the query, 'Am I not your Lord?' (Arabic: '*Alastu rabbikum*'). The *rind* is a topos of Persian poetry and Sufism, who personifies the outwardly unorthodox and inwardly liberated character. In the fifth couplet, the *makam*s, located on specific steps of the general scale, are identified with spiritual stages (*makam*), culminating with *Lâmekân* (lit. 'no place'), the stage of Union with the Divine, in which the stages are transcended. The image is one of constant musical and spiritual ascent. The sixth couplet combines the image of the musician (*sâzende*) tuning his *tanbur* with that of the Sufi teacher (*murşid*) twisting the ear of his indolent disciple. No image could more graphically illustrate the spiritual identity of the musical creator and the spiritually liberated mystic. The following couplet refers to the Simurgh, the magical bird that was credited in Persian Sufi (and earlier Near Eastern) myth with the creation of music (During 1989: 95–102). The final couplet creates a Sufi image of gnosis as the Ocean which surrounds the world, likened to the bubbling cup of wine, which, in turn, is likened to musical melody.

Ayni's poem offers a rare glimpse of the brilliant mixture of mystical and courtly aesthetic that flourished in Karamanid Turkish culture, centred in their capital Konya. Later, the symbolism of the *ney* came to dominate the poetic expression of musical thought among the Mevlevis of the Ottoman era, as I explain in chapter 4, 'The Ney in Mevlevi Music'.

2

THE MEVLEVI PHENOMENON

The biography of Jalaluddin Rumi, his crucial relationship with the enigmatic Shams of Tabriz, the activities of his son Sultan Veled, his grandson Ulu Arif Çelebi and the next generations of leaders of the Mevleviye, have been presented lucidly in English by Franklin Lewis (2001), based largely on the basic research of Abdülbaki Gölpınarlı (1953). The Turkish historian Ekrem İşın has researched many primary Ottoman sources and presented the most nuanced history to date of the Mevlevi, but İşın's publications are available only in Turkish. His work makes clear that the intellectual and artistic history of the Ottoman Empire became increasingly bound up with the history of the Mevlevi Order.

The bibliography of works in English and French on Rumi himself is voluminous. The novelist Elif Shafak popularised the life of Rumi even further through her novel *The Forty Rules of Love* (2010). Among the most enlightening contemporary books is the English translation of the Discourses (*Maqalat*) of Shams, published by William Chittick as *Me & Rumi: The Autobiography of Shams-i Tabrizi* (2004). However, the history of the Mevlevi Order in the Ottoman Empire, when its influence was at its highest point – during the seventeenth, eighteenth and earlier nineteenth centuries – has attracted less attention in Western language sources. This is also the case for the important role of the Mevleviye in fifteenth-century Anatolia, which was divided between several Turkish principalities. It is worth stating that the outstanding success of the generations of leaders coming immediately after Jalaluddin in establishing and stabilising a mystical 'tradition' was due both to their and to his extraordinary genius and charisma, and to the unique political and geographical situation in which they found themselves. While the first element is always remarked upon, the second one is not always given its full weight.

It is a melancholy fact that the great Sufi philosopher Yahya Suhrawardi, author of *The Wisdom of Illumination* (Hikmat al-Ishraq), was executed in Aleppo in 1191 by none other than the son of Sultan Saladin. The apparent charge was not only theological, but political; Suhrawardi's philosophy may have rendered him close to Ismaili doctrines that were then opposed by the Sunni states in the region. The pressure of the Crusaders was still palpable, and the Ayyubid and Seljuq governments felt the need for a spiritually united, Sunni ideology in order to confront them in Syria.

Shams-i Tabriz was apparently only a child at the time. But when he visited Rumi in Seljuq Konya in 1244, many realities had changed, so that he was never in real danger from either the government or the ulema. Moreover, the religious situation of Anatolia differed from that in Syria. Orthodox and Armenian Christianity were a major demographic presence, and there appears to have been increasing intellectual communication between the Christian and Muslim elites[2] as well as among the common people. Sufis were well positioned to play a role in this communication. And the appearance of Jalaluddin as a *medrese* teacher, a charismatic Sufi and a major poet all were ideal for the needs of Islam in Seljuq Anatolia. As Yassir Tabbaa[1] has noted in connection with the history of Islamic art: '. . . Sufism was quickly taken over by the Seljuqs and their successors and actively promoted through various acts of patronage' (2001: 15).

Yet another positive opportunity for Sufism resulted from the appearance of the Mongols in Iran and in Anatolia as overlords of the Seljuqs. After a period of internal conflict in Iran, the Buddhist-turned-Muslim Gazan Khan began a period of enlightened rule, starting in 1295. This also worked to the

[1] An enlightening discussion of the Armenian situation may be found in Rachel Goshgarian, 'Futuwwa in 13th century Rum and Armenia: Reform Movements and the Managing of Multiple Allegiances on the Seljuk Periphery', in A. C. S. Peacock and Sara Nur Yıldız, eds, *The Seljuks of Anatolia: Court and Society in the Medieval Middle East* London: I. B. Tauris, 2013, pp. 227–63.

benefit of Sufis, and of the Anatolian Mevlevis in particular. Ekrem Işın has elegantly introduced the background of the appearance of Mevlevism:

> In the cultural history of Anatolia, the thirteenth century was a period of social restructuring in which the confraternities called *tarikat* began to be organised on the foundations of Islamic mysticism or 'Sufi' (*tasavvufi*) thought. The first coherent and enduring example of this restructuring, which was undertaken in the shadow of the Mongol threat to the world of the Seljuk Turks, appeared on the historical stage in the person of Sultan Veled and has come to be known as Mevlevism (*Mevlevilik*). (Işın 2004: 16)

Brief Outline of Mevlana's Career

The broad outlines of the life of Mevlana Jalaluddin Rumi are known, although his enduring legacy comes through his literary output. Here we will follow the brief retelling by Hodgson, Chittick and Işın, among others.

Jalaluddin was born in 1207 in the major city of Balkh in Khorasan – near today's Mazar-e Sharif, in Afghanistan. His father Bahauddin had been an Islamic scholar and a Sufi sheikh of the line of the Central Asian Kubrawiyya. Bahauddin left Khorasan with his family prior to the great Mongol raids of 1220–31 under Chingis Khan and his sons, which decimated the region. The family was welcomed in Konya, then the capital of the Seljuqs of Rum. Jalaluddin studied there and in Damascus. After his father's death in 1231, he continued his education and soon was able to teach in the *medrese* in Konya. He became an acclaimed preacher, and was commonly addressed as 'Mawlana' (Arabic: 'Our Master'; Turkish: 'Mevlana'). Rumi, as he is known in the West, comes from Rum, i.e., Rome, the Muslim term for the Byzantine Empire and hence for Anatolia.

Rumi was only thirty-seven years old when he encountered the Qalandari dervish Shams-e Tabriz, who visited Konya in 1244, 'a wildly unpredictable man who defied all conventions and preached the self-sufficiency of each individual in his search for the divine' (Hodgson 1974: 245). Most stories about Shams come from the hagiographical writing of Eflaki, two generations later. But on the basis of Shams's Discourses (*Maqalat*), published in Tehran by Movahhed and translated into English by Chittick (2004), we now know that Shams, too, was a highly learned man. Chittick described Shams's meeting with Rumi in a Preface to his translation:

For Mawlana it was love at first sight. He devoted himself totally to Shams. He shirked his teaching duties and began to occupy himself with *sama*, that is, listening to music and poetry and dancing along with it. Many of his disciples were shocked at this behavior, which was unbecoming of a respected scholar, and many of them complained, but Rumi paid them no heed. (Chittick 2004: xiii)

After two years Shams left Konya and travelled to Syria. Jalaluddin sent his son Sultan Veled to find him and bring him back. Although Shams agreed to return, the situation for him in Konya was again made so unpleasant by the disciples that in less than a year he disappeared again, never to resurface. While rumours that he had been murdered have circulated, they have never been substantiated. After several years of waiting, Rumi 'took refuge in *sama*, and it was during this period that he was transformed into one of the greatest poets of the Persian language' (Chittick 2004: xiii).

Rumi's literary legacy is found primarily in his *divan*, which he entitled *Divan-e Shams-e Tabrizi*, and whose texts later became the basis for much of the *mukabele/ayin* repertoire, and in his narrative *Masnavi* (*Mesnevi*). Hodgson succinctly characterised this masterpiece:

> Without going very far in the theosophical speculations that had recently been developed by Suhravardi and Ibn-al-'Arabi, it presents, in its many anecdotes, most of the fundamental viewpoints that gave tarîqah Sufism its power. (Hodgson 1974: 246)

One can hardly overestimate the influence that Rumi's *Masnavi* has had throughout the Muslim world, where it has often been referred to as 'The Qur'an in Persian' and was already well established by the time of the great Timurid Sufi poet Abdurrahman Jami (1414–92). While the study of the *Masnavi* became a formal institution among both the Mevlevis and other *tarikat*s within Turkey, the prestige of this seminal work is in no way confined to *tarikat* circles. Of course, this magnificent literary legacy alone would have established Rumi's reputation wherever Persian was read, which is to say, in the entire Persianate zone of Islamdom. But, as I show in some detail below, it would appear that Rumi's son Sultan Veled and his grandson Ulu Arif Çelebi were instrumental in creating an enduring structure through which Rumi's teachings could be integrated into the life of a community, and indeed of a large society and polity. Before we turn to this social and historical phenomenon, let us view Işın's lucid characterisation of the intellectual basis for this structure:

> The mystical foundations of Mevlevism were laid as a result of the fusion of the Khorasan school of Sufism, which began entering Anatolia at regular intervals from the early thirteenth century onward, with Seljuk culture. During the lifetime of Mevlânâ Celaleddin-i Rumi (died 1273), both the Kübrevi (of which his father, Bahaeddin Veled, was an adherent) and the Kalenderi (represented by Şems-i Tebrizi) philosophies became the two quite distinct sources of the ideas that nourished the cultural structure that took shape under the roof of Mevlevism. In addition, one should also note the concept of *Vahdet-i vücud* ('unity of being') systematised by İbn Arabi as another source of influence in the Anatolian cultural sphere. The influence of the school of Andalusian Islamic mysticism, which was embodied in the personality of İbn Arabi, initially did not receive much favour from Mevlana though it would later play a conspicuous role in the subsequent cultural structuring of the Mevlevi Order. In particular, many of the commentaries on Mevlana's *Mesnevi* were undertaken within the framework of this Sufistic systematic. (Işın 2004: 17)

Among the terms introduced above (and in other sections), we may note in particular Kalenderi, *batini* and *rind*. Kalenderi (Qalandari) is a broad term employed in Turkish, not for a specific *tarikat* organisation, but rather for a mystical tendency that de-emphasised ritual practice and sharia law. The word itself is of unknown etymology. In early sources it is associated with Jamal al-Din Sava, an early thirteenth century figure from Iran, who was active in Syria. But there is little agreement on the details of his career. These sources also distinguish the Qalandari path from that of the Sufis.[2] Its practitioners often affected an outward appearance that differentiated them from the majority of Muslim males, in that they shaved their beards, moustaches, heads and eyebrows – the so-called 'four strokes' (Pers. *char-darb*). They tended to travel over large distances. It is often assumed that Shams-i Tabriz represented such a philosophy, although this remains questionable. *Batini* is a mystical-philosophical term for those tendencies in Sufism that emphasised the 'inner'

---

[2] See Ahmet T. Karamustafa, *God's Unruly Friends: Dervish Groups in the Islamic Later Middle Period 1200–1550*, Salt Lake City: University of Utah Press, 1994, pp. 39–44.

(*batin*) over the 'external' (*zahir*) shape of all things, including issues of ritual practice and law. *Rind* is a term for anyone – especially dervishes, poets or musicians – who enjoyed both the pleasurable and the aesthetic aspects of life, at times, but not necessarily, with a suggestion of mysticism.

As Işın noted above, the position of Shams-i Tebrizi within this complex can be interpreted variously. But whatever Shams's personal beliefs and choices, later Ottoman sources refer to the Şems kolu ('arm of Shams') – representing something closer to the Qalandari philosophy and practice – as opposed to the Veled kolu ('the arm of Sultan Veled'). Both of these so-called arms appear in the *Menakib-i Hoca-i Cihan ve Netice-i Can* of Vahidi (1522), and in the writings of the major Mevlevi sheikh-poet Sakıb Dede (1652–1735). Nevertheless, Gölpınarlı tends to view them more as mystical 'tendencies' (*meşrep*) of particular figures within the Mevleviye itself, rather than as distinct social 'groups' (1953: 208–14).

Brief History of the Mevleviye

Before addressing aesthetic and mystical issues, first let us turn to the material basis of the proto-Mevleviye. Throughout the history briefly presented below, political, social and mystical-metaphysical factors will be in continual interaction. A. C. S. Peacock (2013) noted the small space devoted to Rumi and the Mevlevis in earlier histories of Seljuq Anatolia such as those of Cahen (1968) and Turan (1971). By way of contrast, he stresses the importance of the early Mevlevis in any historical understanding of the period: 'The role of court patronage in spreading Sufism and broadening the appeal of groups like the Mevlevis through the provision of financial incentives is a subject that needs further research' (2013: 220).

Both through his father Bahauddin and through his own reputation, Rumi established good relations with members of the Seljuq governing elite, which resulted in *vakf* (pious foundation) monies being laid aside for the needs of his family and some members of his community. Rumi's intentions as to the continuation of his teachings on an institutional basis are by no means clear. Upon his death, in 1273, the remaining students were led by a principal disciple, Çelebi Hüsameddin. It was he who organised the construction of Mevlana's tomb in Konya, and also set aside some of the *vakf* revenues for the maintenance of Mevlana's remaining family. Upon Hüsameddin Çelebi's death eleven years later, Rumi's son Sultan Veled remained under the tutor-ship of his teacher Sheikh Kerimuddin. But on his death in 1292, Sultan Veled took formal control of his father's group, including its finances. Hence-forth for the next six centuries, the central authority would remain with the descendants of Sultan Veled. While the predominant narrative of Rumi's life and those of his close descendants is based on the work of Eflaki, discussed below, Peacock (2013) points to the fact that historians have tended to ignore the documentary evidence preserved in the letters of Mevlana himself and poems with particular addressees by Sultan Veled.

The most notable figure of these early generations was Sultan Veled's son Ulu Arif Çelebi (d. 1320). We are extremely well-informed about his numerous activities, thanks to the writing of the poet Ahmet Eflaki (Aflaki), especially his *Manaqib ul-Arifin*, completed in 1353. Eflaki had accompanied Ulu Arif on many of his major journeys. According to Ekrem Işın's apt characterisation:

> Ulu Arif Çelebi set the mould for Mevlevism in the pre-Istanbul era. His thoughts and his life-style were formed under the influence of the Qalandaris of Anatolia. The affinity that he felt for the heterodox tendencies urged him to create a synthesis between these mystical currents and Mevlevism. One of the most striking aspects was his life-long wandering through Anatolia, and his travelling to Iraq and Tabriz in order to introduce the Sufi conceptions of these regions into the structure of Mevlevism. It is also well known that he drank wine and had a *rind*-like personality. All of these characteristics turned him into a prototype for Mevlevi culture, and left a lasting impression on the Mevlevis later on in Istanbul. (Işın 1994: 423)

During Sultan Veled's tenure the Ilkhanid Mongol state, based in Iran, rep-resented the dominant political power in the larger region. A crucial turning point occurred in 1295 when the previously Buddhist Gazan Khan con-verted to Islam. Wasting no time, Ulu Arif Çelebi represented his father and Mevlana's lineage on a mission to the Mongol Khan in Tabriz. Both his inherited charisma and his evident personal charisma turned this meeting into a complete success. Eflaki's epic account of this mission to the East displays Ulu Arif Çelebi's confidence bordering on audacity. While Sufis of various backgrounds played a role in the Islamisation of several Mongol rul-ers, Gazan Khan became a protector of the Mevleviye in particular.

This protection lent an added authority to the group in Konya. After Sultan Veled's death in 1312, Ulu Arif Çelebi pursued this enhanced status by means of his many journeys through the Seljuq and Mongol territories of Anatolia and Azerbaijan. These included Lârende, Beyşehir, Aksaray, Akşehir, Karahisar, Amasya, Niğde, Sivas, Tokat, Birgi, Denizli, Menteşe, Alâiye, Antakya, Bayburt, and Erzurum, several of which became Mevlevi centres. After Ulu Arif Çelebi's death in 1320, he was succeeded in Konya by his descendants.

The second branch of Mevlana's family were the descendants of Sultan Veled's daughter Mutahhara Hatun, known as the *inas*, or female line. Two sheikhs of the female line from Sultan Veled's daughter were crucial in establishing the Mevleviye in Anatolia: Celaluddin Ergun Çelebi (d. 1373) founded the Mevlevihane in Kütahya, while Bali Mehmed Çelebi established the Mevlevihane in Karahisar. His son Divane Mehmed Çelebi (d. 1529) was to become one of the major Mevlevi figures both in Anatolia and in the newly incorporated Constantinople/ Istanbul. It is of course noteworthy that the Mevleviye had navigated the transition from Mongol-Seljuq rule through the breakdown of this system, leading to the emergence of the Karaman Beylik (Principality) in the region of Konya, beginning in the mid-thirteenth century and continuing until 1487.

The Mevlevis incorporated many strands of Sufism that were current in Anatolia between the thirteenth and fifteenth centuries. With the expansion of the Ottoman state, and especially after the Conquest of Constantinople, several Sufi *tarikat*s from the East, with customs and beliefs quite different from the Mevleviye, entered Anatolia. At this time, the Mevlevis were so well established under the Karaman Beylik in Central Anatolia that they were somewhat distanced politically and culturally from the emerging Ottoman state. One of the more mysterious episodes in this history is the creation of the Kalendarhane Zaviye out of the Akateloptos Monastery in Constantinople under Mehmed II, the Conqueror. According to contemporary records, the Mevlevi ceremony was performed by a four-piece musical ensemble after the Friday prayers led by a sheikh. Afterwards Rumi's Mesnevi was taught. This enigmatic situation was not long-lasting, but it shows that in this era the Mevlevis could reconcile both orthodox practices and heterodox 'Qalandari' practices with their own core customs.

It was only during the following reign of Bayezid II (1481–1512) that the Mevlevis – along with several other *tarikat*s – found their place in Istanbul. Yet another kind of Mevlevi synthesis emerged in the Mevlevihane founded by Abid Çelebi (d. 1497) in the neighbourhood of the Fatih Mosque in 1494. This was apparently a dual Mevlevi-Naqshibandi institution, in which the Mevlevi *ayin* was celebrated on Thursdays and the Naqshibandi Hatm-i Hacegan ceremony on Fridays.

In this decade the earliest exclusively Mevlevi establishment was created in 1491 on a game farm on the Galata hills belonging to Iskender Pasha. Its first sheikh (*postnişin*) was the outstanding representative of the female Mevlevi line, Divane Mehmed Çelebi, mentioned above. He was both a respected poet and favoured the same type of Qalandari Sufi practice as had Ulu Arif Çelebi a century earlier. Like his predecessor he travelled widely to the East, even making contact with a variety of extreme Sufi groups there. But whereas Ulu Arif Çelebi was able to ingratiate himself with the Mongol Gazan Khan, Divane Mehmed found himself under deep suspicion on the part of the Ottoman Sultan Bayezid, from whom he only escaped due to the influence of Iskender Pasha. Soon after leaving Galata in the hands of his successor, Safai Dede, he returned to Karahisar, where he had inherited sheikhly status from his father. But soon after the death of Safai Dede, in 1533, under Mesnevihan Mahmud Dede (d. 1548), Galata was removed from Mevlevi control, and given to the Halveti dervishes, who then enjoyed greater support from the state.

Thus, during much of the sixteenth century, despite their great dispersion throughout Anatolia, the status of the Mevleviye within Istanbul was not entirely stable. The situation improved later in the century, especially after 1597, when a second major Mevlevihane was built in Yenikapı, closer to the centre of the City. This too was built by a Pasha with high government connections, Malkoç Mehmed Efendi. The first *postnişin* at Yenikapı was Kemal Ahmed Dede, famed for his Turkish verse translation of Eflaki's *Menakibül Arifin*. But Galata was not returned to the Mevlevis until the time of Sırrı Abdi Dede (d. 1631). For unknown reasons the latter was removed from Galata by the Çelebi in Konya and replaced in 1610 by Ismail Ankaravi (see chapter 6). Soon afterwards, however, Sırrı Abdi was able to found another Mevlevihane in the Kasımpaşa neighbourhood. This Mevlevihane was remarkable for two reasons: first, it was not founded by government ministers but rather by

Mevlevis themselves; and second, it tended to keep its leadership among the members of local sheikhly families, rather than appointees from Konya. At the same time, in 1622, yet another Mevlevihane was built by Grand Vizier Ohrili Hüseyin Pasha in the Beşiktaş district of Istanbul. This too became a highly influential Mevlevi centre with close connections to the government.

Understandably, extant historical sources from the end of the fifteenth century onward tend to favour the unfolding of the Mevlevi story within the Ottoman capital, where contacts with governmental figures became closer, and many major sheikhs resided. But the exceptional documentary study of the Konya Mevlevihane (the Asitane), conducted by Sorayya Faroqui (1988) reveals something of the Anatolian situation. The Celali Revolts, intensifying after 1603, and other economic and even environmental factors led to a decline of the rural population and hence a weaker tax base within Anatolia through much of the seventeenth century (Shaw, vol. 1 1976: 186). According to Faroqui's study, the years between 1584 and 1652 show a drastic decline in the functioning of the Konya Mevlevihane. Whereas in 1584 the Asitane was home to eighteen full-time dervishes (*dede*), by 1652 this number had dropped to four. The orchestra (*mıtrip*) also shrank from one *hafiz*, one *naathan*, three *neyzens*, one *kudümzen*, and two *daf* players – a total of eight musicians plus the *semazen* (*devirhan*) – to only three musicians in 1652. Faroqui concludes that 'By the later sixteenth century the order had apparently ceased to expand, and failed to attract the followers of rural background which it had possessed in the earlier stages of its development' (1988: 45). She adds that 'Curtailment of hospitality, and probably even of publicly visible dervish ceremonies, was to make it difficult for an order like the Mevlevis to gain popularity outside of the urban upper class milieu where it had traditionally recruited adherents' (1988: 63).

Thus, while the interaction between the Mevlevihanes of Istanbul and the Çelebi in Konya would continue – and occasionally we hear some news from such Mevlevihanes as Karahisar and Kütahya, Gelibolu and Edirne – Mevlevi history after the early seventeenth century is increasingly focused on Istanbul. New Mevlevihanes were founded in the Arab provinces at the end of the sixteenth century, particularly in Cairo and in Baghdad. Within the first decades of its founding, the Baghdad Mevlevihane became a major centre of manuscript production – including many with miniature paintings – of Mevlevi, general Islamic, and secular topics (Milstein 1990). But most of this production came to an abrupt end in 1624, with Shah Abbas's Iranian conquest of the city, and his annihilation of the Sunni inhabitants. Even after the Ottoman Sultan Murad IV finally retook Baghdad in 1638, it never regained its former importance, although the Mevlevihane continued to function. The Cairo Mevlevihane would assume great importance only in the nineteenth century.

Işın presents the broad lines of the ideological conflicts and syntheses that would be enacted in Istanbul:

> The mystical teachings of the first Mevlevi sheikhs in Istanbul appeared as a synthesis of their own values with the heterodox tendencies that were widespread in Anatolia. Throughout history, this synthesis was gradually loosened, and the tarikat purified itself of the heterodox influences that had taken shelter within it, and would lay the foundations for an understanding of Mevlevism that was particular to Istanbul. (1994: 423)

> During the seventeenth century the Mevlevism of Istanbul lived through a dual cultural process. On the one hand the remnants of *batini* esotericism were removed from the structure of Mevlevi culture, while on the other hand these tendencies were formed once again within the Bektaşi circles and were introduced into Mevlevism. While the Galata Mevlevihane was the centre of this cultural 'cleansing', Yenikapı became one of the main centres for relations with Bektaşiism. (1994: 425)

In order to establish better connections with the Ottoman government, on which the Mevleviye came increasingly to depend, the leadership in Konya evidently felt the need to purify the Istanbul Mevlevihanes of their *batini* and Kalenderi tendencies. During the seventeenth century, the leading figure of this movement was Ismail Rusuhi Dede (d. 1631), from Ankara, who was appointed the sheikh of Galata in 1610, in place of Sırrı Abdi Dede, who then founded Kasımpaşa. Known as the Şarih-i Mesnevi, or 'Commentator on the Mesnevi', Ismail Ankaravi (Rusuhi) was a leading interpreter of the Mevlevi tradition in the light of the philosophy of Ibn al-Arabi. I will speak more about him in chapter 6.

At the same time, Yenikapı was led by Doğani Ahmed Dede (1601–30), who succeeded in establishing contacts and attracting students from among the highest government officials. This might have had unintended negative consequences, as when Murad IV's ruthless Grand Vizier Mehmed Paşa, known as 'Sufi' created a bad reputation among the people for his cruelty. Nevertheless, the somewhat heterodox practices linked to Bektashiism were able to continue in Yenikapı, particularly under the following *postnişin*, Sabuhi Ahmed Dede (d. 1644).

The situation of the Mevleviye, along with the other dervish orders, became truly critical later in the seventeenth century, when the preacher Vani Mehmed Efendi – a sympathiser of the populist Kadizadeli movement – became tutor and sheikh to the mentally unstable Sultan Mehmed IV, with the support of Grand Vizier Fazıl Ahmed Paşa. In 1666 the Mevlevi *mukabele* ceremony was banned, the lodges were raided, and dervishes were murdered. This ban remained in effect for eighteen years, until 1684. This general ban probably had a negative effect on the transmission of the earlier *mukabele/ayin* compositions. Nevertheless, other sources show that this same sultan held the sheikh of Galata, Gavsi Ahmed Dede (d. 1697) in high regard, and he even issued an imperial decree (*hatt-i şerif*) prohibiting anyone from disturbing him (Ari 1995: 4).[3]

The deposition of Sultan Mehmed IV in 1687 hardly resulted in peace and tranquillity in the Ottoman capital, as the following short sultanic reigns and conflicts with Grand Viziers and generals resulted in the major Rebellion of 1703, which led finally to the accession of Sultan Ahmed III (1703–30).[4] But the Mevlevis no longer were the targets of oppression, as they had been between 1666 and 1684. Indeed, one of the most competent statesmen of the era, Köprülü Amcazade Hüseyin Pasha (1644–1702), was a Mevlevi *muhibb* (Shaw 1976: 225), whose private *meclis* gatherings were major cultural events (Abou El-Haj 1984: 89). It may be assumed that these meetings brought together major musicians from within the Mevlevi, other *tarikat*s, and more secular spheres, and contributed to the musical renaissance that occurred in the later seventeenth century.

From the late seventeenth century onward, three major historical tendencies among the Mevleviye are apparent: first, the increasing separation of Istanbul from the smaller and rural Mevlevi settlements in Anatolia; second, the rise of 'sheikhly' dynasties among the four major Mevlevihanes

---

[3] 'Gavsi Dede'ye kimse taarruz eylemesin'.
[4] On this tumultuous period, the classic work is Rifa'at Ali Abou-El-Haj, *The 1703 Rebellion and the Structure of Ottoman Politics*, Istanbul: Nederlands Historisch Instituut, 1984.

of Istanbul, which were de facto independent of the Çelebi in Konya; and third, increasing outreach to the Mevlevihanes of the Balkans and the Levant, in particular to Syria.

The 'long eighteenth century' thus became the era of maximum stability and influence of the Mevlevis throughout the Empire. Part of this stability most likely resulted from the establishment of a small number of sheikhly dynasties that shared in the leadership of all the Mevlevihanes of the capital, sometimes even uniting more than one under the hand of a single sheikh. Frequent marriages among members of these different dynasties often led to the moving of a member of one group into a *tekke* ruled by another. For example, the descendants of Eyyubi Memiş Dede (d. 1732) continued to provide sheikhs for Beşiktaş from 1669 until 1765 – almost a century. From the middle of the eighteenth century until the early years of the twentieth, Yenikapı was guided by descendants of Kütahyalı Ebubekir Dede (1705–75). He was the son of a Halveti sheikh of the Seyyid Nureddin line, yet he also attended talks with the famous Melami Zaim Ağa (Işın 1994: 429).

Two families originating in Tripoli (Trablusşam) in Syria and Lebanon came to dominate the Mevlevihanes of Kasımpaşa and Beşiktaş, and later, of Galata. One of these families consisted of descendants of Musa Safi Dede (d. 1774), who retained control of Kasımpaşa for half a century, from 1722 to 1787. The other was the family of Ahmed Dede (d. 1771), who oversaw first Beşiktaş, and then Galata, from the later eighteenth century to the middle of the nineteenth. Together they were known as the 'Arapzadeler', or 'The Arab Lineage'. Moving ahead to the nineteenth century, Ahmed Celaleddin Dede (1853–1946) from Gelibolu, did his *çile* training at the Mevlevihane of Cairo in 1873. He was then appointed sheikh of the Mevlevihane of Üsküdar, which was basically a *zaviye* housing Mevlevis from outside of Istanbul. Eventually he became the last sheikh of Galata (1910–25).

In addition to the political influence of the Mevlevi, the eighteenth century marked a high point for their involvement with the culture of Istanbul, especially music and poetry. As part of a general renaissance of Ottoman music, the Mevlevi *muhibb* Buhurizade Mustafa Itri (d. 1712) composed in all the elite musical genres, and produced one Mevlevi *ayin* (Segah).

The end of the prohibition of the *mukabele* was symbolised by his composition of the Naat-i Peygamberi in *makam* Rast as a Eulogy to the Prophet. This composition is sung to this day before every Mevlevi *mukabele*. He was also one of the principal music teachers of Prince Cantemir, who cites him as an authority. The only fragment of any of his compositions – a *peşrev* – written down in his lifetime appears at the end of Cantemir's notated Collection, appended to his *Book of the Science of Music* (Wright 2000; Feldman 1996, 2018).

Kutb-i nayi Osman Dede (1652–1730) displayed multifaceted activities. Born in Istanbul in 1652, he became a *neyzen* and then the Chief Neyzen (*neyzenbaşı*) of the Galata Mevlevihane. Osman married the daughter of the sheikh of the Galata Mevlevihane, Gavsi Dede. Upon Gavsi Dede's death, in 1698, Osman Dede was appointed sheikh of Galata, a post that he retained until his death in 1730. Apart from music, he was responsible for teaching Rumi's *Mesnevi*. He founded a sheikhly dynasty through his daughter's marriage to the sheikh of Yenikapı lodge, Ebubekir Dede (d. 1775). In the next generation, three of his grandchildren – Ali Nutki Dede (1762–1804), Abdülbaki Nasir Dede (1765–1820), and Abdürrahim Künhi Dede (1769–1831) became sheikhs of Yenikapı and major composers and music theorists. All three sons of Ebubekir Dede became the sheikhs of Yenikapı in turn. While all were excellent musicians, it was Abdülbaki Nasir Dede who combined the skills of *neyzen*, composer of Mevlevi *ayin*s, and creator of a sophisticated music theory and system of musical notation, which differed in principle from those of his grandfather, Osman Dede, and of Prince Cantemir. It was in this notation that he transcribed a Mevlevi *ayin* for the first time – the Suzidilara of Sultan Selim III (d. 1808) (Uslu, Doğrusöz, 2009).

Selim became a disciple of the poet Muhammed Said Galip Dede (d. 1799), known as 'Sheikh Galip', who trained in Yenikapı and was appointed sheikh of Galata in 1790, thus strengthening the relationship between the palace and the Mevlevihane. Galip was the most outstanding poet of the later eighteenth century, with his own *mesnevi*, *Hüsn ü Aşk* (Beauty and Love), which is considered one of the masterpieces of the entire Ottoman tradition. Işın sums up this period comprehensively:

The Mevlevism of Istanbul became an imperial *tarikat* that transmitted the rich cultural combinations of the Ottoman geography to the daily life of the city. Although its adherents came mainly from the upper classes, it was also widespread among the middle classes. The Mevleviye were in contact with other mystical movements, such as the Bektaşi, Nakşibendi, Halveti, Gülşeni,

Melami and Sadi, and exerted an influence upon them. From the other side, Mevlevism functioned as a school that produced the highest level practitioners of literature, calligraphy and music for the life of the city. (1994: 430)

The history of the Istanbul Mevlevihanes during the nineteenth century is better known through a variety of sources, and is also summarised by Lewis (2001). In particular Yenikapı emerges as a major support of the Tanzimat Reforms, which began in 1839. Osman Salaheddin Dede (d. 1887) guided this Mevlevihane for almost fifty years, and among his *muhibb*s were the two major architects of the Tanzimat, Fuad Pasha (d. 1868) and Ali Pasha (d. 1871). He was also a close friend of the major reformer Midhat Pasha (d. 1883). Naturally Yenikapı was kept under scrutiny by Sultan Abdülhamid II, and it was a centre for many supporters of the Young Turk movement under Sheikh Mehmed Celaleddin Dede (d. 1908). This political role for the Mevleviye came to an abrupt end two years into the Turkish Republic, with the decree no. 677, banning it, together with all other *tarikat*s.

In 1925, with the closing of the *tekke*s in the new Republic of Turkey, the centre of the Order was moved to Aleppo. While this situation was confirmed by the Mandatory Government, it was rescinded by the newly independent Syrian government in 1944. Today, the Syrian Mevlevi groups, while preserving the authentic Mevlevi dress and ritual turning, no longer practice the *mukabele*, its music, and Persian poetry. They have adopted the Arabic-language hymns of other Sufi orders. While they bear a historical relationship to the Mevleviye they are today a synthesis of several mainly local trends of Sufism, and no longer participate in a common Mevlevi culture.[5]

The Mevlevi Centres

While in theory the Çelebi resident in Konya appointed all *postnişin* (sheikhs) in other Mevlevihanes, by the later seventeenth century the rise of sheikhly dynasties, especially in Istanbul, put a certain de facto limit on this authority.

---

[5] Several highly revealing interviews with local dervishes in Aleppo (with some Mevlevi background) were undertaken in 2010 by Amar Chabib for his film *Wajd*. Most of these interviews were removed from the commercially distributed version of the film, released as *Wajd: Songs of Separation,* but still exist in an unpublished version.

Likewise, during periods of economic hardship, as Faroqui had found, even the Konya Asitane had to cut back on its ability to train new dervishes or to present the *mukabele* ceremony fully. But in general, those larger Mevlevi centres known as *asitane* throughout Anatolia and elsewhere in the Empire, were able to sustain themselves and their services. For the Anatolian *asitane*s an added factor tending toward their economic stability was their dual function as a saint's tomb. A good example was Karahisar, the burial place of Divane Mehmed Çelebi (d. 1529), who had served as sheikh there.

As described below, the basis for the Mevlevi training was the 1001-day retreat known as *çile*, which required a number of dervishes to conduct some of the cooking and daily tasks, as well as the *mukabele*, and to supervise the aspirants in their retreats and service to the *tekke*. The other Mevlevihanes were located in smaller towns or villages, and were known as *zaviye*. Within greater Istanbul, even Üsküdar functioned as a *zaviye* rather than an *asitane*, like Galata, Yenikapı, Kasımpaşa, and Beşiktaş. In Anatolia and Thrace, other *asitane*s were Kütahya, Manisa, Eskişehir, Kastamonu, Gelibolu, Edirne, Izmir, and Bursa. In Rumeli the most important *asitane* was Larissa/Yenişehir. A number of important *zaviye*s were founded during the later sixteenth century in the Balkans, principally Salonika, Filibe (Plovdiv), Üsküb (Skopje), Vidin, Niş, Saray-i Bosna (Sarajevo), as well as Buda, in Hungary. The latter ceased to exist following the retreat of the Ottomans in 1699. In the Arab world the same period saw the founding of *asitane*s in Cairo and Aleppo. However, the Haj pilgrimage and the caravan routes rendered a number of the *zaviye*s on the fringes of, or outside, Anatolia of major importance. Among these *zaviye*s were those at Antalya, Ayntab, Antakya, Baghdad, Cyprus, Tripoli, Damascus, Jerusalem, Mecca, and Medina. Although they were not equipped to train dervishes, these urban *zaviye*s retained their importance until the closing era of the Empire. However, starting in the seventeenth century many of the village *zaviye*s were gradually reduced to little more than part of the *vakf* basis for the maintenance of the larger centres, in addition to being centres of prayer and *sema* for the rural Mevlevi population.

The role of the major provincial Mevlevihanes such as Edirne, Izmir, and Salonika as centres of musical pedagogy is well documented. However, the lives of several major recent Turkish musicians, including the *tanbur* master Necdet Yaşar (1930–2017), the *kemençe* virtuoso Ihsan Özgen, and the vocalist Dr Allaeddin Yavaşça, point to a residual musical development in the southeastern regions of Kilis and Nizip, thanks to the Mevlevi *zaviye* in Kilis.

Women Sheikhs and Dervishes

The sources reveal a drastic deterioration in the status of women dervishes from the generations of Mevlana, his children, and grandchildren to the situation during the seventeenth century and thereafter. Rumi himself is frequently recorded as having conversed with women – both within his family and among his female followers – on serious topics. In the following generation, Eflaki notes that Sultan Veled's daughter Şerife Hatun was a sheikha with many dervishes. Another woman dervish from Konya, Arife-i Hoş Likaa, became a *halife* in Tokat, attracting many prominent male dervishes. Eflaki also records that Ulu Arif Çelebi conversed with women and allowed women dervishes to participate in his *sema* (Gölpınarlı 1953: 279).

Gölpınarlı concludes, on the basis of several early Mevlevi narrative sources, that 'Women became *khalifes*, and were considered greater than many of the men who became their dervishes' (279). These women wore the Mevlevi elements of dress – the *hırka* and *küllah* headgear – and led the *sema*, in which both men and women participated.

How can we interpret this remarkable situation? No doubt several factors must have been responsible. Some impetus surely came from decisions made by Rumi himself as well as by his son and grandson. There may also have been social factors originating in the status of women in earlier Turco-Mongol society. As I noted in a much earlier study of the Chaghatay-Timurid poet Navai, the female presence at the court of Sultan Husayn Bayqara (1459–1506) in Herat was quite prominent (Feldman 1999: 269–75). This finding accords with earlier research stressing the Turco-Mongolian heritage of the Timurids (Subtelny 1979; Manz 1992), in which women held a much more public role than was usually the case in the Arabic- or Persian-speaking areas within Islamdom.

Concretely, several Anatolian Alevi groups emphasise the equal participation and at time the centrality of women in their *semah* ceremony. Among Kurdish Ahl-e Haqq Sufis in Iran, women from sheikhly families might become leaders of the order even in the twentieth century. Thus, the role of women dervishes suggests that this Turkic heritage, along with other probably indigenous Anatolian and Kurdish features, may be relevant to the evolution of the Mevlevi *sema*. Specific kinetic relationships between some Alevi *semah* movements and the development of the Mevlevi *sema* will be outlined in the following chapter.

In Karahisar, Güneş Han, a fourth-generation descendant of Divane Mehmed Çelebi (d. 1529), became the sheikh and *halife* of this major Anatolian Asitane. A Mevlevi male poet named Dervish Yakiyn wrote the following poem of praise to her. To understand its imagery, we must recall that *güneş* is the Turkish word for 'sun':

> *Zihi saʾdüs-suʾud-i tali-u baht-i Güneş Hani*
> *Ki etti pertev-i lutfiyle ihvani sena-hani*

> Behold the joyous, felicitous sunrise of Güneş Khan!
> Whose radiance causes dervishes to sing the praises of her kindness.

> *Zihi şemʾ-i şebistan-i vilayet kim kerametle*
> *Pür etti dairen madar bezm-i heft eyvani*

> Behold the lamp of sainthood,
> Whose miracles illuminate every corner
> Of the feast 'neath the seven vaults!

> *Zihi nahl-i tecelli kim zuhur-i şuʾle-i sırrı*
> *Seray-i vahdet etti hankah-i heft erkani*

> Behold the date-palm of Divine Unveiling –
> The flame of her Secret turns the four-pillared convent
> Into a Palace of Divine Unity!

Güneş Khan proved to be among the last generation of female leaders of any of the Mevlevi *asitane*s or in the *sema*. Nevertheless, in the Kütahya Asitane women dervishes still maintained a degree of influence and respect into the eighteenth century. Thus we learn that the appointment of the noted poet Sakıb Dede (d. 1735) as sheikh of Kütahya was in part through the influence of Fatima Hanım, who came from the line of Küçük Arif Çelebi (d. 1421). Soon thereafter Sakıb married Fatıma Hanım's niece Havva Hanım. Thus, in

Kütahya several dynastic as well as cultural factors seem to have preserved the status of the women dervishes to a certain degree.

Elsewhere in Anatolia there is evidence for the literary creativity of women dervishes well into the nineteenth century. One of the rare published examples is the *divan* of Tevhide Hanım (1847–1901), a female dervish in the southwest Anatolian town Manisa. One of her surviving verses seems to reflect the loneliness of her position as a female dervish:

> *Geçip ağyar ü yarinden kılıp dil mülkünü tenha*
> *Yuyup gönülden masivayı devran surelim biz bize*

> We left both Beloved and the Other,
> In the Heart's realm we stand alone.
> Erasing from the Heart all but the One,
> Let us whirl around ourselves.
>
> (Pehlivan and Bayram (eds) (2007: 107)

In Istanbul and elsewhere, during the course of the seventeenth century and thereafter, the status of a woman sheikha seems to disappear from the sources, and from living memory. By the nineteenth century women sheikhs or *halifes* are unheard of, although women dervishes – in particular members of the families of sheikhs – still appear. But they were no longer welcome in the general *sema* ceremony, which they could only watch from a gallery or through a screen. All-female *mukabele* ceremonies within the harem seem to have occurred at times, but little concrete information survives about them.

The reasons for this social change are probably varied. The Mevlevi move to Istanbul, and their increasing contact with members of the Ottoman government – which became more pronounced during the seventeenth century – obligated the *tarikat* to observe more of the social norms current in the Ottoman court, at least on the level of gender. The purification of esoteric *batini* practices observed in the Galata Mevlevihane under Ismail Rusuhi Dede (d. 1631) may have also had a role in this increasing gender division (see chapter 6). The recovery from the period of violent attacks on dervishes between 1666 and 1684 – when the *sema* was banned – may also have pushed the Mevlevis in the direction of caution in the face of fundamentalist and populist rage.

The social and economic decline of much of Anatolia, which weakened many of the smaller Mevlevi *zaviye*s, may also have contributed to the extinction of earlier rural Turkish practices among them. In addition, the building of several *asitane*s and *zaviye*s in Arabic-speaking provinces, such as Syria, Iraq, and Egypt, and their increasing interaction with Konya and Istanbul, may well have induced the Mevlevi leadership to avoid gender practices that would appear anomalous in Arab society. But it is unlikely that the available sources will ever prove rich and detailed enough to answer this question in anything like a comprehensive manner.

Basis of Mevlevi Training and Education

At the beginning of the eighteenth century the sheikh of Kütahya, Mustafa Sakıb Dede (1652–1735), put down some of the basic principles of the Mevlevi path as well as a reconstruction of the history of the Mevlevi Order in his book *Sefine-i Nefise-i Mevleviyan*. He was also a major Mevlevi poet, who wrote *mesnevi*s dedicated to the *sema* and to the *ney*. He was a profound student of the works of the great Sufi philosopher Muhyiddin ibn-al-Arabi (1165–1240). Sakıb Dede was also apparently part of the movement of Mevlevi leaders working to combine this more esoteric philosophical interpretation of Islam with the more overtly Sunni practices of the Naqshibandi *tarikat*. In his book, he uses as a model Pir Adil Çelebi (d. 1460), who enunciated the basic doctrines and principles that would characterise the Mevleviye many centuries hence. Sakıb Dede expressed these as the 'Words' of Pir Adil Çelebi (Ambrosio et al. 2006: 95). The first six are attributed to the practices of Shams-i Tabriz, namely:

Ecstasy (*vajd*)
Joy (*safa*)
Spiritual Dance (*samā'*)
Spiritual State (*hal*)
Divine Attraction (*jazba*)
Love (*ashq*)

To these six principles Sakıb Dede added seven more, which he seems to have taken from the tradition of Pir Adil Çelebi. With the exception of the *samā'*, the terms attributed to Shams are much broader principles of the mystical life, rather than specific practices. The seven terms that Sakıb Dede sees as emanating from Adil Çelebi are concerned with applying these broad principles to a spiritual discipline:

Control of the Breath (*khush dar dam*)
Consciousness of the Gait (*nazar dar kadam*)
The Journey to the Spiritual Homeland (*safar dar vatan*)
Solitude within the Multitude (*khalvat dar anjuman*)
Remembrance (*yād kard*)
Return to God (*bāz gasht*)
Observation of the Self (*negah dāsht*)

No doubt it is for this reason that Adil Çelebi, who instituted much of the discipline actually put into practice within all the Mevlevihanes large enough to conduct full-time training, was considered to be the Second Saint (Pir-i Sani) of the Mevleviye. Indeed, the more formal organisation of the ecstatic *samā'* as the ritual of the *mukabele* was attributed to him.

Gölpınarlı (1953), and following him, Yazıcı (1964), describe the training of a Mevlevi dervish in some detail. The Mevlevi education and training had been structured according to a two-tiered system: on one tier, a more elementary discipline needed to become a novice or general follower of the Order, called a *muhibb* or *nev-niyaz*, and on the other tier, a more rigorous discipline whose mastery signified a fully trained dervish, known as a *dede*.

A *muhibb* could be initiated by going through a short ritual in which the sheikh placed the *sikke* headdress on his head and he submitted to training in the *adab ve erkan* (manners and rules) under the supervision of a *dede*. If he wanted to, the novice could learn *sema* and then come and participate in the *sema* ceremonies at the *tekke*, first going through the 'beginners *sema*' (*mübtedi mukabelesi*). If he possessed musical talent he could be instructed in playing the *ney*, the percussion instruments, and singing parts of the Mevlevi vocal repertoire.

In the case of a very young *muhibb* aspirant, his parents' consent would be obtained first. During the 1001-day period of *çile* he was not allowed to spend even one night away from the *tekke*; if he did so, this was known as *çile kırmak* (breaking the *çile*), and the novice would have to begin over again from day one. The novice was known as a *can* (soul), and he would be given over to one *dede* at the *tekke*, who was then responsible for his training and his behaviour. The training of the aspirant dervish had to maintain a balance between, on the one hand, his inner, spiritual development and increasing sensitivity to the needs of others on both the material and psychological levels and, on the other hand, his acquisition of a degree of relevant knowledge and mastery of the arts that were part of the spiritual path.

One aspect of the *çile* thus consisted of elementary service to the other dervishes, such as cooking, serving food, preparing the table, waiting at table, laundry services, shopping, and, finally, cleaning the latrines. In this way, a novice would learn the manners and conduct of the dervishes. This included everything from posture and speech to a broad delicacy and sensitivity to the feelings of others, and even a concern for inanimate objects – a book, a pen, a musical instrument, clothing, or opening and closing a door.

The novice's training proceeded in discrete stages. At the beginning he had to spend three days in the kitchen, seated on his knees, as he watched the dervishes going about their tasks. As he advanced to various levels over time, his *dede* and various dervishes intoned specific prayers and incantations connected with the Mevlevi Order. As Gölpınarlı pointed out (1953: 393), some of these show relations with incantations of the Bektashi Order, another old Anatolian Order with which the Mevleviye had interacted over centuries.

Another part of the novice's *çile* training consisted of both intellectual and musical instruction, as well as training in the *sema*. While music and singing depended largely on the innate talents of the novice, all novices were expected to advance in their basic Islamic literacy (in Qur'an and Hadith as well as law), and to acquire enough of the Persian language to understand the *Mesnevi*. If indeed they displayed talent in this latter sphere, they could eventually advance to the level of expounding the meaning of this foundational text. They might also be instructed in calligraphy, and in some times and places, in miniature painting, although this seems to have been much rarer.

When his 1001 days had been completed, the novice once again returned to his kneeling position in the kitchen. That night an elaborate candlestick with 35 or 70 branches was lit. A ceremony ensued, including the intoning of the ritual *gülbenk* of the Order. Then the novice was assigned a specific cell (*hücre*), which would be his. All the *dedes* visited him there, and left him various gifts. He did not leave his cell for the next three days. After this time the *meydancı dede* would bring him to the sheikh of the *tekke*, who performed various rituals and accepted his initiation (*bay'at*) into the Mevlevi Order. He then returned to his cell for another 18 days, for what is called the *hücre çilesi* (trial of the cell), during which he engaged in prayer and meditation. At the end of this period, the sheikh of the *tekke* dressed him and placed the tall hat (*sikke*) of the dervish upon his head; he had now acquired the status of dervish or *dede*. He would also be eligible to teach those skills at which he excelled to the incoming novices. Over time he might be chosen to become a sheikh or a *halife* of the Mevlevi Order.

3

DEVELOPMENT AND CULTURAL
AFFINITIES OF THE MEVLEVI *AYIN*

While the cultural significance of the Mevlevi Order was by no means confined to their musical ceremony, the *ayin-i şerif* held crucial importance within the life of the order, and was perhaps the most characteristic feature in shaping how the Mevlevis were viewed from the outside. This ceremony developed over the course of centuries, and many features can certainly not be traced back to the time of Mevlana himself, beyond a general preference for a mystical dance in which music and poetry both played a role. From the early descriptions of his circle and followers, it is clear that Mevlana's *samā'* was a spontaneous and ecstatic event. Even a superficial acquaintance with Mevlana's writings and biography raises doubt that he would have approved of his descendants many centuries later continuing to perform a faithful version of his mystical dance.

Musical sources on the ceremony per se do not predate the end of the eighteenth century. All other sources are either literary, artistic, or come from an oral tradition of musical transmission traceable in some form since the mid-seventeenth century, with the exception of a handful of somewhat earlier short musical transcriptions, which, of course, have great value. Several mystical tendencies were combined within the emerging Mevlevi Order and even within the separate Mevlevihanes of Anatolia and, later, of Istanbul. The seventeenth century was both a time of great creativity and political challenges for the Mevleviye, culminating in the prohibition of the *ayin-i şerif* ceremony for eighteen years, from 1666 to 1684. It is not unlikely that this blow, along with the general economic malaise of the era, which caused a reduction of musicians in the Mevlevi centres, may have caused the loss or fragmentary preservation of ceremonial music composed earlier. Nevertheless, this relatively brief period of economic dislocation and political repression was not sufficient to scatter the bearers of the Mevlevi tradition, nor to prevent them from maintaining a coherent mystical and musical practice.

The Possibility of a Historical Approach to the Mevlevi Ceremony

Musical and choreographic practices – loosely termed *samā'* (*Turkish: sema*) – were employed continuously from the lifetime of Jalaluddin Rumi in the thirteenth century up until the twentieth century. While certain technical questions concerning the development of these practices can be answered more or less empirically, in most cases a synthesis of available sources yields results that are more suggestive than conclusive. These sources include the following:

- Hagiographical writing about Mevlana and his immediate circle from shortly after his lifetime.
- Poetic works of a didactic and ideological nature that attempt to explain the deeper significance and symbolism of the Mevlevi practice, written from the beginning of the sixteenth to the eighteenth century and beyond.
- Visual depictions, beginning with internally produced Mevlevi and other Ottoman painting of the late sixteenth century and extending to European and Turkish painting of the eighteenth to early twentieth centuries.
- Written descriptions by European travellers, beginning in the seventeenth century.
- Early notated documents of the Mevlevi *ayin*.
- Early twentieth-century transcriptions in Western staff notation of the entire existing repertoire compiled by Turkish Mevlevi scholars.
- Broader comparisons with existing *sema* practices of rural Anatolian groups with a focus on movement.

Drawing on these sources, the following stable structure of the *mukabele* can be ascertained from the later eighteenth century onward:

1. *Na'at-i Peygamberi* (Hymn to the Prophet): a pre-composed rubato form
2. A *taksim* on the *ney* (*baş taksim*)

3. The Sultan Veled Devri, performed to a *peşrev* in the newer form of *usul devr-i kebir* (28/4)

4. The *ayin* proper and the turning of the *semazen*s, beginning with:

5. *Selam-i Evvel* [First Selam] in *usul devr-i revan* (14/8) or *düyek* (8/4)

6. *Selam-i Sani* [Second Selam] in *usul evfer* (9/4)

7. *Selam-i Salis* [Third Selam] beginning in *usul devr-i kebir* (28/4) and continuing in *usul sema'i* (6/8)

8. *Selam-i Rabi'* [Fourth Selam] in *usul evfer*

9. *Taksim* on the *ney*

10. *Son* (final) *peşrev* in *usul düyek*

11. *Son yürük sema'i* (6/8)

In the form it assumed from the early eighteenth century onward, the distinctive features of the *mukabele* include the following:

- The composer of an *ayin* was free to choose any *makam* or modulations from one *makam* to another. No *makam* was more typical of the *ayin* than another, and no particular *makam* was required for the constituent *selam*s. By the later seventeenth century an *ayin* that began the First Selam in a particular *makam*, and which consequently gave its name to the entire *ayin*, might then modulate into different *makam*s within each successive *selam*.

- Each *selam* was largely defined by its *usul*. A canonical series of selections from an older Persian and Turkic system of *usul* rhythmic cycles as well as the later Ottoman system of *usul* had to be employed for each *devir* or 'selam' in the *ayin-i şerif*.

- While the rhythmic (*usul*) system of Ottoman music underwent profound changes over the course of the eighteenth century, usually in the direction of tempo 'retardation' coupled with melodic 'elaboration', the Mevlevi *ayin* shows a preference for older and simpler forms of *usul*. The newer, expanded *usul*s make only very discrete appearances in specific sections of the *ayin* and the *mukabele* as a whole.

- Distinctive compositional techniques in each *selam* create irregular relationships between melody and *usul*.

- Unique compositional forms were created for each *selam*. None of these forms have close parallels in the courtly Ottoman repertoire.

- Within the *ayin*, a distinctive ordering of the *usul*s characterises each *selam*. Unlike in the courtly *fasıl*, these do not proceed from longer and slower *usul*s to shorter and quicker ones. Rather, the *ayin* displays an idiosyncratic series of transitions from short to long and back to short *usul*s.

- Certain archaic rhythmic and melodic patterns, and even specific melodies, are retained, particularly for the Second Selam and for the second part of the Third Selam. The Second Selam sometimes shows allusions and quotations from the Mevlevi repertoire extending from the middle of the nineteenth century back to the early seventeenth century.

Many of the distinctive features described above concern the rhythmic structure of the successive *selam*s within an *ayin*. Ottoman music as a whole contains an extremely rich and varied system of rhythms with a fixed number of beats. The resulting rhythmic cycles are called *usul*s, and they may be grouped into short, medium, and long categories. Each *usul* generally has a characteristic range of tempos. In the past century, by convention these have been expressed according to the choice of eighth, quarter, or even half notes. Thus the *usul devr-i revan* in the First Selam will be written as 14/8. The opening of the Third Selam had employed another fourteen-beat cycle played at half the speed of *devr-i revan*. This was known as *devr-i kebir*, the 'great cycle'. In the course of the eighteenth century and thereafter, a process of rhythmic 'retardation' developed, so that an original medium tempo *usul devr-i kebir*, which could be written in Western notation as 14/4, gradually expanded to the point that it might be expressed as 14/2. As the melody over the *usul* became more elaborate and longer, and the tempo still slower, it became accepted to write the *usul* pattern – and the melody composed over this pattern – as 28/4. This issue will be discussed in more detail in chapter 7.

Perhaps the most obvious distinctive feature of the *ayin* is that it is predominantly a vocal genre, composed by a single Mevlevi composer. The instrumental *peşrev* preceding it (now used for the Sultan Veled Devri procession) and the final *peşrev* are less integral to the musical genre of the *ayin*. Both of these *peşrev*s were sometimes taken from non-Mevlevi sources. Nevertheless, unlike the *peşrev*s, the instrumental *sema'i* melodies that appear later in the *mukabele*, in the *Selam-i Salis* (Third Selam) and *son yürük sema'i*, may be of considerable antiquity, hence they probably point to an early stage in the development of the Mevlevi *sema*.

The instrumental *peşrev*s used in the processional section of the *mukabele* share only a single characteristic: they must be composed in the *usul devr-i kebir* in 14/4 or 28/4. Some, but not all, of these *peşrev*s were composed by Mevlevi musicians specifically for the *mukabele*. But the *peşrev*s could be replaced with relative ease. For example, in Rauf Yekta's 1931 edition of the Beyati Ayin of Mustafa Dede, the *selam*s are preceded by a *peşrev* attributed to the sixteenth-century *mehter* musician Nefiri Behram. But by the time of Heper's edition (1979), this non-Mevlevi composition had been replaced by the famous *peşrev* of Emin Dede Yazıcı (d. 1945).

In addition, Qur'anic recitation (*tecvit*, *tajwid*) and Sufi hymns (*ilahi*) may be performed, but these are not part of the musical structure of the *ayin*. Apart from the *peşrev*, the other components of the *ayin* had been in place since the later sixteenth or early seventeenth centuries.

According to the more recent Mevlevi tradition, which was established in the mid to late eighteenth century, following the *baş-taksim* the dervishes assemble for the Sultan Veled Devri to a *peşrev* in the modern form of *devr-i kebir* (see Feldman 2001). This procession was followed by the music of the *ayin* proper, beginning with the First Selam, usually in the rapid *usul devr-i revan* in 14/8. This First Selam is the longest individual section of the *ayin*, and, as such, offers an extended demonstration of the techniques and the vision of the composer. The Second Selam (*selam-i sani*) of the 'ancient' Pençgah and Dügah Ayins is in *usul evfer*, which uses nine beats, written today as 9/4. The use of this moderate *usul* in the Second Selam is preserved in all subsequent *ayin*s. The Second Selam is considerably shorter than the first. *Evfer* was considered a lighter *usul*, and it was commonly used in the Persianate *naqsh* (Turkish: *nakış*) genre. After the end of the seventeenth century, *evfer* was no longer used in the courtly *fasıl*. Thus its permanent position in the Second Selam indicates that the model had to have been created before, and, in all likelihood, considerably before, that time. Looking for a probable model for this rhythmic usage, we may note that *evfer* is also the *usul* of the folk dance known since the nineteenth century as *zeybek*, which is widespread throughout southwestern parts of Anatolia, from the Aegean to a considerable way inland, including Karahisar, an old Mevlevi centre. But since *zeybek* does not appear in earlier Ottoman musical descriptions, or even in the notations of folksongs in various languages by Ali Ufuki Bey (in Paris Turc 202; see Haug 2019), this is not a likely source of the usage in the Second and Fourth Selams. In the later sixteenth and seventeenth centuries, however, the *naqsh* might have texts in either Persian or Turkish, and thus served as a link between these musical cultures (Wright 1991). Thus, the Mevlevi preference for *usul evfer* may reflect a connection to the secular vocal form *naqsh*, in which it had been a common rhythmic cycle. The Second Selams of the unattributed Dügah Ayini, Beyati Ayin of Mustafa Dede, and Saba Ayin of Ismail Dede are discussed in more detail in an online appendix, 'Note on the Second Selam' (website).

The Third Selam (*selam-i salis*) is always created from two *usul* cycles, the first usually in a form of *devr-i kebir* in 14 or 28 beats, which changes, sometimes with a short instrumental transition, to the second – an ancient Turkic Sufi rhythm known as *sema'i*, in 6/8. This transition is always introduced by a hymn in the Turkish language. Thus, in the *sema'i* section of the Third Selam, an ancient compositional nucleus has been preserved. This fragment of antiquity is repeated in every *ayin* composition of whatever historical period from the later seventeenth century onward, and is used as the introduction to an increasingly complex and sophisticated musical development. I will discuss this development at length in chapter 9.

The Fourth Selam (*selam-i rabi*) employs the same *evfer usul* as the Second Selam, and often the same text as well. It is generally the shortest *selam* of the *ayin*, and may, with small variations, reprise the Second Selam. These short and restrained melodies in the *evfer usul* in a moderate tempo lead directly into the final *ney taksim*. In modern practice this forms a striking, transcendental moment, as the *semazens* continue to whirl, but without the support of any rhythmic structure, to the flowing melody of the *taksim*.

The notated *ayin*s as they exist today constitute a rich field for stylistic and structural analysis. In the following paragraphs, I offer some general observations about the characteristics of the *ayin* and certain features of its musical transmission. Musical features of the *ayin* are presented more fully in chapters 7–9.

The movement (*sema*) performed during the music of the *ayin* is a smooth rotation that is essentially the same in each *selam*. It does not include any dance-like steps that would need to be synchronised with the rhythmic cycle (*usul*) of each *selam*. The arm position is likewise constant and does not vary from *selam* to *selam*. This forms yet another large contrast with the *zikr* practices of other Turkish Sufi orders. In these, although there is no 'dance' step per se, the overall body movement and breathing are synchronised with the rhythm and tempo. This feature is charmingly suggested in the poem by the Halveti poet Dai (d. 1659), praising the *tekke* musician Zakiri Hasan (Feldman, in Lifchez 1992: 191):

> He is the joy of the people of rhythm;
> He is the truth of the people of Union.

The rhyme juxtaposes *ehl-i usul* (people of rhythm) and *ehl-i vusul* (people of [Divine] Union) thus suggesting how the sensual intoxication of music and rhythmic movement may, under the proper conditions, lead to divine ecstasy. It is not at all unlikely that the earliest Mevlevi *sema* had a similar approach. But even in Dai's generation, the far greater complexity of the rhythmic cycles used in the Mevlevi *sema* probably suggested a more internalised practice.

The clearest summary of the extant sources on the earliest period was provided by Evrim Binbaş (2001: 67–71). These include Faridun bin Ahmad Sipahsalar (d. 1312), who presented a description of the *samā'* of Mevlana and his immediate circle of followers. This Persian text includes a brief characterisation of the physical movements and their spiritual significance. Sipahsalar's primary interest is in the latter. He begins by stating that 'All the movements emanating from the mystics during the *samā'* symbolise a point or a truth' (Binbaş 2001: 68). This joining of the 'point' (*noqta*) with 'Truth' (*haq*) will be taken up prominently by Divane Mehmed Çelebi in his writing on *samā'* almost two centuries later. Sipahsalar mentions four movements of the *samā'* by name: *charkh zadan* ('whirling' or 'circling'), *jahadan* (jumping), *pā kuftan* (stamping the foot) and *dast afshāndan* (opening the arms). The latter movement seems to be connected with 'embracing a saint' (*aziz*) and 'dancing together' (2001: 69).

In a general sense 'whirling' and 'opening the arms' still characterise the Mevlevi *sema*. But at least since the end of the eighteenth century, the *sema* has no place for 'jumping' or 'stamping the foot'. Eflaki's *Menakib al-'Arifin* contains several similar descriptions (Yazıcı 1964: 135–50). These references collectively offer strong evidence that the *sema*, as it has been known in recent centuries, has some continuities but predominantly, many differences from the *samā'* of the first generations after Mevlana. A partly similar collection of movements is mentioned in a later text, the Turkish-language *Risale fi Beyan al-Sema'*, preserved in more than one fifteenth-century manuscript, but attributed to the early Turkish Sufi poet Aşik Paşa (1272–1333). In this treatise rhythmic bodily movement emerged out of the 'divine melodies' (*nağamat-i Ilahiye*). These melodies had twelve pitches (*oniki perde*), and four movements, or 'dances' (*oyun*), emerged out of these twelve notes: *çarh* ('whirling' or 'circling'); *raks* ('vibrating' or 'dance' in general); *mu'allak* (hanging), and *pertav* (jumping). These four types are subsequently connected with the four seasons.

The 'whirling' (in Sipahsalar, *charkh zadan*) is still part of Mevlevi practice, under the same term in its Turkish form: *çarh atma*. But the other three terms probably are unrelated to modern usage; nor is the nature of 'hanging' entirely clear. At that point in the text a mystic 'clad in blue' (*sufi-i azrak-puş*) enters the dance, thus leaving little doubt about the Sufistic environment the author is describing. Since Aşık Paşa was a grandson of the famous Turkish Sufi Baba Ilyas, these movements may form part of the common heritage originally shared by the followers of Mevlana and other Anatolian Sufi movements, very likely including the Qalandari. As Ahmet Yaşar Ocak stated succinctly:

> A cette époque, la Kalenderiyya trouva des conditions favorable parmi les Turcs d'Asie Centrale, notamment en Transoxiane, et s'y répandit assez vite. Elle n'a connu presque aucune difficulté, grâce à son caractère syncrétiste, pour s'adapter au milieu turc; et au début du XIII siècle, plusieurs baba turcomans, derviches hétérodoxes, s'étaient déjà faits kalenderis. (Ocak, in Popovic and Veinstein, 1995: 56)

On the other hand, the greater centralisation of the Mevlevi Order, especially during the fifteenth century, led to an increasing formalisation of the *sema*, in contradistinction to earlier Qalandari practices. Gölpınarlı had posited that the formalisation of the *sema* into the *ayin* was the work of Adil Çelebi (d. 1460), who was awarded the title of Pir, generally given to the founder of a dervish order, because of his establishment of a fixed ritual for the Mevlevi *sema*.

The major poetic description of the Mevlevi *sema* by Divane Mehmed Çelebi (d. 1529), which appears later in this chapter, divides the ceremony into three sections, called *devir*s, a term that he also used in connection with, but not synonymously with, *selam* (see below in this chapter). This division into sections assumes a degree of formalisation in the structure of the *mukabele*. Divane Mehmed was a major propagandist for the Mevleviye, similar in that respect to Ulu Arif Çelebi two centuries earlier. Hence it is not unlikely that Mehmed Çelebi put some of his ideas about the *sema* into practice, either in Istanbul or in Karahisar, where he was the sheikh. Some sources credit the seventeenth-century Hüseyin Çelebi (d. 1666) with putting the *mukabele* into something close to its present form (Inançer 1994: 420).

The division of the *ayin* into four sections is only securely documented since the early eighteenth century – in the *mecmua* anthology of 1704 and in the *Sefina-yi Nefise-yi Mevleviyan* (The Elegant Ship of the Mevlevis) of Sakıb Dede (d. 1735).[1] The latter claims to have found this information in a fourteenth-century treatise by Celalüddin Ergun Çelebi (1301–73), sheikh of Kütahya, and a descendant of Mevlana's granddaughter Abide Mutahhara Hatun. However, Görpınarli reasonably asserts that this is a misattribution (Binbaş 2001: 71). Due to the centralised nature of the Mevlevi Order it would seem that once new practices became established in Konya and Istanbul they were instituted in all Mevlevi *tekke*s throughout the Empire. We do not have access to the details of this process, however. It must be stressed that the changes and evolution within the *mukabele* and the music of the *ayin* represent an internal Mevlevi process in which the order relied on its own resources to alter its practices according to the perceived needs of the times. Neither in their music nor in their *sema* were the Mevlevis dependent on any external dominant influence or model, except to the extent that they shared some of the Qalandari and other Anatolian Sufi practices mentioned above. But in time, even these practices underwent deep transformations.

I take as a working hypothesis that the underlying symbolism of the *mukabele*, its expression in the use of space, the physical movement within the *sema*, and its musical accompaniment, all developed to a certain extent independently. They interacted in various ways over time, and under the influence of several major Mevlevi leaders, within the separate traditions of a number of Mevlevi centres. Despite the ultimate authority of the Çelebi in Konya, it would be an anachronism to attribute all the modern Mevlevi practices even to such major figures as Pir Adil Çelebi or Divane Mehmed Çelebi. In order to reach the form of the *mukabele* that has been known since

---

[1] Konya Müzesi. Dated Zilhicce 1114 (1704).

the nineteenth century, many generations of development were needed, and a gradual consensus had to be reached.

In this connection it is best to treat the movement within the *sema* separately from its musical structure, as the kinds of available evidence are different, though at times with a degree of overlap. I will also present some evidence for the internal symbolism of the ceremony, as developed by Mevlevi thinkers.

Movement within the *Sema*

We are fortunate in having several Ottoman paintings of the *sema* dating from the later sixteenth century. The earlier is the 'Visit to Hazret-i Mevlana in Konya', from the *Nusretname* by Mustafa Ali, dated 1581. This lavish edition of the 'Book of Victories' contains one miniature of the *sema* as performed in the Mevlevi Asitane in Konya. In the upper section of the painting, Mustafa Ali, the author of the book (written on his figure as '*müellif-i kitab*') is seen presenting it to his patron Lala Mustafa Paşa (d. 1580), while the Mevlevi Celebi apparently is speaking to them.

The elegant painting shows twelve dervish *semazen*s performing the *sema* to the music of a *mutrıp* ensemble, who are seated on their knees in a corner. The *mutrıp* consist of two *neyzen*s, one *kudümzen* and the *ayinhan* (vocalist), who is also playing the *daire;* naturally enough the *ayinhan*'s head is turned toward the *neyzen*s. This ensemble is a smaller version of the *mutrıp* that was actually documented in the Asitane records, which, even then, had only a single *ayinhan* and a single *kudümzen* (Faroqui 1988). Very likely this slight reduction was caused only by the overall layout of the picture, which needed to accommodate the 12 *semazen*s. Especially with the figure of Mustafa Paşa, this would seem to be a depiction of the kind of formal *ayin-i şerif* where a visiting dignitary was present.

It is most remarkable that none of the *semazen*s hold their arms in the currently accepted posture of '*lam alif*', with arms extended and the right palm turned upward and the left downward.

In the miniature, the central dervish figure, wearing a shawl over his shoulders, appears to be the *semazenbaşı*. The movements of the dervishes are depicted with great care and individuality. All of the *semazen*s are wearing a form of the basic Mevlevi robe; but seven are in brown, two in blue, two in white and one in a kind of grey. Such variety was not known in later centuries.

Image 3.1 'Visit to Hazret-i Mevlana in Konya', from the *Nusretname* by Mustafa Ali (1581). Topkapı Sarayı Müzesi (H1365), 36a.

Image 3.2 Performance of the Mevlevi *sema* with 'standard' posture, Galata Mevlevihanesi. Photo by Ara Güler. Courtesy of Ara Güler Doğuş Sanat ve Müzecilik AŞ.

One dervish (on the lower right) actually has his arms folded before him. Another is holding his right and left hands, while his elbows extend outward. One dervish holds his right hand upward, while two extend their left. Two of the dervishes appear to be clapping their hands to the music. One of the dervishes has removed his *sikke* headgear, and holds it in his left hand. It would seem that the artist chose to depict the most ecstatic moment toward the end of the ceremony – perhaps while the final *sema'i* melodies were being performed. While a certain amount of individuality in the movements of the *semazen*s might be explained by artistic licence, from the perspective of modern practice, there is a striking disconnect between the evident familiarity of the *mutrıp* ensemble and the near total exoticism of the *semazen*s' motions. The subject was not a provincial *Mevlevihane* where, in this period, there may still have been female *semazen*s or other particular or idiosyncratic practices, but rather the central Asitane in Konya. As most of the Mevlevihanes of Istanbul had not yet been built, this Asitane was still the most established Mevlevi centre in every way. We cannot know for sure whether the artist had seen the ceremony in Konya, and the Mevlevis were not yet prominent in Istanbul.

As noted in chapter 2, the Mevlevi-Kalenderi *tekke* in Fatih had been closed, Galata was in Halveti hands during this period, and neither Yenikapı nor Beşiktaş *tekke*s had yet been founded. Still, some form of the Mevlevi *sema* was apparently performed in a number of places within the capital. And it is unlikely that Mustafa Ali himself, who had been to Konya, would have approved of a grossly inaccurate depiction of the *sema*. Thus the total absence in this painting of the posture of the Mevlevi *sema*, as it was known in later centuries and as it is still known today, suggests that such postures had not yet been instituted. This absence may also offer indirect affirmation of the tradition that attributes to Hüseyin Çelebi the formulation of the *mukabele* in something like its present form. Incidentally, this sheikh passed away in Konya in the same year (1666) that the Mevlevi *sema* was prohibited by the Ottoman state. But this was over two generations later than Lala Mustafa Paşa and Mustafa Ali's viewing of the *sema* in Konya.

Another nearly contemporary painting, in the *Sevakib-i Manakib* from 1599, is of a different character for two reasons. First, it was painted by Mevlevis in Ottoman Baghdad, and second, it attempts to depict the *samā'* in the time of Mevlana.

That the model for the painting comes from earlier phases of Sufism can be seen from the character and even the postures of the musicians: there is one *neyzen*, two *dairezen*s, but no *kudüm*, and no one is clearly an *ayinhan*. And, perhaps most significantly, they are all standing. Mevlana is depicted as the tallest figure in the middle, wearing a turban around his *sikke*. The other five dancing figures are wearing *sikke*s, but otherwise there are no Mevlevi costumes. Rather, the figures are dressed in Persian outer robes, with their characteristic long sleeves. During their dance, several of them wave their arms, with their sleeves covering their hands entirely, something that is completely unacceptable to later Mevlevi practice. We cannot, of course, be certain about the Mevlevi customs in Baghdad during the period of Ottoman rule in the sixteenth century. It is not impossible that some earlier Iranian Sufi practices of the *sema* may have persisted there. But it would seem more likely that the artist was not attempting to portray contemporary Mevlevis, but, true to the goal of the Sevakib text, to 'reimagine' Mevlana's *samā'* in Konya more than three centuries earlier. For purposes of this study, it is the painting from the *Nusretname* of 1581 that most reliably illustrates

Image 3.3 A *samā'* scene during the lifetime of Mevlana. *Tercüme-i sevakıb-i menakıb* (The Shining Stars of the Feats of the Mystics), fol. 21v. Probably Baghdad between 1590 and 1599. The Morgan Library & Museum. MS M. 466. Purchased by J. Pierpont Morgan (1837–1913) in 1911.

Image 3.4 A *samā* during the leadership of Rumi's successor, Husam al-Din, *Tercüme-i sevakıb-i menakıb* (The Shining Stars of the Feats of the Mystics), fol. 159r. Probably Baghdad between 1590 and 1599. The Morgan Library & Museum. MS M466, fol. 159r. Purchased by J. Pierpont Morgan (1837–1913) in 1911.

the development of the Mevlevi *sema* movement in Ottoman times. Another painting in the Sevakib depicts a *sema* session in the time of Hüsameddin, Mevlana's successor (in Elias 2017: 192).

Interestingly, the *mutrıp* ensemble seems more formal – there is an *ayin-han*, they are seated, and there is also an oud among them, but the *ney* is absent. All musicians and the *semazen*s appear in the tall headwear known as the Mevlevi *sikke*, but no other elements of later Mevlevi costume. The motions of the six *semazen*s are as broadly ecstatic as in the previous painting; two of the dancers even hug one another affectionately, and one waves his *sikke* in the air. These delightful paintings from Baghdad would seem to be the Mevlevi present imagining the Mevlevi past.

Before describing the later tradition of the Mevlevi *sema*, I should note the enigmatic position of the ecstatic movement of the Alevi *sema* (or *semah*) within this entire complex. The groups known as 'Alevi' in Anatolia share a tradition that combines elements of Sufism, especially in its Qalandari manifestation, Shiism, and, probably, earlier Gnostic movements, perhaps in Christian form. Links were established between these rural and tribal Turkish groups and the Bektashi *tarikat* already in Ottoman times. Both revere the figure of Haci Bektaş Veli (1209–71), a major Turkish saint who had probably emigrated from Khorasan to Anatolia and was a contemporary of Mevlana Rumi. A different lineage of the Alevi-Bektaşi movement can be traced through the Guran-Yarsan-Ahl-e Haqq complex of Iranian Kurdistan and Northern Iraq. As Martin van Bruinessen showed with his suggestively titled article 'When Haji Bektash Still Bore the Name of Sultan Sahak' (in Popovic and Weinstein: 1995), through their belief in reincarnation, these Kurdish groups see the Turkish saint as an 'avatar' of their own founder Sultan Sahak. Sultan Sahak is shrouded in even more legend than is Hacı Bektaş. Moreover, his name is Armenian – only in that language does 'Sahak' stand in for Yitskhaq (Isaac); it is not the Islamic form 'Ishaq'. This in turn suggests origins among the Paulician Gnostic heretics within Armenian Christianity, who had flourished in Eastern Anatolia between the seventh and middle of the ninth century, before the arrival of the Seljuq Turks.

What can be documented today is the choreographic practices of the various Alevi groups in modern Turkey. They term their ritual movement *semah*. While the many subgroups are independent of one another, some common features include a dance-like movement around a circle of individual male and female 'couples'. In certain groups a single female occupies the centre of the circle. What is most striking in the context of the fourteenth-century descriptions of the Sufi *sema* in Persian and Turkish quoted above is the centrality of the positions named *charkh zadan* ('circling' or 'whirling') and *dast afshandan* ('opening the arms') to the female participants. For example, among the Alevis of Hubyar, near Tokat (in North Central Anatolia), the women practise a continual whirling motion, with their arms lifted upward.[2] The male movement is quite different, featuring sharp flailing motions of both arms without the constant whirling. It is perhaps not too far a stretch to recognise a kindred motion to the widespread Persian visual depictions of 'dancing' Sufis, and even to the Baghdad *Sevakib-i Menakib* from 1599. This consanguinity also accords with Ahmed Sipahsalar's linking of the Mevlevi *sema* practices to Şems-i Tebrizi, described in chapter 2 (Binbaş 2001: 68).

Western European Sources

Western European travellers of the seventeenth and eighteenth centuries left several verbal and visual descriptions of the *mukabele* as they had seen it in Istanbul, which are crucial in establishing a chronology for the development of the ceremony. As Bülent Aksoy (1994) has stressed, in this broad period European observers still had a real curiosity about and even admiration for certain forms of Ottoman music. Among these the ritual music and *ney* playing of the Mevleviye were usually among the most appreciated. This is particularly true of the Italian and French travellers, whose countries often had close relations with the Ottoman State. As Aksoy also notes, it would be most inaccurate to attribute the growing 'colonialist' and 'Orientalist' attitudes that developed during the nineteenth century to earlier observers, particularly from these two Mediterranean countries. That said, contemporaneous use of the 'Turk' as a figure in eighteenth-century European opera, even in France and Italy, usually admitted very little input from evidence provided by travellers. Here the 'Turk' was an established figure of exoticism

---

[2] I thank Judit Frigyesi Niran for pointing out this striking similarity, on the basis of many YouTube videos of the Hubyar Alevis that she had collected.

within a long Christian and European tradition. In a sense this use of the Turk corresponded to the occasional appearance of Western European figures in Ottoman burlesque performances, such as the Album of Ahmet I (ruled 1603–17) from the earlier seventeenth century. In these performances, the serene entertainment of the Ottomans contrasts with the boisterous performance of figures wearing tight leggings, slippers and conical European hats with brims. The dancers' faces are hidden by masks with long noses, moustaches and beards, while their hands gesture nervously.[3] These dancing figures are probably meant to represent Italians, whose speech gestures were seen perhaps to be as comical to their Turkish contemporaries as they would later be to Anglo-Saxon observers. Thus, we should not confuse these internally-focused representations of the 'Other' – whether Christian or Muslim – with eyewitness reports of travellers, whose information was held in some esteem by important segments of their home public.

Several European travellers of the seventeenth century, such as the English comical writer Thomas Coryate (1577–1617), the Roman composer and musicologist Pietro della Valle (1586–1652), and the French merchant Jean Antoine Sieur du Loir, describe a sequence of movements during the Mevlevi ceremony that include the rapid turning motion of the *sema* divided into several discrete sections. Of these, the most precise description, published in 1654, was written by Sieur du Loir, who had accompanied the French ambassador de la Haye to Istanbul in 1639. Sieur du Loir attended a Mevlevi ceremony, probably in Galata, and noted the following key points:

> The giver of the sermon then sings some verses from the Kuran. After the sermon ends, the singers and *ney* players who are seated on a gallery, similar to the one used for the organ in churches, begin to sing the hymns . . . The ceremony begins with the beating of the drum.

> The sheikh is at the *qibla*, seated on a decorated camel skin. As soon as the second section begins, he puts his hands together and all the dervishes stand on their feet. The one who is closest to the sheikh goes to him and stands, he

---

[3] Ettinghausen, Eyuboğlu and Ipşiroğlu, *Turkey: Ancient Miniatures,* New York: New York Graphic Society, 1961: Pl. 26); Feldman 1996: 155.

bows to the ground and greets the sheikh with his head, and then begins to whirl with such speed that the eye cannot follow it. Those behind follow him, and thus thirty or forty dervishes repeat the same motion. After this circular dance goes on for seven or eight minutes, the one who began the dance makes a sign and suddenly stops. The dervishes stand in place without moving a muscle, waiting for a new sign from the sheikh. This dance which stops and begins again four or five times, can go on for over an hour, as the dervishes' breathing expands and the rhythm speeds up. For this practice the dervishes wear wide skirts, similar to what women wear in France, which expand in the air as they turn. (Sieur du Loir 1654; Aksoy 1994: 35–6)

Sieur du Loir's detailed description from 1639 would appear to be the earliest confirmation of the existence of a *mukabele* ceremony and 'dance' movement that more or less resembles later practices. The prescribed behaviour of the *semazenbaşı* in relation to the sheikh (*postnişin*) and the other dervishes is indeed a close predecessor of the movements known from the nineteenth century. The special architectural space for the *mutrıp* ensemble is evidently an innovation within seventeenth-century Istanbul. In particular, the author's eloquent depiction of the *semazenbaşı*'s whirling 'at such speed that the eye cannot follow it' would seem to be a close antecedent of the turn as it was known to Mevlevis in the twentieth century. This is no longer the older Sufi *charkh zadan* and *dast afshandan*, which could fit older Mevlevi practice as well as current (female) Alevi ritual movement. It is rather a highly specialised technique, requiring years of training. On the other hand, the author's words about the visible exhilaration of the *semazen*s toward the end of the *mukabele* is confirmed by both the earlier Ottoman and somewhat later European visual depictions. Perhaps the only item that might be questioned is the dance stopping and starting 'four or five' times, where we would expect only four distinct cycles. But du Loir, who could distinguish cycles of 'seven or eight' minutes was evidently a keen observer. Another important detail that can be gleaned from du Loir's description is that the whirling to the separate *devir* sections of the *ayin* began immediately following the *ney taksim*. There is no Sultan Veled Devri, the circumambulation to the music of an instrumental *peşrev*. As explained in chapter 7, the existence of such a movement seems extremely unlikely until the fundamental decrease in tempo in instrumental music began to assert itself in the course of the eighteenth century.

Among the clearest of the early European visual sources for the *mukabele* is the gravure of Jean-Baptiste van Mour completed in 1712. Van Mour had been commissioned by Charles de Ferriol, the French Ambassador to the Ottoman Empire between 1699 and 1711. This artistic and frequently reproduced print faithfully shows the *mutrıp* gallery of Galata, with the *neyzen*s peering down at the *semazen*s below. The scene is fairly tumultuous, most probably a depiction of the final *sema'i* section of the Third Selam, with the *semazen*s moving their arms in various manners, particularly the *dast afshandan* with open arms, among other positions. Several of these actually resemble the Ottoman painting from the *Nusretname*, rather than current practice. Recall that the extremely rapid whirling of the *semazen*s was noted by du Loir already in 1639, hence these loose postures could not have characterised the entire *mukabele*.

Image 3.5 *Les dervich[e]s dans leur Temple de Péra, achevant de tourner*, Jean-Baptiste Vanmour, in Charles Ferriol, *Recueil de cent estampes représentant différentes nations du Levant*, Paris, 1714. The Miriam and Ira D. Wallach Division of Art, Prints and Photographs: Art & Architecture Collection, The New York Public Library. The New York Public Library Digital Collections. https://digitalcollections.nypl.org/items/510d47d9-69c7-a3d9-e040-e00a18064a99

Spatial Structure and Movement

Apart from any architectural beauty of the medieval stone or the post-eighteenth-century wooden Mevlevihanes, the most crucial feature of the space of the Mevlevi performance – the *semahane* – was the division of the floor into two sections. The line between them was known as the *hatt-ı istivâ*, the 'equator line', extending from the edge of the post to the entrance door, which divided the *semahane* into two halves and which no one except the sheikh could walk on (Tanrıkorur 2004). This line was never painted, but was rather imaginary – in Mevlevi terms '*mevhum*'. At one end was the *mihrab* and the sheikh's mat (*post*). At the other end stood the outer door of the *tekke*. Symbolically the side of the *semahane* with the *mihrab* and post represented the Divine; the other end near the door represented the human. At the exact middle of the 'equator line' was the pole, or *kutb*. This was the place of the Perfect Human (Insan-i Kamil), here represented by the sheikh, the *postnişin*. The following descriptions of the spatial movement of the *sema* will always refer to these fixed positions.

In the developed movement of the *sema*, the arms and hands have the following fixed positions:

1. The opening and closing of the *sema*, with arms folded over the chest and the two hands touching the shoulders. This is the *niyaz* position that can lead into a ritualised bowing.
2. Before the beginning of the *sema* movement the hands are pointed downward.
3. The elbows are brought upward with the hands still pointing downward.
4. The backs of either hand are rubbed to the sides of the face.
5. The arms are stretched outward, with the right palm turned upward, and the left facing downward. This position is known as '*lam-alif*', standing for '*La Illahe ilallah*' (*There is no god but God*), and is the standard arm position for the movements of the *sema*. Throughout the *sema* the eyes of the *semazen* must be focused on the downward-turned left thumb (Tanrıkorur 2004: 33).

The foot position corresponding to (1), *niyaz* or entreaty, is the *ayak mühür-leme*, the 'sealing of the feet', leading into the bowing of the head. The foot positions for each part of the revolution of the *semazen* are entirely fixed, and indeed are part of their prolonged training, formerly within the *çile* period. In this training the big toe and the second toe of the left foot 'hugged' a nail that had been inserted into the floor of the training space of the *tekke*. During the entire revolution these two toes had to remain in contact with the nail, so that the aspiring *semazen* would not lose his (or her) balance. Incidentally throughout the last centuries of the Mevleviye, this barefoot practice during the *sema* training was continued in the actual *sema*. The light ritual prayer boots (*mest*) used in today's public performances of the *ayin* were not part of the Mevlevi practice of the *sema* in any documented period.

Only the general postures indicated by these arms and leg movements are in evidence in Van Mour's gravure of 1712, certainly not the specific directions of the two hands. By the end of the century, however, all of the representations, such as d'Ohsson's, in 1790, depict both the *niyaz* posture and sometimes the *lamalif*, but not entirely consistently with each *semazen*. Perhaps the visual representation with the most exact correspondence to modern Mevlevi practice is the early twentieth-century postcard depicting the *semahane* of Cairo, after a well-known painting by Edward William Lane (d. 1876).

Image 3.6 Postcard of the *Semahane* of Cairo. Painting by Edward Lane (1801–76).

While it is certainly possible that some of the vagueness in the depictions of the hands of the *semazen*s may be due both to artistic licence and to lack of attention to detail, it is also very likely that ritualisation and uniformity of every movement of the *sema* increased by the end of the eighteenth century and throughout the nineteenth, and was not actually practised earlier.

As du Loir had described in 1639, the *mukabele* began with the lesson from the *Mesnevi*, and the chanting of the Qur'an. By the end of the seventeenth century a hymn to the Prophet with words by Rumi, the *Na'at-i Peygamberi*, composed by Buhurizade Itri (d. 1712), had been added (see chapter 7). The beginning of the *ayin* proper, with the opening Sultan Veled Devri as it has been performed since perhaps the late eighteenth century, is described in detail by the contemporary Sufi authority Tuğrul İnançer:

> As soon as the *naat* is finished, the *kudümzenbaşı* beats a few strokes on the *kudüm*, and the *neyzenbaşı* or another *neyzen* begins the *taksim* known as *post taksimi*. As soon as the *taksim* is over the *peşrev* begins. With the first beat of the *peşrev* the sheikh and the *semazen*s hit the ground strongly with the hands and stand up on their feet. The *neyzen*s also stand up and play the melody of the *peşrev*. The now standing *semazen*s approach one another, moving toward the right. At that point the sheikh arises from his sheepskin mat (*post*), bows his head and greets the dervishes, and the same greeting is repeated by all. Then the sheikh turns toward the right and, to the tempo of the *peşrev*, steps onto his right foot while dragging his left, and then does the same on his left foot. Then the *semazen*s begin to walk with the same movement. When the chief cook (*aşçıbaşı*) or the *semazen* who is behind the sheikh comes before the skin mat (*post*), he places his feet together in the 'sealed' position (*mühürleyip*), bows his head, and passes over without touching the imaginary line known as the *hatt-i istiva* lying between the edge of the *post* and the door, and on which no one other than the sheikh is permitted to step. Without turning his back toward the *post*, he faces in the direction of their coming, crosses his feet, and again waits. Behind him the *semazen* who is approaching the post also crosses his feet. The two dervishes before the *post* look at one another's face, eyes and especially at the space in between their brows. Under their *hirka* cloaks they bring their right hands to their hearts, greet and pray for one another. The *semazen* to the right of the mat (*post*), without turning his back toward the *semahane*, walks while turning toward the right, and makes the same movement toward the *semazen* directly behind him. In this manner everyone greets each other.

> On reaching the extension of the imaginary line dividing the *semahane* behind
> the mat, they again cross their feet and bow their heads, before moving on . . .
> When the *semazen*s have crossed around the *semahane* three times, it is known
> as the *Devr-i Veledi* ('Cycle of Sultan Veled'). (Inançer 1994: 420)

Apart from the other ritualised motions, we should note especially this point: 'The two dervishes before the *post* look at one another's face, eyes, and especially, at the space in between their brows'. Underlying this apparently simple gesture of greeting is a wealth of Sufistic theory as well as folkloric Sufi practice. These are connected with the human face as both a 'mirror' of the Divine and the actual locus of an indwelling Divinity. Divane Mehmed Çelebi speaks of the former, while the latter underlies the Bektashi-Alevi poetic and visual imagery of the calligraphed face, with the name 'Ali' extended into the lines of the human visage.[4]

This image is extended into practice among various Alevi groups during their *semah* ceremony. The long association of Galata and Yenikapı (in different periods) with Bektashi, Melami, and Kalenderi ideas and individuals explains how the ritualised gesture of greeting in the *sema* became an allusion to various heterodox strands of Sufism among the Mevlevis as well.

The majestic 'cycle' around the *semahane* set to the instrumental music of the *peşrev* leads directly into the motion of the *sema* proper:

> After this *peşrev*, the first *selam* of the *ayin* starts and, except for the *semazenbaşı*,
> the *semazen*s leave their dark *hırka* cloaks behind and move towards the
> sheikh. The sheikh kisses each dervish's *sikke* as the *semazen* kisses the sheikh's
> hand in return. Then he moves under the direction of the *semazenbaşı*, who
> uses only his feet, eyes, and head to indicate the direction that the *semazen*
> should start to whirl. The *semazen*s follow an orbital pattern of movement
> around the *meydan*, following each other while pivoting around their own
> individual axes, just like the planets in the galaxy in their orbitary movements
> around the sun. The *semazenbaşı* directs these movements by walking around
> the *meydan* in between the whirling *semazen*s. (Tanrıkorur 2004: 29)

This modern *sema* practice is well documented in both video and photography. As I have indicated, most of these postures and movements are less closely

---

[4] Illustrated in Malik Aksel, *Religious Pictures in Turkish Art*, Istanbul: Elif, 1967, p. 88.

connected to any possible response to music than to an underlying philosophy and its many metaphoric expressions. And it is to these that I now turn.

Symbolism of the Mevlevi *Sema*

One of the most evocative explanations of the symbolism of the Mevlevi *mukabele* was penned by a non-Mevlevi Ottoman author, Vahidi, in his 1522 *Menakib-i Hoca-i Cihan*, a survey of spiritual practices among Sufis (Karamustafa 1993):

> *Sema* is occasioned by the efforts of the Mevlevi to return to his father, who is the sky, itself in constant rotation (the mother is earth). The decree that obliges the Mevlevi to dance is issued to them through the sound of the reed-flute, and the spirit, which is intoxicated by this sound, then ascends to the sky. (trans. Binbaş 2001: 71)

Perhaps the richest literary source for the symbolism of the *mukabele* is the *mesnevi* poem by Divane Mehmed Çelebi (d. 1529). As discussed at length in chapter 2, coming from the female Çelebi line in Karahisar, Divane Mehmed was briefly the *postnişin* of Galata, but spent the latter part of his life as sheikh of his native Mevlevihane in Karahisar. Having travelled widely to the East, as far as Khorasan, he was a leading and radical thinker of the Mevleviye. What he describes as 'A Treatise or Mesnevi Concerning the Mevlevi Mukabele' (*Mevlevi Mukabelesi Hakkında Risale yahut Mesnevi*) contains much of the mystical philosophy and its metaphors that underlie the Mevlevi whirling ceremony in its later development.

The framing story of the opening of the poem is a dialogue between a sultan and a dervish, but after the first ten couplets, this dialogue is more or less abandoned as the mystical doctrines appear in close succession (Gölpınarlı 1953: 473–4):[5]

> A sultan to a dervish said
>   'What is that robe, and that tall cap on your head?'
>
> 1. Quoth the dervish: 'oh my Sultan of exalted line,
>   That robe is my tomb and on my head I wear its stone'.

---

[5] The full original text is available on the website that accompanies this book.

After this introduction, with its familiar imagery, the combination of technical Sufistic language and literary metaphor becomes quite dense. Among the key terms are: mirror (*mir'at*); names and qualities (*esma ve evsaf*); essence (*zat*); point (*nokta*); movement (*seyr*); to circle (*devr etmek*); potentialities/possibilities (*mümkinat*); circle (*daire*); appearance (*zahir*); secret (*batin*); origin (*asıl*); return (*rucu'*); emergence, derivation (*furu'*); cosmos or creation (*kainat*); remainder (*masiva*).

Knowing these terms, we can begin to read Mehmed Çelebi's poem. As its author describes it, it is both a narrative poem (*mesnevi*) and a treatise (*risale*), and thus inhabits the interface of poetry and mystical doctrine:

17. For Man is the True One's mirror – look you well!
     See the True One's Names and Qualities.

18. For that pure essence is defined in a point
     From its swift movement all potentialities emerge.

19. All of existence lies within that circle
     around which move Man and Jinn and all that is possible.

20. Know that this circle divides into two –
     Observe that one is right, the other left.

21. On the right – the World of Appearances,
     On the left – the World of Secrets.

22. Straight across resides the level of Humankind
     And Man is the mirror for the Merciful One.

Couplet 18 presents several ideas and terms that are crucial to an understanding of the *mukabele*. The Divine Essence is located within a single point (*nokta*), but the energy of this point, as it were, lies in its 'swift movement'. In the previous couplet we had seen the human as the mirror of the Divine. Couplets 21–2 present spatial imagery of right and left, signifying what is apparent (*zahir*) in the universe, as opposed to its hidden meaning (*batin*). Whether in Mehmed Çelebi's own time, or perhaps somewhat later, this spatial imagery became concretised on the floor of the actual *semahane* where the *mukabele* was performed.

23. That point encompasses the circle;
    Returning to itself, the point encircles.

24. Because that point to its origin returns,
    And all that has emerged becomes erased.

25. Thus potentials are all one point –
    Beyond that lies all creation besides the One.

26. Once potentialities have returned to their origin
    All is pure essence – nothing beside remains.

The 'point' then performs a 'circle', and by doing so it is able to return to its true Divine origin. It is also significant that in couplet 18, Mehmed Çelebi stresses the 'swiftness' (*sur'at*) of the movement of the point. This is surely the thought underlying the extreme rapidity of the turn, which had so impressed Sieur du Loir in 1639. Technically this movement pattern is far beyond the *çarh atmak* whirling of the Alevi women, and, presumably, of the medieval Sufis – including Mevlana's circle of disciples and family.

27. Then is God's name Peace,
    And to his servant He grants Revelation.

28. 'Peace unto you oh servants –
    Then from all doubts you will be free!'

29. My unity you will know with eyes of certainty –
    Peace be unto you, oh Believers!'

The poet then repeats the word 'peace' (*selam*) in many couplets. There can be little doubt that this usage lies behind the later adoption of the word *selam* for each constituent cycle of the *mukabele*. But to Mehmed Çelebi the standard word was still *devir*, as in couplet 31:

Dinle ol ikinci devrin remzini
Diyeyim sana o raksın remzini.

Listen to the allusion of the second cycle (*devir*);
I will tell to you to what that dance (*raks*) alludes.

Couplet 36 reveals the third and, for this author, final, cycle of the *mukabele*:

> *Dinle ol üçüncü devri iy güzin*
> *Ana derler aşikan hakkul-yakiyn*

> Oh chosen one, listen to the third cycle
> The lovers call this the Ultimate Truth!

In the remainder of the poem the poet praises his master, Jalaluddin Rumi, and closes:

> *Ol cemalin nuruna pervaneyem*
> *Gece gündüz yanaram Divane'yem*

> I am the moth to the light of his beauty
> I am Divane who burns by night and by day!

Although more could be said about the various allusions and metaphors in this short *mesnevi*, the above should suffice to demonstrate the close connection between Divane Mehmed Çelebi's thought and the known structure of the *mukabele*. We will probably never know the extent to which Divane Mehmed shaped these later structures, or whether he was essentially commenting on a structure that had already been put into place by Pir Adil Çelebi a generation before him. It is very likely he did some of each.

With this background in place, I will turn (in chapter 6) to an examination of the written discourse of the Mevleviye concerning music as a whole, and to the role of Mevlevis within music. This background is perhaps even more crucial to understanding the later development of the music of the *ayin*. Moreover, a presentation of the musical tradition of the Mevlevis must be introduced by a discussion of the multifaceted role of the reed-flute *ney* within that tradition.

4

THE *NEY* IN MEVLEVI MUSIC

Aesthetics of the *Ney* in Mevlevi Literature

The reed-flute called *ney* in Turkish and Persian (Arabic: *nai*) is one of the most ancient instruments of the Near East. Its construction is so simple that it is impossible to state confidently where and when it developed. In Islamic culture the *ney/nai* has functioned simultaneously as an instrument of courtly music, popular music, and Sufi *samā'*. Even before the lifetime of Mevlana, the *ney* was mentioned by the Persian Sufi poets Sanai and Attar and had a status among Sufis as the preferred musical instrument for *samā'* sessions with anything other than vocal music. Rumi immortalised the *ney* in the opening verses of the *Masnavi-i Ma'nevi*, in which the wailing of the reed-flute, cut off from the reed-bed, symbolises the lament of the soul, cut off from its heavenly source.

> *Bishnevez ney chun hikāyat mikonad*
> *Az judāyihā shikāyat mikonad*

> Now listen to this reed-flute's deep lament,
> About the heartache being apart has meant.

Rumi continues his 'Song of the Reed' (lines 9–10):

> It's fire not just hot air the reed-flute's cry,
> If you don't have this fire, then you should die!

Love's fire is what makes every reed-flute pine,
Love's fervour thus lends potency to wine;
> (Rumi, *The Masnavi, Book One*, trans. Jawid Mojaddedi, pp. 4–5)

By opening his *Masnavi* with these lines, Rumi announces the unique potency of the sound of the *ney* to remind humanity both of its tragic separation from its divine source (the 'reed-bed') and the absolute need for passion leading to Love, in order to trace our way back. While we will never know much about the style of *ney* performance in Rumi's own time, he used the *ney* as a central image that was subsequently taken up by virtually every poet of the Mevlevi Order. Moreover, most of the composers of the Mevlevi *ayins* – from Kutb-i Nayi Osman Dede (d. 1730) to Ismail Dede (d. 1846) and beyond – were also ne*yzen*s. While Mevlevis played other instruments, and the music of the Mevlevi *ayin* is mainly vocal, the *ney* both as an actual producer of sound, and as a symbol and metaphor contains many meanings.

The sources mention that Rumi had a *neyzen* around him, named Hamza, who was called the 'Kutbünayi' – the 'world axis' of the *ney* (Qutb-i Nayi) – a title that would be used for later *neyzen*s of the Mevleviye (Gölpınarlı 1953: 455). Osman Dede (Cantemir's 'Derviş Osman', d. 1730) was also known as Kutb-i Nayi, thus indicating his pre-eminence among *neyzen*s. The use of the term *kutb* (*qutb*), a borrowing from classical Sufism, draws the analogy of the *qutb* as the axis or pole that supports the moral universe, and the cylindrical *ney*, shaped like a 'pole', which supports the music of the spheres. This term is a sign indicating the existence of a developed oral tradition of the significance of the *ney* and its music, which has continued among Mevlevis into the present.

Taking Mevlana as his starting point, Sheikh Galib (d. 1799) introduced 'fire' into one of his three *gazels* on the subject of the *ney*:

Aşk ateşiydi deştde berk-i kiyah-i ney
Şerer-i ah saçar şu'le-i endamından
> (Duru 2007)[1]
Lightning strikes the desert from the *ney*'s fire of love;
Burning, it scatters spark-groans from its flame.

---

[1] Most of the Turkish verse quotations in this chapter are taken from Duru's article 'Mevlevi şairlerde ney metaforu', in *Uluslararası Mevlana Sempozyumu Bildirileri* [Proceedings of the International Mevlana Symposium] 1, Istanbul: Motto, 2007, 359–84. All English translations are my own.

Necip Fazıl Duru introduces the *ney* in the writings of Mevlana and in the Turkish Mevlevi literature in the following way:

> Because the *ney* won the friendship and love of Hazret-i Pir [Mevlana], it achieved a distinction from all the other instruments; it proclaims God's existence 'Hu', and at the same time it is a dervish chanting 'Hu' in the *zikr*. It is a mysterious and incomparable power that can temporarily return the souls who have emigrated from there back to the World of Divinity.[2] (Duru 2007: 382)

In the following discussion of the *ney* in Mevlevi literature, I quote verses from several poets associated with Sufism and the Mevleviye.

The above-mentioned Sheikh Galib appears with several couplets, along with Sakıb Dede (1652–1735), the *post-nişin* at the Kütahya Asitane, and the author of the poetic biographical dictionary *Sefina-yi Nefise-yi Mevleviyan* (The Elegant Ship of the Mevlevis). Their contemporary, Yahya Nazım Çelebi (1651–1739), was known primarily as a composer and vocalist. Nazım became a *muhibb* of the Mevleviye, apprenticing himself to the noted Mevlevi sheikh and poet Neşati (d. 1674) at the Mevlevihane of Edirne. He is also remembered for his eulogies for the Prophet, the *na'at*, some of which were set to music by contemporary musicians. Ahmed Fasih Dede (d. 1699) left a government bureaucratic position to undergo a full Mevlevi training under Gavsi Dede of Galata, and became a noted Mevlevi poet. Abdülbaki Nasir Dede (1765–1821) was a *neyzen* and musicologist who became the sheikh of Yenikapı Asitane after the death of his older brother, Ali Nutki Dede, in 1804. Not as well known was the poet Ibrahim Hanif (d. 1802), who left a bureaucratic position, travelled to Mecca, and then returned to Istanbul to lead a reclusive life as a Sufi poet and writer.

Perhaps the least typical of the contributing poets, as well as the oldest chronologically, is Hemdemi (d. 1658), who was primarily known as a musician, both for the Janissary orchestra, the *mehterhane*, and for the Ottoman court. He became a *nedim* ('boon-companion') of Sultan Murad IV (d. 1640), and was a highly respected performer on the panpipes *mıskal*.[3] His twenty-nine

---

[2] Duru divides images of the *ney* into several categories. Some of these are also explained independently by Beşir Ayvazoğlu, who adds his own emphasis. See Beşir Ayvazoğlu, *Neyin Sırrı*, Istanbul: Kapı, 2007.

[3] A *nedim* (Eng. 'boon-companion') was regularly invited to accompany and entertain a sultan in a variety of private and public occasions. See Pakalin 1971, *Osmanlı Tarih Deyimleri*, Istanbul: Milli Eğitim, vol. 2, p. 667.

notated *peşrev* compositions under the name 'Solakzade' (a Janissary title) constitute the largest corpus surviving from any composer of the first half of the seventeenth century. Apart from his *gazel* with the poetic monorhyme (*redif*) '*ney*', his possible connections to the Mevleviye are not known.[4]

Myths and Metaphors

In Mevlevi poetry the *ney* is consistently described as a revealer of secrets. This role as 'revealer' often refers to two different sets of images, based on two different myths. One of them has a pan-Islamic background, with probable deep roots in the ancient Mediterranean world, while the other is a product of the history of early Sufism.

In its Islamic version, the first myth is related to the return of the Prophet Muhammad to earth following his Ascent to Heaven (Mi'rac; Mi'raj), and his description to Hazreti Ali of what he had seen there. In one variant, he received 90,000 words from Allah. Of these, 30,000 were to be spread widely, 30,000 were destined for a spiritual elite, and 30,000 were for Ali alone. Ali receives these Divine words, and though the Prophet cautioned him from revealing them to any human being, Ali, unable to keep them to himself, goes to an entirely deserted pit and speaks the words there. The power of the words caused a reed to grow on the edge of the pit, and from the reed a passing shepherd made himself a flute. Before long the Prophet heard his very words floating through the air. When he questioned Ali on how this had happened, Ali claimed that he had spoken the words to no living creature. In that case, the Prophet decreed that this reed, the *ney*, would reveal the Divine secrets until the end of time (Duru 2007: 373). In another version of the story, what the Prophet reveals to Ali are the manifestations of the Divine Beauty that he had witnessed during the Mi'raj (Ayvazoğlu 2007: 27). Sheikh Galib seems to refer to this latter variant in his verses from his *gazel* with the *redif* '*ney*':

> *Envar-i Mah-i Nahşebidir şu'le-i sada*
> *Ayn-i Ali'den aldı nazar çünki çah-i ney.*
>   (Duru 2007)

---

[4] As a poetic term, *redif* (from Ar. *radaf* 'to follow') is a repeating word at the end of a poetic line, as distinct from a rhyme, which is *kafiye*.

Flames of Divine Light were revealed as sound,
When the reed-pit caught the glance of Ali.

There is yet another level of cultural transmission within this story. As modern Turkish writers have pointed out, the story of the *ney* bears an uncanny resemblance to the legend of the Phrygian King Midas, as related in Ovid's *Metamorphosis* and other classical sources (Ayvazoğlu 2007: 27). In a brief retelling, King Midas becomes one of the judges in a musical contest between the gods Apollo and Pan. While everyone else favours the majestic lyre playing of Apollo, Midas prefers the flutes of Pan. Outraged, Apollo turns Midas's ears into those of a donkey, since only a donkey could have such low musical taste. In this legend, it is not difficult to discern the longstanding conflict within ancient Greek culture between Apollonian and Dionysian forms of musical expression, and all that this conflict implies. Mortified, King Midas hides his new ears under his ample Phrygian cap. But in time his barber becomes aware of this transformation, and, unable to keep this news to himself, he speaks them to an empty pit. A passing shepherd cuts himself a reed from the pit, and fashions a shepherd's flute from it. Sure enough, the King himself, along with his entire kingdom, come to hear of this unhappy metamorphosis.

There would seem little doubt that some form of this legend remained current within the broader Anatolian and Syrian regions, and that probably by purely oral means it was transformed into the sacred myth of the Prophet and Ali. But the interpretative transformation is also of interest. Music does not appear at all in the preamble to the story. In its Islamic guise, what is at stake is a secret Divine teaching, or a privileged vision of the Divine Beauty. The resolution of both the antique and the Islamic versions is almost identical, however. And it is noteworthy that the musical priorities of the Ancients and of the Muslims – in this case, the Sufis – are rather different. The lyre of Apollo had represented the high art of sobriety and social aristocracy within the *polis*, while the pan-pipes represented the irrational and the rural. In the Islamic Sufi transformation, it was precisely this unconventional irrationality that recommended the humble reed-flute as the bearer of the weightiest of Divine Secrets.

The other myth of the secrets comes through the figure of Mansur al-Hallaj (858–922), an Arabic Sufi writer of Persian origin, whose life and teachings have been the subject of controversy throughout the centuries. His best-known work is the *Kitab al-Tawasin*. It is an historical fact that Mansur was first imprisoned and then ordered to be skinned alive by the Caliph Al-Muqtadir in Baghdad. The immediate trigger for the death sentence was his saying *'Ana al-Haq'*: 'I am the Ultimate Truth'. This was a form of ecstatic mystical utterance, known as *shathiyat*.[5] However, the deeper reason for this harsh sentence was evidently hidden in the multiple theological and political conflicts that beset the Caliphate at that time. One of the contested issues both during al-Hallaj's lifetime and afterwards, was his refusal to confine himself to a Sufi environment, and his public preaching, which often used expressions that were likely to be misunderstood by the common people. Even Rumi in his *Masnavi* could not avoid the political implications of the case:

> *Chun qalam bar dast-e ghadari buved*
> *La jurm Mansur bar dāri buved*

> Whenever the pen [of authority] is in the hand of a traitor
> Though guiltless, Mansur is on a gibbet.
>   *Masnavi*, trans. Nicholson, 1977

Nevertheless, in the later Mevlevi tradition, the *ney*, like Mansur, acted as the revealer of the deepest level of unity linking God and humankind. And, by implication, the Sufi ceremony of *sema*, in which the *ney* played a prominent role, was likely to be misunderstood and condemned by narrow-minded religious and political authorities. Fortunately, apart from the period from 1666 to 1684, discussed in chapter 2, the Mevlevis could generally avoid such blanket prohibitions. Taking their lead from Mevlana, the Ottoman Mevlevi poets developed the image of Mansur and the *ney*. As the Mevlevis developed a set of *ney*s in different pitches, it seems perhaps only coincidence that the lowest-pitched one was called 'Mansur' ('granted victory by God'), yet this

---

[5] The concept, as well as the example, of al-Hallaj were discussed lucidly by Carl Ernst in *Words of Ecstasy in Sufism*, Albany: State University of New York Press, 1985, pp. 102–10.

name strengthened the link between the quintessential Mevlevi instrument and the quintessential Sufi revealer of secrets.

Durmayıp her bar ene'l-Hak söyler ol Mansur gibi
Itdiğiçün sırrı ifşa asılur dara ney
    Hemdemi, quoted in Duru (2007)

Ceaselessly the *ney*, like Mansur, repeats 'I am the Ultimate Truth'.
He reveals the secret and is hanged on the gallows.

Sırr-i 'acibe-i dil-i Mansuru şerh ider
Her dem zeban-i hal-i mü'essir-eda-yi ney
    Fasih, quoted in Duru (2007)

Without pause the *ney*, through its impressive tongue,
explains the wondrous secret of Mansur's speech.

Neyi divan-i raza terceman-i gayb itmişler
Zeban-i hal-i bal olmış reh-i imada her parmak
    Sakıb, quoted in Duru (2007)

They appointed the *ney* as hidden interpreter for the *divan* of secrets,
His every finger gestures with a winged tongue.

With such a literary heritage deeply influencing the intellectual and spiritual life of Ottoman Turkey, we should not be overly surprised to see Refik Halid Karay (1889–1965), one of the founders of twentieth-century Turkish literature, gesturing to both the *ney* and, by implication, to Mansur al-Hallaj: 'I am here alone, listening to the *ney* . . . I feel that my soul has been washed in warm water, that it is being lathered with the fibres from angels' wings. I have been so much cleansed that I fear that soon I will prostrate myself to myself as a sacred creature' (Karay 1939: 123).

Several other common metaphorical images are the staff of Moses (Musa), the trumpet of the Resurrection (*mahşer*), the Sufi guide (*mürşid*), and the master of music. Apart from any Mevlevi usage, the staff (*asa*) of Moses appears in Ottoman poetry with Sufi leanings. A good example comes from the *divan* of

Na'ili (d. 1666), an outstanding poet of Halveti affiliation who was also a friend of Cevri. Both of these poets were known as consummate masters of what would come to be called the Indian Style of Ottoman poetry:

Maruz ki asa-i kef-i Musa'da nihanüz
Mar anlama muruz ki teh-i pada nihanüz
   (Ipekten 1968)

We are the snake and in the staff in Moses' hand we're hidden
Say not snake, but rather ant, and under foot we're hidden.

Within this couplet Moses' staff is transformed, first into a snake, and then into an ant. Many transformations of this basic image ensue in the remaining seven *beyt*s. But the poetic relationship between staff and snake is determined by the Biblical and Qur'anic opposition of the staff of the prophet and the snake into which it is transformed before Pharaoh's magicians. The Mevlevi *muhibb* and musician Nazim brings the image into a more Sufistic and Mevlevi context:

N'ola Firaun-i nefs-i münkire ejder-nüma olsa
Kef-i Musa-yi 'Işk-i Hak'da guya kim asadır ney

It is the *ney*, appearing as staff in the hand of the Moses of God's love;
It turns into a dragon before the God-denying soul of Pharaoh.

Pharaoh (Firaun) is now not only the figure of the Biblical Exodus story, but represents the lower human soul, the *nefs*. The lower soul denies God. This denier (*münkir*) is theologically akin to the 'ungrateful' unbeliever (*kafir*). As such he deserves to be terrified not just by a worldly snake (*mar*) but by a dragon (*ejder*). Surprisingly, however, the staff undergoes yet another transformation – this time into a *ney*. This does not terrify, but is rather a symbol of God's love, thus underscoring the poem's quite dense theological and Sufistic message. Without the image of Moses, Nazim then paints the *ney* as a Sufi master. Here the link between musical instrument and spiritual teacher is the image of the breath:

'Aceb mi ehl-i aşkı bir nefesde eylese irşad
Ki zira mürşid-i sahib dem-i rah-i Hudadır ney

Is it any wonder that with one breath it provides guidance (*irşad*) to the
people of Love?
For the *ney* is the breath-giving Master on the path to God.

Fasih Dede also envisages the *ney* as providing guidance, but now on the 'path
of inner meaning'. And in this couplet it is the long shape of the *ney* that acts
as the teacher's finger, pointing to the truth:

Reh-i ma'naya ney engüşt-i işaret dile bes
Gayrı kimden nefes ümmid idüp irşad ister

The *ney* points the finger to the path of inner meaning;
From whom else would the heart seek guidance?

The Mevlevi sheikh Sakıb Dede creates an image of sound, here a camel-bell
indicating the way to those lost in the desert of their own indolence:

Ser-geşte karban-i beyaban-i ğaflete
Menzil-nüma-yi zinde-nefesdür dera-yi ney.

To all those lost in the wastelands of indolence,
The *ney*'s bell-like tone shows the way toward the breath of life.

From the spiritual guide we move naturally to the master of music. Sheikh
Galib presents a whimsical picture of a group of aspiring *neyzen*s trying to
imitate the 'sighs' coming from the *ney* of their teacher:

Nayin ki tifl-i mektebdür saff-i musikar
Üstad önünde verziş-i ah-u enin eder

The *ney* is the school teacher, where the rows of child musicians
Exercise their sighs and moans.

The *neyzen* and actual teacher of music at Yenikapı, Abdülbaki Nasir Dede (1765–1821), almost repeats what he had written in his musical treatise *Tetkik ü Tahkik* (1796), where he presents the *ney* as the model instrument. Here, however, it has not only a musicological but a spiritual interpretation:

> *Mukteda-yi rah u ahenk oldu cümle saza ney*
> *Guş ururlar başlaya ta ibtida avaza ney*

> The *ney* sets the example for harmony's road to all the instruments;
> Before setting out, first they must turn their ears to the voice of the *ney*.

To conclude this selection of verses, I offer two *beyt*s from the great twentieth-century poet (and friend of Ahmed Hamdi Tanpınar), Yahya Kemal Beyatlı (1884–1958), in his poem 'Ismail Dede'nin Kainatı' ('The World of Ismail Dede Efendi'):

> *Mesnevi şevkini eflake çıkarmış nayiz*
> *Haşredek hem-nefes-i Hazret-i Mevlana'yız*

> *Şems-i Tebriz hevasıyle sema üzre Kemal*
> *Dahil-i daire-i bal ü per-i Monlayız.*
>   Eski Şiirin Rüzgariyle (1974: 95)

> We are the *ney*, whose passion raises the *Mesnevi* up to the Heavens.
> Until the Day of Resurrection we will never leave Mevlana's side!

> Oh Kemal! Entering the *sema* with Shams-e Tabrizi
> Within that circle, like Mevlana, let us fly!

For Yahya Kemal in the mid-twentieth century, these lines were part of his homage both to the great Ottoman composers, like Dede Efendi and Buhurizade Itri, and to the literary tradition of the Mevlevis. The delightful verse of Nasir Dede forms a bridge from poetic metaphor to the development of the *ney* as an actual musical instrument. In the next section, I briefly note its appearance in the antecedent Timurid musical culture, and then its development among the Mevlevis within the Ottoman Empire.

Technical Development of the *Ney*, and the *Ney* as the Mevlevi Instrument

We have no way to assess how the *ney* was used in the Sufi environments of Rumi's own time. No clue survives as to which musical genres were deemed most appropriate for solo performance on the *ney* or for its use as an accompanying instrument. Given the dearth of descriptions, it is of some interest to learn how the *ney* might have been employed within a courtly, rather than a Sufi, context. One source consists of remarks in the *Baburnama* that concern a *nay* player at the court of the Timurid Sultan Husayn Bayqara (ruled 1469–1506), fully two centuries later than the lifetime of Mevlana:

> Another was Şayxi Nayi. He also played well on the *'ud* and the *ghiççak*. Apparently he had played well on the *nay* since his twelfth or thirteenth year. On one occasion at the gathering (*suhbat*) of Badiuzzaman Mirza he performed a *kar* (*bir işni*) beautifully.
>
> (Babar/Babur 1905: fol. 182, trans. Annette Susannah Beveridge)

Şayxi (Şeyhi) was apparently a secular musician, with neither Sufi nor ulema associations. Here he uses the *nay* as a solo instrument on which to perform a courtly vocal composition, a *kar*. In this fifteenth-century Timurid musical environment, the *nay* was a respected solo instrument. But the *nayzen* Şayxi also performs professionally on the oud and on the fiddle *ghiççak*. These three instruments dominated music at the court of Husayn Bayqara, in addition to the harp *chang*, and the psaltery *qanun*.

The *ney* itself may have gone through several developments in technique but its construction seems to have remained quite constant throughout the Near East. The major technical innovation was created by the Ottomans, in all probability by the Mevlevi dervishes, who took the step of adding a mouthpiece and creating sets of identical *neys* to be played in different keys. The mouthpiece, called in Turkish the *başpare* ('head-piece'), is a conical piece of bone placed over the opening of the reed. This piece is approximately equal to the diameter of the mouth and it enables the player to produce the maximum sound with the minimum of breath.

It also makes possible the use of long *neys* that produce the notes A_3 (called Mansur) or B_3 (called Şah). *Neys* producing these lower tones, which allow the *ayin*s and *taksim*s to be pitched in a lower range, are characteristic only of Ottoman musical culture. They are particularly common in Mevlevi practice, for unlike the courtly *fasıl* suite, the *ayin* must be pitched in the lower register. Aspiring Mevlevi *ney* students always had been trained first on the low-pitched *ney*s before being allowed to learn the higher ones (Cem Behar, 2003).

This newer form of *ney* did not remain confined to the Mevlevi convents. By the seventeenth century it had also become the new standard for *ney* playing at the Ottoman court. As Ottoman court music developed as a highly differentiated musical practice and repertoire – not before the last third of the seventeenth century – the *ney* took its place along with the newly developed lute, the *tanbur*. Prince Cantemir, in his description of the Ottoman concert (c. 1700), specifies that only the *ney* and *tanbur* had fixed positions in the instrumental ensemble, namely, directly behind the vocalist (*hanende*), so they could furnish the principal accompaniment (*peyrevlik*). In a symbolic sense this duet of *ney* and *tanbur* represented the fusion of the secular Turkic lute with the Sufi reed-flute, and thus, of the two elements that predominated in the creation of Ottoman Turkish music.

Without claiming a historical connection, it is also striking that within the Japanese Zen tradition a form of bamboo flute occupies a position somewhat analogous to the Mevlevi *ney:*

> The quiet, meditative *syakuhati* [shakuhachi] music of the Huke sect was strongly influenced by Zen. This music was originally religious, and the *syakuhati* was not considered a musical instrument but was called *hoki*, indicating an instrument of ritual or religion. Mendicant priest-flutists – *komuso* 'priests of nothingness' – described playing the *syakuhati* as *suizen* 'blowing-meditation' or 'playing-meditation', a term analogous to Zen *zazen* 'sitting-meditation'. (Shimosako, 2002: 549).

Out of the ten eminent Istanbul *neyzen*s mentioned in the 'Book of Travels' (*Seyahat-name*) of Evliya Çelebi (d. 1682), six are Mevlevi dervishes, including the sheikh of a major *tekke* – Beşiktaş. Elsewhere in the *Seyahat-name*, Evliya Çelebi connects the *ney* with the Mevlevi tradition: 'The *ulema* (clergy) of Turkey (Rum) showed great favour toward this instrument because it was played in the assembly of the Sultan of the Ulema (Behauddin Veled) and

Hazret-i Mevlana, and it is played now in the Mevlevihanes' (Evliya Çelebi in Özergin 1972, trans. Feldman 1996: 137).

'Sultan of the *Ulema*' was an honorary title of Behauddin, the father of Rumi. By noting that the *ney* was played in the assembly of both Behauddin, who was a noted *alim* (clergyman), and of his son, who became known primarily as a Sufi rather than as an *alim*, Evliya was probably referring obliquely to the controversies about Sufi practices that had become violent in the seventeenth century. This controversy had been instigated by Kadızade Mehmed b. Mustafa (d. 1635), but the effects of the Kadızadeli movement were felt for generations after. Although Evliya's patron, Sultan Murad IV, cooperated with Kadızade on certain issues, he patronised the Mevlevi sheikh Doğani Ahmed Dede (d. 1630), and was generally supportive of traditional Sufi ritual practices.

Bobowski/Ali Ufuki mentioned the *ney* as one of the instruments 'which they use to accompany the delicate songs', but he cites it only toward the end of the list of instruments (Bobowski 1665). The distinctive mouthpiece of the Ottoman *ney* was apparently first described by the Englishman John Covel in 1670: 'There is neither a fipple above, nore noze in the mouth, but the head is a horn sloped up and brought to a very fine edge, which leaning sideways to the mouth, gives the sound, as boyes (with us) used to whistle in acorn cups, this plaghiaulos, whence our flageolet' (Covel, 1670: 168). Iconographic evidence suggests that the mouthpiece appeared only in the mid to late sixteenth century. The continuing Persian influence over Ottoman *ney*-playing in the earlier sixteenth century is demonstrated in the *cema'at-i mutriban* list of Sultan Süleyman's musicians (1525), where none of the *neyzen*s are Ottoman Turks; all are evidently Iranian Azerbaijanis. This list includes no dervish *neyzen*s. In many Turkish illuminations of the sixteenth century the *neyzen*s are dressed in courtly and not dervish clothing. An illustration to the *Süleymanname*, dated 1558, still shows two *ney* players in secular courtly costume playing long, thin Iranian *ney*s without mouthpieces. Mustafa Ali, in his *Kava'id ül-Meva'id* (written in the 1590s), still mentioned the *nay-i Irakiye*, which was probably the older Iranian *nay* without a mouthpiece. Whereas in the early sixteenth century court Iranians and their students had been the principal *ney* players, they are not mentioned at all in the following century.

Starting in the later sixteenth century there is a tendency to represent the *ney* as slightly wider than previously shown, and the mouthpiece begins to make its appearance. The *Sur-i Humayun* manuscript of 1582 shows both secular and dervish *neyzens* playing in a variety of contexts. All of the *neyzens*, however, are playing the newer type of *ney* with a mouthpiece. Thus, the sixteenth century iconographic and literary evidence indicates that the wider *ney* with a mouthpiece came into existence some time after the middle of the century. During this time it coexisted with the older Iranian *ney*, but by the last quarter of the century the newer *ney* with mouthpiece became dominant. Van Mour included a lively painting of a casual, social performance of Mevevi *neyzens* in the Galata Mevlevihane in 1712.

In the illustrated *Surname* manuscript of Vehbi (1720–30), the *neyzens* are dressed either as Mevlevi dervishes or as secular musicians. Occasionally a *tanbur* (long-necked lute) player may also be depicted wearing the Mevlevi felt hat (*sikke*). By the later seventeenth century, the *ney* had achieved pre-eminence

Image 4.1 *Dervishes Sharing a Meal.* Jean Baptiste Vanmour (1671–1737). Riksmuseum SA-K 1999. Depiction of *neyzens* in Galata Mevlevihanesi.

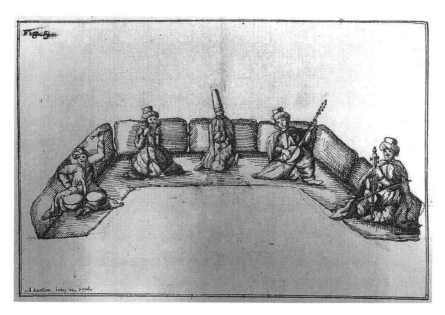

Image 4.2 Ottoman *Ensemble*. Charles Fonton, *Essai sur la musique orientale comparée à la musique européenne*. Paris, 1751. Bibliothèque nationale de France, MS. 4023, figure 5.

over all the *makam* instruments except for the *tanbur*. By 1751, the French dragoman Charles Fonton wrote that 'the *ney* is the principal instrument of the Orientals'. When he illustrated a typical aristocratic instrumental performance – what Cantemir had termed the *fasıl-i sazende* – he features only five instruments. These are the *ney*, the panpipes *mıskal*, the *tanbur*, the Ottoman form of the *ghıççak* (then termed '*rebab*'), and the kettledrum *kudüm*. The *neyzen* is dressed in the Mevlevi costume and he sits in the middle of the divan, between the *tanbur* and the *mıskal*. Other than the *neyzen*, the musicians wear secular costumes. And, of course, it is no accident that here the *neyzen* is a Mevlevi dervish.

Cantemir had considered the *tanbur* to be the 'most perfect instrument', but at the end of the eighteenth century, Abdülbaki Nasir Dede, in his theoretical *Tetkik ü Tadkik* from 1796, described the *makam*s in terms of their performance on the *ney* for his patron, Sultan Selim III, who performed both on the *ney* and the *tanbur*. Such a status for the *ney* was totally without precedent in other *makam* musics, even in the older practice of Turkish music.

It serves as a testament to the prestige that the Mevlevi Order of dervishes brought to the science of music (*'ilmül musiki*), and to the prestige Mevlevi musicians had acquired within secular Ottoman music.[6] During the eighteenth and the first half of the nineteenth century, the aristocratic amateur musicians who upheld much of the repertoire and style of Ottoman music performed either on the *ney* or on the *tanbur*.

A painting of an Ottoman concert at the British Embassy in Istanbul on February 22, 1779, reproduced below, shows three Muslim vocalists (playing *daires*) and nine instrumentalists. Of the latter, two are *neyzens* in Mevlevi costumes, while one is a *neyzen* dressed as a Greek or Armenian. There is also a Christian playing the *mıskal* panpipes, as well as a Muslim and a non-Muslim (probably Jewish) *tanbur* player. Also shown are single performers on the *santur*, *kemançe* (*rebab*), and Western violin, all of them Greeks or Armenians (Pekin 2003: 1032). In the following generation, a leading *neyzen* was the Armenian Oskiyam (1780–1870), also known as a *tanbur* player who had studied the instrument with the Jewish Tanburi Isak Fresco-Romano (d. 1814).

By the middle of the eighteenth century, several post-Byzantine notated collections of Ottoman secular music had appeared, as well as the Greek-language comparative theories of Panagiotes Chalatzoglu (1724) and Kyrillos Marmarinos (1749). By their time, knowledge of Ottoman music was becoming *de rigueur* for the *psaltes* cantors of the church (see Popescu-Judetz and Ababi Sirli 2000). Petros Peloponneseios/Lambatharios (d. 1778) had a substantial reputation within Church music, but he was also said to be a tutor of Mevlevi dervish musicians. It was also said, perhaps hyperbolically, that 'no one composed in the Ottoman capital without his approval' (Apostolopoulos 2005: 41). His remarkable career is in part a result of the strong influence of Mevlevi teachers on the instruction of the Muslim educated classes, which emphasised the quest for a deeper reality beneath the surface of doctrinal and ritual differences between religions (see chapter 6).

The Mevlevi emphasis on larger and lower-pitched *neys* to accompany the composed *ayins* increased the variety and audibility of the instruments' overtones. Not accidentally, the newly developed *tanbur* was also characterised by

---

[6] Much of the material on the previous two pages appeared in Feldman, *Music of the Ottoman Court*, Berlin: Verlag für Wissenschaft und Bildung, 1996, pp. 136–8 ('The *ney*').

Image 4.3 Ottoman Concert 1799, British Embassy, Istanbul. Copy by an unknown Greek painter of a Turkish miniature painted for Sir Robert Ainslie, British Ambassador to the Porte. Collection of King Stanislas Poniatowski. Purchased for the University Library in Warsaw, 1818. Print, Royal Collection T. 171, no. 647.

a robust system of overtones, and hence the two instruments playing together produced a wide spectrum of sound. The same was true in a different fashion of the combination of several *ney*s played during the *mukabele*. This emphasis on overtones and timbre may have had purely internal explanations, but it is difficult to avoid the possibility that there was also an underlying connection with a 'timbre-centred' music that was characteristic of Turkic cultures in a wide geographical swath that extends from Tuva, in South Siberia, to Bashkortostan, in the Urals. In the latter region, in particular, the endblown flute *kurai* is a major musical vehicle for timbre-centred musical expression (see Levin 2006). There seems little doubt in the case of the *tanbur* that this was not the product of recent contact with Central Asia, but rather of the reemergence of a Turkic musical aesthetic that subsisted within Turkish Anatolia. In the case of the *ney*, there was probably a dual process that emerged both from this Turkic heritage and from the internal practices of the Mevlevis as their musical tradition crystallised in more recent centuries.

Fonton (1751) described the mouthpiece of the Turkish *ney* in greater detail:

> The upper end of the *ney*, where the embouchure is, is a piece made of horn or ivory, whose shape resembles on the outside that of a truncated cone. Its interior is hollowed out and forms the same shape but smaller, and turned upside-down in relation to the exterior cone, such that the section ABC of the exterior cone serves as the base of the interior cone, which is cut out from the inside along points DEF, the base of the exterior cone . . . One can see the difficulty of this embouchure. It is often necessary to blow for years to get it just right, and even then it is only possible for extremely strong and vigorous lungs. (Fonton [1751] 1988–9: 100)

Fonton also described the construction of the *ney* and mentioned the *ney*s of different sizes:

> The material of which it is made is a 'noded' cane, of which the best species grows in Syria, especially around Damascus, in a marsh called Ainazare. The length of the *ney* is normally 24–25 inches. However, there are larger ones called *şah mansur* to distinguish from *the küçük mansur*. Their difference is one tone or even a semi-tone, lower in the former and higher in the latter. Another which differs from the preceding two is called *davud*; the sound of it is less high than either, and it is slightly longer. (Fonton [1751] 1988–9: 100)

Evliya had averred that there were twelve types of *ney*, and he names eight: *battal düheng*, *girift*, *mansur-şah*, *bolaheng*, *battal*, *davud*, *serbeng*, and *süpurga*. The modern system has the following twelve *ney* sizes (Öztuna 1974: 79):

Mansûr - A	*mansûr mabeyni* - B♭	*şâh* - B♭
dâvûd - c	*dâvûd mabeyni* - c♯	*bolahenk* - d
bolahenk mabeyni - e♭	*sipürde / ahterî (süpürge)* - e	*müstahsen* - f
müstahsen mabeyni - f♯	*kızneyi* - g	*kızneyi mabeyni* - g♯

Of these, the seven that are pitched to six degrees of the fundamental scale plus *'acem* (f) are in most common use (*dügah, segah, çargah, neva, hüseyni, gerdaniye, 'acem*). There is no *ney* pitched to *rast* (G). In the nineteenth century the *girift* (mentioned by Evliya as a kind of *ney*) was considered to be a different instrument because it employed a different playing technique. *Girift*s could be made for *çargah* (c) or *rast* (G). They came to be viewed as non-Mevlevi, secular instruments (*Türk Musikisi Ansiklopedisi* [hereinafter TMA] 1, 1969). Although Toderini called the *girift* a 'smaller version of the ney' (Toderini 1789: 231), the fact that he mentions none of the other seven to twelve versions of the *ney* indicates that he viewed the *girift* as a different instrument.

The Sufi aesthetic of the *ney* became increasingly integrated into that of Ottoman courtly music. The prominence of the *ney* in secular music implied

Image 4.4 *Ney.* Fonton (1751), *Essai sur la musique orientale comparée à la musique européenne.* Paris, 1751. Bibliothèque nationale de France, MS. 4023, figure 1.

much more than organological symbolism, and should be seen as symptomatic of a reconceptualisation of the entire issue of music, which must have affected many other musical spheres, such as intonation, timbre, tempo and rhythm. It seems clear that the performing style of the Mevlevi *neyzen*s constituted one of several disparate elements that were welded into a coherent musical whole during the eighteenth century.

Ney and *Taksim*

There is no doubt that the Mevlevi *neyzen* played the *peşrev* and *semai* compositions of the *fasıl-i sazende.* In addition, like any instrumental soloist, he would perform the 'improvised' (or 'performance-generated') genre known as *taksim*. To the Frenchman Fonton, this was a 'caprice', and he describes it as follows:

> This caprice [i.e. the *taksim*] must be in the same mode as the air which will be played and in fact serves as a kind of transition to it. It is played by only one of the musicians assembled for the concert, while the others play a kind of drone by playing continuously the tone on which the *taksim* is based. There are some who succeed perfectly in these *taksim*s, which they prolong for whole hours entirely in the same mode, which they embroider in a hundred different ways. It is in these caprices that the talent of the musician develops. It is not constrained by measure, as are the *peşrev*s, because he may change it at will and because the *taksim* must not follow any of the *usul*s of which we have spoken. (Fonton [1751] 1988–9)

To Fonton this 'caprice' is a major component of the Ottoman concert. To Cantemir it was perhaps even more crucial. The centrality of the *taksim* to Cantemir's musical thought can be seen from the position that his verbal description of *taksim* holds in his treatise. The treatise commences with some general definitions of musical terms, and then proceeds to explain the principles of Cantemir's system of notation. The use of notation was certainly an important aim of Cantemir's treatise and Collection. However, the treatise continues to present a classification of the entire *makam* system, including a brief definition of every existing modal entity. This catalogue constitutes the bulk of the treatise (Chapters 3 to 6), but it is followed by a broader attempt to explain 'consonance' (*ünsiyyet*) in music (Ch. 7). Cantemir concludes his chapter with a verbal description of a *taksim* that modulates through-out the entire *makam* system. Cantemir seeks here to explain the nature of musical consonance by demonstrating how different *makam*s can be joined together to form a musical whole. He originally ended his book after describing the *taksim* in chapter 7: 'In this way the science of music according to the alphabetical and numerical notation, and the treatise of music according to my own theory has come to an end' (c. 1700: 7: 67). Of course, neither the Moldavian Prince Cantemir nor the Frenchman Charles Fonton were Mevlevi dervishes, yet the centrality of the *taksim* genre was obvious to both of them.

Moving ahead to our own time, we can observe a similar phenomenon in relation to the *ney*. A recent (2004) anthology of *ney* performances, as part of Kalan Records' *Masters of Turkish Music* CD anthology, features sixteen *neyzen*s. Nine of them are clearly the product of Mevlevi education in one form or another, while the remaining seven seem to have arisen more through the secular music schools of Republican Turkey. The two CDs include thirty-eight items, and every one of them is a *taksim*. Thus, it is striking that to the compiler, the *neyzen* Aziz Filiz Şenol, a student of Niyazi Sayin, the potential of the *ney* can be heard at its fullest in the performance of the *taksim*. Of course the other CD anthologies, for example the two CDs for the preeminent *tanbur* virtuoso (and my teacher) Necdet Yaşar (1930–2017), feature many *taksim*s, but there are also several *peşrev*s and *saz sema'i*s.

The improvised vocal and instrumental genre called *taksim* was developed during the later sixteenth century. By the first quarter of the seventeenth cen-tury, the term *taksim* first takes on the meaning of 'improvisation'. No literary reference connects the early *taksim* specifically to the Mevlevis, but in modern Mevlevi practice, the *taksim* is very prominent, and a highly specific form of *taksim* has been developed for the *ney*. The specificity of this *taksim* lies in its rhythmic conventions and pulse and in the tone and pitch of the instrument. Part of this aesthetic is an emphasis on the overtones emitted from the *ney*, and the function of the breath of the player. Some Mevlevi *neyzen*s are articulate about this connection. For example, the late Aka Gündüz Kutbay (1934–79), in his conversations, used to view the breath of the *neyzen* as a symbol of the mystical syllable *Hū*, which articulated the fact of divine existence in the universe. While some of the Sunni *tarikat*s employed several singers to create a vocal overtone system during the *zikr*, the Mevlevis preferred to use the *ney* for this purpose. The *ney* could express these timbral relationships both in solo playing and through the use of drones (*demkeş*) held by the accompanying *neyzen*s. This practice imparted a distinctive sound both to the performance of *peşrev*s and *taksim*s. The *neyzen*s could also perform the *taksim* apart from the *ayin* ceremony. The great *neyzen*s of the mid to late twentieth century – Neyzen Tevfik, Halil Can, Halil Dikmen, Ulvi Erguner, Aka Gündüz Kutbay, Niyazi Sayin – were known for their extended *taksim*s, whose long duration and leisurely pace set them apart from the *taksim*s of the masters of the other instruments, which are usually valued for their compression of material into a smaller space. Dr Mehmet Eröz wrote the following elegant description of an extended *taksim* performed in his private office by Halil Dikmen – then the director of the State Painting and Sculpture Museum in Istanbul – and a former student of Emin Dede:

> Then he closed his eyes and began a *taksim*. Passing from *makam* to *makam* this feast continued for half an hour. Perhaps he would not have found such inspiration, nor would he have been able to demonstrate such a performance at any private gathering. Gazing out at the blue waters of the Bosphorus from this Ottoman palace, my soul took wing and I flew away!' (quoted in Ayvazoğlu 2007: 78)

Turning to the recent practice of the Mevlevi *mukabele*, in the early twentieth century, it was regarded as long-established that the order of the ritual music featured the rubato Eulogy (*na'at*) to the Prophet, composed in *makam* Rast by Mustafa Itri. This would be followed by the *baş taksim* (lead *taksim*) by the principal *neyzen* in the *makam* of the *ayin*. While secular *taksim*s acquire added value by demonstrating multiple, often momentary, modulations through single note alterations and transpositions, the *baş taksim* generally remains in a single *makam*. Its nature is highly meditative, as it prepares the dervishes for the opening of the composed *ayin* music.

While the traditional *mutrip* ensemble for the *ayin* would be led by the *neyzenbaşı*, his most outstanding role was as a performer of the improvised *taksim* in a flowing rhythm. Although I have treated the *taksim* earlier (Feldman 1993 and Feldman 1996), it is helpful to reiterate some of these points also in this Mevlevi context, in which the *ney* is so central.

The Origin of the *Taksim*

Starting in the early seventeenth century, Ottoman texts employ the term *taksim* (Ar. *taqsim*, 'division') to refer to a performance-generated melody in a non-metrical, 'flowing' rhythm, which might be performed either vocally or instrumentally. While *taqsim* occurs as a non-musical term in Arabic and many other Muslim languages, studies of Arabic and Persian sources have not attested its musical use as an improvised, non-metrical genre prior to the nineteenth century. In fifteenth-century Turkish *mecmu'a* anthologies, *taksim* had been 'a section setting the first verse block' (Wright 1992b: 316). This section was a part of the composed, metrical genres within the *nauba*, i.e., the *qawl*, *ghazal*, *tarana*, and *firudasht*. Very likely the *hanende* would have sung an improvisation using the first *misra'* (hemistich) of the *gazel* or *ruba'i* of the *beste* with which he would then begin the *fasıl*.

The *taksim* as it is known in modern Turco-Arabian music is defined by four major characteristics, which are not present as an ensemble in any other non-metrical genre within the core Muslim world (including the Maghreb and Transoxiana):

- Performance-generation ('improvisation') that precludes learned, tune-like models
- Specific rhythmic idioms in an overall flowing-rhythm context
- Codified melodic progressions (*seyir*)
- Modulation

The first necessary element in the *taksim* was performance-generation. Although neither Cantemir nor other Turkish theorists had any term for this concept, in his seventh chapter Cantemir makes clear that the prior learning of any section disqualified a melody from being considered a *taksim*. Cantemir used a single term to describe both instrumental improvisation and vocal improvisation that used a secular *gazel* poem as text: 'The instrumentalists' *taksim* is not different from the vocalists' *taksim*, so there is no need to describe it' (c. 1700: X: 102).

In the medieval Middle East some of the non-metrical genres were apparently used as preludes, particularly where cyclical performance arrangements were accepted. It is likely that the use of non-metrical vocal genres in the beginning of the modern Moroccan *nauba*, the Kashmiri *sufiyana kalam*, and the Uyghur *muqam* relate to a similar medieval Muslim musical practice (Pacholczyk 1992). In contemporary Moroccan practice the leading vocalist may insert non-metrical passages between the composed genres of the *nauba*. However, in these modern Muslim art musics, as in their medieval predecessors, the role of performance-generation and 'flowing rhythm' is far less significant than that of the metrical composed genres. In modern times it is only in Iran, Azerbaijan, and Iraq that non-metricity of the melodic line is the rule in art music repertoires. Research by Iranian-American musicologist Amir Hosein Pourjavady (2005) suggests that this dominance of non-metricity is the indirect result of the break in transmission of the vocal repertoire in the long *usul* cycles, which occurred after the middle of the eighteenth century, with the fall of the Safavid Dynasty.[7]

It is unlikely that the four critical elements of the *taksim* had coexisted for a long time prior to the earliest literary references to the genre. As has been known almost since its creation, the *taksim* relies heavily on a codified melodic progression (*seyir*). This emphasis on *seyir* overshadows other possibilities for musical variation, such as those used by the Persian *avaz*, e.g., repeated ornamentation of single tonal centres and neighbouring tones, vocal trills, and other ornaments (especially in the *tahrir* section), or rhythmic variations reminiscent of poetic metres. All of these elements are either not essential or completely absent in the *taksim*, especially as practised in Turkey. These possibilities for musical interest, which were taken up and developed in the Persian *avaz*, were excluded from the *taksim*. Something akin to the Persian *avaz* seems to have existed in Iran in the seventeenth century, but, as Cantemir notes (in his Chapter 7), this was fundamentally distinct from the *taksim*.

Cantemir's brief characterisation of the Persian '*taksim*' focuses on a characteristic feature that distinguishes the modern Iranian and Turkish conceptions of variation and 'improvisation'. To Cantemir, the distinguishing characteristic of the Iranian '*taksim*' was its segmentary and largely pre-composed nature.

---

[7] This topic is treated further in chapter 6 of the present work. See also Feldman, 'The Musical "Renaissance" of Late Seventeenth Century Ottoman Turkey: Reflections on the Musical Materials of Ali Ufki Bey (c. 1610–75), Hafiz Post (d. 1694) and the "Maraghi" Repertoire', in *Writing the History of 'Ottoman Music*', ed. Martin Greve, Würzber: Ergon, 2015, pp. 87–138.

Iranian musicians, both vocalists and instrumentalists (*hanendeleri ve sazen-deleri*), compose (*beste eylemişler*) their *taksim*s 'in the form of a *peşrev*' (*peşrev şeklinde*). They teach the *taksim* (*talim virirler*) to their students part by part (*terkib terkib*). Cantemir never uses the verb *beste eylemek* ('to compose') in reference to the Turkish *taksim*. This verb and *tasnif olmak* ('to be composed') are used for both instrumental and vocal compositions. The usual verb for the *taksim* is *icra olunmak* ('to be performed').

The second characteristic by which Cantemir defined the *taksim* was its use of modulation. The *taksim* was the principal means by which 'conso-nance' or 'agreement' (*hiss-i ünsiyet*) was achieved in music. For this reason, modulation was as essential to the seventeenth-century conception of *taksim* as it is to its modern descendant. Cantemir stressed the role of the individual musician in creating 'melodies which are brand new and entirely his own', and that the highest type of *taksim* could be performed only by 'one or two musicians' (c. 1700: 7: 67). To Cantemir, the major significance of the *taksim* lay in its ability to create musical 'agreement' or 'consonance' by uniting the separate modal entities of the *makam* system through modulation. Today's *taksim* may contain sections which consist of a single *makam*, but a *taksim* that remained in one *makam* for more than a few minutes would be judged to have little aesthetic value (Signell 1977: 66).[8]

In looking for generic relatives of the *taksim*, there are several reasons for introducing the *tajwid* (*tecvit*) form of the Qur'anic chant. The Qur'anic *tajwid* and the *taksim*, both in the Arab countries and in Turkey, have simi-lar attitudes toward performance-generation, avoid fixed rhythmic cycles and compositions (although their specific rhythmic idioms differ), and modulate. In addition, it should be noted that the *tajwid* form of Qur'anic chant (as opposed to the *tartil*) is based on the same *makam seyir*s as is the *taksim*. There is not enough musical information about the practice of Qur'anic *tajwid* in past centuries to trace possible influences of the *tajwid* upon the *taksim*, or vice versa. However, given the relative novelty of both the *taksim* and the codified *seyir*s on which it is based, it is not unreasonable to suppose that *seyir* had already developed in the *tajwid* before it became the basis of the *taksim*. If one views the Qur'anic *tajwid* as one of the most stable

---

[8] This topic is discussed further in Chapter 7, 'Modulation'.

elements in Muslim musical cultures, then it is possible that the development of *seyir* within the *tajwid* could well have been worked out by the Qur'anic cantors long before the need was felt for such a usage by the secular courtly singers whose repertoire consisted primarily of rhythmic composed genres. The position of the Qur'anic cantors in Ottoman courtly music, which became established only in the later sixteenth century, furnishes the social context in which such a transference of musical practice becomes likely.

In the chapter on 'Professionalism' of my 1996 monograph *Music of the Ottoman Court*, the ulema figure prominently (1996: 80–4). Indeed, the earliest biographical dictionary of 'secular' musicians and composers was created in the 1720s by Es'ad Efendi (1685–1753), who was the Ottoman Shaykh al-Islam (Şeyhülislam), the highest dignitary in the official religious hierarchy. No other Islamic society, including the Timurids, demonstrated such a deep involvement of the Muslim clergy with all areas of secular artistic music. This historical phenomenon should be understood both as part of the history of a particular social class, and as a symbolic representation of the relations between secular and religious culture in Ottoman Turkey. In the seventeenth century the higher ulema were part of the Ottoman state bureaucracy, which caused many of them to view their social role as somewhat comparable to that of other Ottoman bureaucrats. Due to the Ottomans' maintenance of a strong commitment to the secular traditions of the earlier Turco-Muslim courts as well as to the increased acceptance of Sufi models for music and *samā'* that characterised the ruling classes, the ulema created a sonic expression for their newly enhanced role as guardians of the religious legitimacy of the state. By the seventeenth century this novel interface of three formerly highly disparate social groups – court musicians, ulema müezzins, and dervish *zakir*s and *neyzen*s – and their respective symbolic visions of musical art led to an equal legitimation of the principles of metrical pre-composition and non-metrical performance generation.

While the Mevlevi *neyzen*s cannot be credited with 'inventing' the *taksim*, they quickly became prominent in its performance. Part of the meditative discipline of the 1001 days of seclusion (*çile*) for the aspiring Mevlevi dervish was learning to produce a sound on the *ney*, beginning with the lowest tones. No other instrument in Ottoman musical culture was as deeply focused on the most 'abstract' understanding of sound and pitch. As the *taksim* genre developed, it naturally attracted the masters of the *ney* to explore the possi-bilities of musical consonance (*ünsiyyet*), thus enriching the potential of both the *taksim* and the *ney*. Particularly in the *baş-taksim* during the *mukabele*, the Mevlevi *neyzen*s have developed a highly idiomatic style of *taksim* play-ing, which has less emphasis on modulation, and a very specific approach to rhythmic idioms and pulse. Many of the recorded *baş-taksim*s of the twenti-eth century feature a pulse that is strikingly similar to that of the *kontakion* hymns sung at the Patriarchal Cathedral in Fener. This has not yet been a topic for serious scientific research. But we might well recall the deep con-nection of several Greek *psaltes* with the Mevlevi dervishes, of whom the most illustrious was Petros Peloponnesios (d. 1778). As noted earlier in this chapter, Petros was both a student and a tutor of the Mevlevi dervishes in Galata. As we will see in chapter 7, the appearance of the *baş-taksim* directly following the Na'at of Itri – with its evident Neo-Byzantine musical connections – renders this stylistic similarity all the more likely.

We have very few descriptions of Mevlevi *ney* performance outside the context of the *mukabele*. But, when they do begin to appear, touching such later nineteenth and early twentieth century figures as Aziz Dede (d. 1905), Emin Dede (d. 1945), and Neyzen Tevfik (d. 1953), the *ney taksim* outside of a specifically Mevlevi ritual context is also very characteristic. For this reason, the musical culture of the Mevleviye and the *ney* must be viewed both from the perspective of its metrical compositional mega-form, the *mukabele*, and from the perspective of improvised performance not bound to any metre or poetic text: the *taksim*.

5

THE MEVLEVI *NEYZEN* AS AN IDEAL REPRESENTATIVE OF OTTOMAN CULTURE

The Mevlevi *Neyzen* and the Transmission of Ottoman Music

Among the various instruments used in Ottoman music from the early nineteenth century to the present, the *ney* has had the strongest continuous lineage of transmission from master to student – this despite the closing of the Mevlevihanes in 1925. The reasons for the *ney*'s pre-eminence in twentieth-century Turkish art music are well worth examining.

The musical lineages of almost all the professional *neyzen*s of the second half of the twentieth century, which included Ulvi Erguner (1924–74), Aka Gündüz Kutbay (1934–79), Selami Bertuğ (1924–2004), and Niyazi Sayın (b. 1927), trace back to such well-known *neyzen*s as Aziz Dede (1871–1905), and Yusuf Paşa (1821–84), and before them, to Yusuf Paşa's father, Mehmed Sait Dede, of the Beşiktaş Mevlevihane (1803–60), and his student Salim Bey (1829–85), as well as to the remarkable Armenian *neyzen* and *tanburi* Kuyumcu Oskiyam (1780?–1870), who was apparently the student of Deli Ismail Dede (d. 1860). Most of the leading *neyzen*s in the twenty-first century, such as Ömer Erdoğdular, Yavuz Akalin, Sadrettin Özçimi, Arif Erdebil, Salih Bilgin, and Ahmet Şahin, had been the students of Niyazi Sayın. The brothers Süleyman and Kudsi Erguner are the sons of Ulvi Erguner and the grandsons of the *hafız* and *neyzen* Süleyman Erguner (1902–53). Ekrem Vural (b. 1945) had been the student of Selami Bertuğ, whose teacher Hayri Tümer (1902–73) had been the student of Türbedar Halid Dede (1872–1940) as well as of a line of teachers reaching back through Muallim Kazim Uz (1872–1938) to Zekai Dede (d. 1896) and Ismail Dede Efendi (d. 1846). Later, Uz had studied with Emin Dede as well. Despite his Mevlevi connections, Tümer attained a secure position in the National Press (*Matbuat-i Umum*) and Radio Ankara. Understandably he worked in the National Press during the period when Turkish music was removed from the radio (on Tümer, see Behar 2005: 117–34).

In order to appreciate the reasons for the strength of the *ney*, we must look at the tumultuous history of Ottoman music, and its instrumentation, in the last century of the Empire. The middle and late nineteenth century constituted a period of crisis for Ottoman music, similar in some respects to the musical crisis of the early seventeenth century. The violent elimination of the Janissary Corps in 1826, and with them the entire *mehter* musical ensemble, also constituted a musical crisis for the Ottoman court. Mahmud II followed his destruction of the *mehterhane* with the creation of the Muzikayi Hümayun orchestra, a mixed Western and Turkish military band, under the leadership of Giuseppe Donizetti, who became known as 'Donizetti Pasha'. While the sultans of the Tanzimat, Abdülmecid and Abdülaziz, continued to have an interest in Ottoman music along with Western music – indeed, Abdülaziz was a Mevlevi *muhibb* – the social conditions did not favour much new creativity within the courtly genres. In 1846, during the reign of Abdülmecid, the great composer of the era, the Mevlevi Ismail Dede Efendi, left the court and went on the Haj, saying that 'this game has lost its flavour'. And during the long reign of Sultan Abdülhamid II (1876–1908), who succeeded Abdülaziz, the sultan showed little interest in any music.

After the middle of the nineteenth century this situation led both to the influence of various forms of lighter Western music at the court, and to the creation of a 'middlebrow' version of the older courtly concert, which gradually usurped its name: *fasıl*. Especially after 1876, this new form of *fasıl* was performed mainly in the alcohol-serving nightclubs (*gazino*), usually run by members of the Greek or Armenian communities. The nightclub '*fasil*' was essentially based on a succession of *şarkı* songs in varying *usuls*, usually beginning with the slow *ağır aksak* (9/4) and closing with the dance-like *aksak* (9/8), as well as popular regional dances, such as the local Greek *sirto* and the imported Romanian gypsy/klezmer *longa*. Lower class versions of these *gazino* clubs in different neighbourhoods featured only *şarkı* and *türkü* songs in short *usul*s, as well as improvised music for the Gypsy *çifte telli* erotic dance.

The Instrumentarium of the Late Ottoman Empire

One of the leading composers for the new *gazino*s was the Armenian violinist Tatyos Efendi (1858–1913). Tatyos also composed instrumental *peşrev*s as well as *şarkı*s for the clubs. According to an existing photograph, his ensemble was still relatively conservative, featuring two *tanbur*s as well as his violin and a *daire* frame-drum for percussion. But later in the nineteenth century the newly imported oud quickly took the place of both the *tanbur* and the semi-rural lutes *tanbura* and *bozuk*, which had also long been used in the cities for popular and folk music. The oud had been displaced from Ottoman urban music, along with the now extinct *kopuz* and *şeşhane*, since the later seventeenth century (Feldman 1996: 152–3). But now the oud's tonal versatility – its fretless neck was equally at home with urban *makam* or with rural folkloric modalities – together with its rhythmic dynamism and relatively greater volume rendered it more appropriate in situations where a purely artistic repertoire was not required.

Tanburi Cemil Bey (1873–1916) played several instruments. He revolutionised the technique of the *tanbur* by giving it a more dynamic right-hand plectrum stroke, and the following generation of *tanburi*s usually adopted his technique. The older *tanbur* technique was apparently preserved by Kuyumcu Oskiyam, who had learned it from the court musician Tanburi Isak Fresco-Romano (d. 1814). The *tanbur* held its own, but largely due to a major change in technique effected by Tanburi Cemil Bey, who was also the most prolific maker of 78 rpm recordings of any of his contemporaries of comparable musical and social status.

Thus, through most of the nineteenth century, instruments of courtly music other than the *ney* were either dropped or replaced. The *santur* was replaced by the *kanun*, the *kemançe* by the violin, and then, in the twentieth century, by the *lyra/kemençe*.[1] By the early twentieth century the *tanbur* continued to survive, but its place was more often taken by the oud, whose

---

[1] The modern Turkish urban *kemençe* is the Constantinopolitan Greek *lyra politikas*. The *kemançe* had been a different instrument. I discuss this at some length in *Music of the Ottoman Court*, pp. 128–33.

initial performance models were either from the southeast of the country, as exemplified by the oud player Udi Nevres Bey, or from the local Roma/gypsy community, represented, for example, in the style of oud player Yorgo Bacanos. In the mid-twentieth century a few creative oudists, such as Rüsdü Eriç and Cinuçen Tanrıkorur (1938–2000), developed a 'classicising' style that combined influences from the above-mentioned styles with a resonance coming from the *tanbur*.

Paradoxically, despite the cultural and musical dislocations of the second half of the nineteenth century, the situation was vastly more favourable for the *ney* than for any other Turkish instrument. This was because Istanbul alone had five major Mevlevihanes, each of which trained and employed a number of professional *neyzens*. And nearby was the active Mevlevi *zaviye* in Gelibolu. While we are usually less well-informed about them, smaller Mevlevi *zaviyes* throughout Anatolia and parts of the Balkans continued to produce *neyzens* of quality. A high technical and aesthetic level was maintained, and the discoveries and techniques of the most creative *neyzens* always had students and imitators. While the *mukabele* was indeed banned after 1925, the performance of the *ney* as such was not. Throughout the twentieth century, an abundance of sources document the musical and social influence of the *neyzens*, who not only retained specific performance techniques that encapsulated musical knowledge no longer as accessible on other instruments but also exemplified the cultural achievements of Ottoman civilisation more broadly (see Şenay 2020). The following section presents short profiles of several of the most influential Mevlevi *neyzens* in Istanbul and adjacent areas over a long historical span, from the seventeenth to the earlier twentieth centuries, focusing both on their careers and their creativity.

The Leading *Neyzens* in History

The status of the *ney* among Mevlevis was such that it was not uncommon for an eminent *neyzen* within a Mevlevihane to be appointed as a sheikh there or in another *asitane* or *zaviye*. Indeed, the Mevlevi *neyzen* could be considered almost an ideal representative of Ottoman culture, often with a high hierarchical position within a Sufi Order. This was a remarkable innovation of the Ottomans that had no close analogue in any other Islamic culture, and it was the *ney* alone that could claim this distinction – even in cases where Mevlevi musicians also played other instruments. While the high appreciation of the *ney* was undoubtedly based on earlier Persianate Sufistic cultural patterns, only among the Mevlevis during the Ottoman period does the *neyzen* attain this status. As I observe below, to some extent this status even survived the demise of the Mevleviye as a formal institution. The veneration of the *neyzen* can be found, for example, in the depiction of Emin Dede (1883–1945) by the Turkish modernist writer Ahmet Tanpınar in his novel *Huzur* (1949). It is also apparent in the biographies of Mevlevi *neyzen*s who were active following the closure of the *tekke*s in 1925 (provided by Ayvazoğlu 2007 and others), which show these men to be crucial in transmitting the musical heritage of both the Mevleviye and the Ottoman court as well as an ideal of the behaviour and ethics (*ahlak*) of a refined Ottoman. The human qualities of individual *neyzen*s emerge more clearly in biographical material from the later nineteenth and twentieth centuries that extend beyond descriptions of their compositions, poetry, and careers as sheikhs.

The earliest description of a historical Mevlevi *neyzen* was penned in the seventeenth century by Evliya Çelebi, in his *Seyahatname*: 'The most eminent of these *neyzen*s is the sheikh of the Beşiktaş Mevlevihane. He is Mevlevi Derviş Yusuf. The heart of anyone who hears him is softened and he is brought to tears' (Özergin 1972 and Feldman 1996: 136). Dervish Yusuf (d. 1669) had a most unusual musical career. He is generally referred to as Çengi Yusuf Dede, and he combined the skills of *neyzen*, *çeng* (*harp*) player, musical theorist, and poet. The fullest biographical information comes from the poetic *tezkire* of Safayi (Behar 2010: 177).

Yusuf began his career in Konya, where he underwent the *çile* with Bostan Çelebi. Travelling to Istanbul, he then learned the *ney* in the Galata Asitane. Sultan Murad IV heard his *ney* playing by chance in the Istavroz Gardens, and immediately invited him to the palace, giving him a position in the Treasury Department. In the 1630s he was described as a performer of the *ney* in the sultanic ensemble (see chapter 6). At some point Yusuf Dede evidently learned the *çeng* well enough to be considered a known performer on the instrument. On the sultan's death in 1640, he left the palace and established himself as a *neyzen* in the Beşiktaş Mevlevihane. Around 1645–55 he wrote a *Risale-i Edvar*, a short treatise on the science of music, one of the very few such attempts in the seventeenth century (Uslu 2015). He also wrote poetry, including a poetic 'response' (*nazire*) to Rumi's *Masnavi*, and is therefore included in Safayi's biographical dictionary. He married the daughter of the sheikh Hasan Dede of Beşiktaş, and between 1663 and 1669, he was the sheikh of the Mevlevihane. In the next generation the most illustrious figure among the Mevlevi *neyzen*s was Osman Dede (1652–1730), known as Kutb-i Nayi ('The World Axis of the Ney'), whose career within the *tarikat* and as sheikh of Galata was presented in the previous chapter.

Osman Dede was one of the most brilliant and creative musicians of the Mevlevi Order. Born in Istanbul in 1652, he became a *neyzen* and then the chief *neyzen* (*neyzenbaşı*) and eventually the sheikh of the Galata Mevlevihane. His artistic fame rested on a number of factors: (1) his great virtuosity on the *ney*; (2) his composition of four Mevlevi *ayin* ceremonies; (3) his composition of the *Mi'raciye*, a religious oratorio that is the most extensive and complex piece in the entire Ottoman repertoire; (4) his composition of secular instrumental music; (5) his use of a system of musical notation of his own invention; (6) his writing of a book of musical theory (7) his great mastery of calligraphy; (8) his religious poetry, under the names 'Osman' and 'Nayi' (Feldman: 2021). Some translations from his writing appear in chapter 6. Apart from music, Osman Dede was responsible for teaching Rumi's *Masnavi*. He founded a sheikhly dynasty through his daughter's marriage to the sheikh of Yenikapı lodge. In the next generation three of his grandchildren – Ali Nutki Dede, Abdülbaki Nasir Dede, and Abdürahhim Künhi Dede – became sheikhs of Yenikapı and major composers and music theorists.

Osman Dede's system of notation – based on Arabic letters and numerals – is very close to that of Prince Cantemir (1673–1723), but which one has priority is unclear. Osman Dede appears to have been the first Ottoman Muslim musician to use notation enthusiastically, and according to his contemporary Salim Efendi, he used it for both vocal and instrumental music. Salim Efendi describes in amazement how Osman was able to write down any *murabba* or *kar* that he heard, and then sing it immediately from his notation. As these items were complex pieces using long *usul*s, Osman's sight-reading was surely astonishing at the time. Osman's surviving notated collection, however, contains only instrumental pieces, similar to Cantemir's Collection.

Osman's magnum opus, the *Mi'raciye* (Arabic: *Mi'rajiya*), which relates the heavenly Ascent of the Prophet Muhammad with the Angel Gabriel – was rescued from oblivion after the closing of the Sufi lodges in 1925, by Dr Subhi Ezgi, Sadettin Arel, and Ahmed Irsoy, who transcribed its sections from several Qur'anic reciters and müezzins. This unique work features Turkish religious poems by the composer-author as well as several Persian poems by Rumi, and by the Halveti sheikh Nasuhi Muhammed (d. 1717). Apparently composed following a dream vision that Osman Dede had at the *tekke* of Sheikh Nasuhi in Üsküdar shortly after the latter's death, the *Mi'raciye* contains six large sections (*bahir*) that use many different *makam*s and their modulations. Each *bahir* is composed in a different long rhythmic cycle (*usul*), and is divided into successive solo and choral sections. While other *Mi'raciye*s had been composed in the Ottoman era, only Osman Dede's survived to the twentieth century.

Osman Dede composed four Mevlevi *ayin* ceremonies – in *makam*s Rast, Uşşak, Çargah, and Hicaz. Internal analysis of these four *ayin*s shows that they illustrate many common features of early eighteenth-century compositional techniques. All four are still performed for the Mevlevi ceremony.

Osman Dede was also a major composer of instrumental *peşrev*s and *sema'i*s. His own notated manuscript, which is still in private hands and was unavailable to scholarship until very recently, contains several of them, and two were notated by his contemporary Prince Cantemir (*Hüseyni Fahte, Neva Çember*). His many other elegant *peşrev*s and *sema'i*s, preserved in posteighteenth century notated sources, have been thoroughly modernised, and are remote in style from anything that Osman Dede might have actually composed (Wright 1988: 47–61).

During the second half of the eighteenth and well into the nineteenth century, Yenikapı became a major centre of musical performance, composition and musical theory. The three sons of Kütahyalı Abubekir Dede, mentioned in the previous chapter, became the sheikhs in succession: Ali Nutki Dede (1762–1804), Abdülbaki Nasir Dede (1765–1821), and Abdurrahim Künhi Dede (1769–1831).

Ali Nutki Dede was a poet who compiled the Mevlevi *mecmua* anthology *Defter-i Dervişan*. He was also a fine calligrapher. His prestige was such that both the leading Mevlevi poet Galib Dede and the leading Mevlevi composer of the following generation, Ismail Dede Efendi (d. 1846), undertook their *çile* under him in Yenikapı. He died childless, and his one surviving composition, the magnificent *Şevkutarab Ayin*, was performed one week before his death, in 1804.

Ali Nutki's brother, Abdülbaki Nasir Dede, combined the talents of *neyzen*, composer and musicologist. He served as the *neyzenbaşı* of Yenikapı and composed two Mevlevi *ayin*s in *makam*s Isfahan and Acem-Buselik. He also composed two major works of musicology, the *Tahririye* and *Tetkik u Tahkik*. The last of these brother sheikhs of Yenikapı was Abdürrahim Künhi Dede. Known for his beautiful voice, he became the *kudümzenbaşı* of Yenikapı. In 1791 he composed a well-respected *ayin* in *makam* Hicaz. Unfortunately his *ayin* composition in *makam* Nühüft was lost.[2]

The musical development within the Yenikapı Mevlevihane reached a culmination in the career of Ismail Dede Efendi (1778–1846), known also as 'Hammami-zade'. His rather peculiar patronymic, which means 'son of the bathhouse owner', does not imply any kind of guild background. His father Süleyman Ağa, who was of Janissary origin, had purchased a bath-house (*hammam*) after his retirement in Istanbul, following a long career as the seal-bearer (*mühürdar*) of the Governor of Lebanon, Ahmed Cezzar (Jazzar) Pasha. As an adolescent, Ismail was registered in the Office of Accounts (*muhasebe kalemi*), but he began to study music at the nearby Yenikapı Mevlevihane. At the age of twenty he decided to leave his office work and enter the Mevlevi three-year retreat (*çile*). During the second year of his service he composed a *şarkı* song *in makam* Buselik that was eventually sung to Sultan Selim III by his imperial singer. This led to Sultan Selim requesting Ismail's service at court. Ismail's superior, Ali Nutki Dede, shortened his *çile* service by one year so that he could begin to attend the imperial *fasıl*s twice a week. Ismail completed his *çile* in Yenikapı in 1799, and went on to become the *neyzenbaşı* there.

As a dervish he received the title of *dede* and continued to teach and compose in his cell in the *tekke*. In 1802 Ismail Dede married a woman of the court and left the *tekke* to live with her in the Akbıyık neighbourhood. They had one son, who died in 1805. Ismail withdrew from the court during the troubles resulting from the assassination of Sultan Selim III in 1808, but with the accession later that year of Mahmud II (ruled 1808–39), he entered the most productive period of his career. He attained the posts of 'imperial companion' (*musahib-i şehriyari*) and chief-müezzin. It was in this period that he composed

---

[2] More information about these brothers appears in chapter 6.

seven Mevlevi *ayins*: Saba and Neva (1823), Bestenigar (1832), Saba-Buselik and Hüzzam (1833), the lost Isfahan (1836), and Ferahfeza (1839). He also completed a *fasıl* in *makam Ferahfeza* (1834) (see Öztuna 1996).

Dede Efendi's somewhat younger contemporary 'Deli' Ismail Dede (1808–60) became the *neyzenbaşı* at Galata. While not known as a composer, his performance on the *ney* was at such a high level that Hemdem Çelebi in Konya decreed that he could be the *neyzenbaşı* of all the Mevlevihanes of Istanbul. For a time he was invited to Egypt by the ruler Abbas I (1848–53), where he became the *neyzenbaşı* of the Cairo Mevlevihane, and was granted a salary and the income from a farm. He eventually returned to Istanbul and taught the *neyzen* and *tanbur* player Sheikh Abdülhalim Efendi (1824–96) and the Armenian Tanburi Oskyiam (d. 1870). His nickname, Deli ('Mad'), originates with his evident capriciousness and wilfulness, which did not seem to interfere either with his artistry or with his Mevlevi and secular career.

The Beşiktaş/Bahariye Asitane produced several creative musicians through the nineteenth century.[3] In the first half of the century the most illustrious of these was the *neyzenbaşı* and later sheikh Said Dede (1803–53), who was the son of Mahmud Dede from Tripoli (Trablusşam). He was the teacher of Salim Bey (1829–85), the *neyzenbaşı* in the Üsküdar Mevlevihane, and a member of both the Mevlevi and the Sadi *tarikat*s, as well as an official in the Ministry of Commerce. He was also known as a poet, a composer of *ilahi* hymns and of instrumental *peşrev*s and *saz sema'i*s, of which his *Hicaz Fahte* is probably his best known. Salim's younger brother was Hacı Faik Bey (1831–91), who played the *ney* but did not become a Mevlevi *neyzen*, and was known as a classical singer. Faik Bey was perhaps the last major composer in the serious classical vocal genres, the *kar* and *beste*, with a prodigious output. His Mevlevi *ayin* in Dügah is also much appreciated. In his professional life he had been the director of a girls' craft school in Aksaray and of the hospital in Haseki.

Said Dede's younger brother, Salih Dede (1818–88), also underwent the *çile* in Beşiktaş, and became the *neyzenbaşı* at both Bahariye and Kasımpaşa.

---

[3] Originally founded in Beşiktaş in 1613, this Mevlevihane was demolished and moved several times. During the reign of Abdülaziz (1861–76) it was rebuilt in the Bahariye section of the Golden Horn.

He did not become sheikh because he was accepted into the official ensemble Muzikayi Hümayun, and rose to the military rank of *kaymakam*, or lieutenant colonel, hence he is also known as Salih Bey. Salih Dede composed an *ayin* in Şeddaraban, as well as *peşrev*s in *usul Devr-i Kebir* for the *ayin* ceremony. Of these his *peşrev*s in Acem-Aşiran and in Pençgah are still in the performed repertoire. His *saz sema'i* in Uşşak is considered a masterpiece of the genre and was frequently played by Tanburi Necdet Yaşar (see Feldman 2017: 159–62).

Said Dede's son Yusuf Paşa (1821–84) is considered the most important composer of instrumental music of the nineteenth century. He also underwent his *çile* in Beşiktaş and became a *dede* as well as the *neyzenbaşı* there. But in 1840, at age 19, he, too, joined the Muzıkayi Hümayun. Quite early on he caught the attention of the new Sultan Abdülmecid (1839–61), and became both a companion and a courtier (*mabeynci*). Later he became the *ney* teacher to Sultan Abdülaziz (1861–76), and rose to the rank of *miralay* (general). All of his *peşrev*s are composed in the *usul Devr-i Kebir* so that they can be used in the Mevlevi *ayin*. His son Celal (Iyison) was also an officer in the Muzikayi Hümayun, learning both Turkish and Western music on the cello. Two of his three daughters, Destine and Vediya, were musicians and became music teachers at prestigious girls' schools in Istanbul.

The last great musician/*neyzen* of Beşiktaş was Hüseyin Fahrettin Dede (1854–1911). The son of Hasan Nazif Dede (1794–1862), the Mevlevi sheikh of Yenişehir, in Thessaly, he was born when his father had already taken up the position of *postnişin* in Beşiktaş, following the death of Said Dede in 1853. Fahrettin was only seven years old when his father passed away, and while a titular sheikh, he received a varied education under the tutorship of Hacı Raşid Dede. This included lessons in Sufism and poetry given by the famous poet Yenişehirli Avni Bey and many other illustrious figures of the time. Fahrettin Dede soon became the most respected *neyzen* of his generation, a fine singer and a major composer and teacher. He was also an instructor in the *Masnavi* and the Persian language. Among his students in the theory of music were Rauf Yekta Bey, Dr Subhi Ezgi, and Sadettin Arel, who were the founders of modern Turkish musicology. Despite his great fame and centrality in the culture, his Ayin in Karcığar was lost, while his Acem-Aşiran Ayin was notated by Rauf Yekta Bey, and thus survives.

Aziz Dede (1835–1905) was a crucial figure in the transmission of the *ney* from the nineteenth to the twentieth centuries. Regarded as one of the greatest *neyzen*s of any period, he also united a wide variety of Mevlevi centres and musicians. Born in Üsküdar to a bureaucratic family, he moved to Gelibolu when his father took up a position there in the Ministry of Commerce. His early musical experiences are related somewhat differently according to his various students (Ayvazoğlu 2007: 35). At some point in his youth he travelled to Egypt and learned the *ney* in the Mevlevihane of Cairo. But by high school age he returned so that he could register in the *rüşdiye* school in Gelibolu. Soon after he completed high school, his father finally accepted his urgent desire to enter the Mevlevihane in Gelibolu, where he continued his study of the *ney*, and finally completed his *çile* under Hüsameddin Dede. Aziz Dede served as *neyzenbaşı* in Gelibolu for almost twenty years, and his fame reached Istanbul. When the position of *neyzenbaşı* in the Galata Asitane became vacant, the *postnişin* at the time, Ataullah Dede (served 1871–1910), wrote to the Gelibolu *zaviye*, requesting the services of Aziz Dede. Apparently the latter gladly accepted the opportunity to return to Istanbul. However, once he found himself in this refined musical environment of the urban Mevlevis, he could not but observe certain limitations in his own playing. To remedy these, he approached the Sadi and Mevlevi, Salim Bey (d. 1885), who was the *neyzenbaşı* in Üsküdar. He was also a bureaucrat in the same ministry in which Aziz's father had worked. According to later anecdotes, Salim Bey initially could not see why Aziz Dede needed to study with him. But eventually they established a good relationship, and Salim reportedly took great pleasure in hearing his own compositions in his student's performance.

Aziz Dede was known for his extraordinarily rich tone on the lower-pitched *ney*s, and for his long and inventive *taksim*s. He also performed on many occasions outside of the Mevlevihanes, and after one of these *taksim*s, Tanburi Cemil Bey (d. 1916) kissed his hand and told him 'I will never forget the spirituality (*ruhaniyet*) of this day for the rest of my life!' On another such occasion Prince Abdülhalim Paşa was visiting from Egypt, and after hearing Aziz Dede, he provided an apartment for him in his own waterfront mansion (*yalı*). The Pasha took Aziz under his wing in every respect, paying him a pension, finding him a suitable bride, and then setting up their household in Üsküdar. During this period Aziz also served as *neyzenbaşı* in Kasımpaşa and Yenikapı, while he was replaced in Galata by Hakkı Dede (d. 1918; Öztuna I: 90).

In his later years Aziz Dede opened a shop in Üsküdar, where he taught students. Among them were the composer and musicologist Rauf Yekta, and the outstanding *neyzen* Emin Dede (Yazıcı). However, despite his favourable relationship with Yekta, he was adamantly against the use of notation, insisting on the exclusive use of oral musical transmission. It may be in part due to this attitude that only seven of his compositions have survived. These include a Hicaz Devri Kebir *peşrev*, and six *saz sema'i*s, of which the *saz sema'i* in Uşşak is widely considered a masterpiece.

Transition to the Early Republic

A treatment of all the *neyzen*s who were active in Istanbul and in some of the other major Turkish cities in the transition from the Ottoman era to the Turkish Republic would require a separate monograph. Here I will characterise the careers of three major figures: Emin Yazıçı (1883–1945), Tevfik Kolaylı (1879–1953), and Halil Dikmen (1906–64). Each of these men exemplified the challenges and possibilities offered by the significantly transformed conditions of post-1925 Turkey. Of the three, only Emin Dede had the opportunity to study the *ney* consistently from major *neyzenbaşı*s at a functioning Mevlevihane. He was thus a link between the great *neyzen*s of the nineteenth century and the generation of *neyzen*s who reached maturity after the closing of the Mevlevihanes.

Emin Dede

The writer and scholar Ahmed Hamdi Tanpınar had known Emin Dede (1883–1945) personally, and Ayvazoğlu and other contemporary writers view him as a tragic figure who was at the same time the archetypal bridge between a functioning Mevlevi culture and the culture of the new Turkish Republic. Tanpınar refers to him by name in his novel *'Huzur'*, written in 1949, where he lavishes a unique description on him:

> Emin Dede was one of those men whom a civilisation had chosen to be one of its highest instruments. He had an appearance that might be said to be more delicate than his reed-flute . . . He projected an attitude that seemed to say:

'Is this him, this tiny man, is he the person who is the last guardian of all of the treasures of the past, whose head is the golden hive filled with the buzzing of six centuries, and through whose breath an entire civilisation lives?' . . .

It was as though he had no personal side, apart from some little substance, half melted in the warmth of his inner sunlight. And even this substance was hidden and disappeared in every moment under a pile of manners, honorific behaviour, his education to view everyone as his equal, a bashfulness – that seemed most strange to us – and which denied everything personal. Looking at him, Mumtaz recalled the couplet of Neşati:

Ettik o kadar ref'-i ta'ayyün ki Neşati
Ayine-i pür tab-i mücellada nihanüz

'Oh Neşati, all manifestation we have rejected, so much so that
In the flame of the polished mirror's brightness we are hidden'.
(Tanpinar 1949: 310–11)

In order to describe such a figure, Tanpınar's character resorts to a verse by Neşati (d. 1674), a leading poet of the seventeenth-century Indian Style, who was also a Mevlevi dervish and sheikh. As the scene progresses, Tanpınar demonstrates the continued relevance of the Mevleviye through the *ney* and the Mevlevi philosophy of music well over twenty years after the Order itself, along with its liturgy, had been banned. Here Emin Dede is performing the *ayin* in *makam Ferahfeza* by Ismail Dede Efendi (d. 1846) for a secular social gathering:

> Not only did Emin Bey speak of the old musicians and saints as though they were living people, he would erase the distance between him and the times of their deaths, and their personalities, by calling them 'our Master', 'our Patron Saint', or 'our Efendi'. In this way he himself, the time in which he lived, and the person of whom he spoke and the actual time of his death became joined.
> (Tanpinar 1949: 320)

This work of fiction is not meant to be taken as indicative of the attitudes toward music of all the mid-twentieth-century upper-class characters in

Tanpınar's novel, nor of the real Turkish readers of Tanpınar's work, who belonged largely to the same upper-class as Tanpınar and his characters. For the people in question, as for Tanpınar himself, Ottoman classical music had become, in his words, 'the old music'; it was not the only music in their lives.

Emin Dede's education and career exemplifies the complex religious, cultural and economic situation in the transition from the Empire to the Republic. He was born in 1883 in the Tophane neighbourhood of Istanbul, where his father, Hafız Eyüb Sabri Efendi, was the preacher (*hatib*) at the Hirka-i Şerif Mosque. The family does not seem to have had any close Sufi connections. Emin and his older brother, Ömer Vasfi, were given both religious and secular educations at the local elementary *mekteb, rüşdiye*, and *idadi* (*lise*) schools. Both brothers shared a great talent for calligraphy, but by age 13 Emin was already studying the *ney* with Neyzen Aziz Dede, in Üsküdar. Anecdotes relate his great persistence in studying with this irascible teacher, even after Aziz Dede had ejected him for the offence of using musical notation.

Emin's formal education continued at two schools of higher Islamic learning, but these were interrupted in 1902, when his father enrolled him as an assistant in the Post and Telegraph Office. Three years later he began to take lessons with Hüseyin Fahrettin Efendi at the Beşiktaş (Bahariye) Asitane. By 1908, he had advanced at the Post and Telegraph Office to the level of *müsevvid*, making rough drafts of formal letters. From 1914 and throughout the First World War, he remained in Istanbul as a map calligrapher for the War Office. Nevertheless, he continued to study the *ney*, as well as music more widely, with such masters as Bolahenk Nuri Bey. By 1918 he was appointed the *neyzenbaşı* of Galata and also of Üsküdar, although his professional duties had not allowed him to undergo the *çile* training. But thereafter he was nevertheless known as 'Dede'. He continued in these capacities until 1924, shortly prior to the official closing of the *tekke*s.

Emin Dede lived for many years in a house in Tophane together with his older brother, Ömer Vasfi. After the closing of the Mevlevihanes, Emin Dede was appointed to the Darülelhan Conservatory, but the following year (1926) the teaching of Ottoman music was prohibited there. Two years later, in 1928, the Arabic/Ottoman script was replaced by Latin letters, thus rendering both his and his brother's calligraphic work obsolete. This proved to be too heavy a blow for Ömer Vasfi, who did not survive the year. When the Press Section of the War Office moved to Ankara, Emin (who had taken the surname 'Yazıcı' – the calligrapher) asked to retire. He spent the remainder of his life among his many students, among whom were Hakkı Suha Gezgin (1895–1960), Süleyman Erguner (1902–53), Halil Can (1905–73),

Image 5.1 Photograph of Emin Dede Yazıcı (d. 1945) Photographer and year unknown. Collection of Uğur Derman.

and Halil Dikmen (1906–64). Emin Dede did not compose widely, but several of his *peşrev*s in *devri kebir* are still well known. In particular his Beyati Peşrevi has come to replace the much older *peşrev* that had been played before the Beyati Ayin of Köçek Mustafa Dede (d. 1683).

Emin Dede finally married late in life. The major Mevlevi poet Tahir Olgun (1877–1951) composed this chronogram on his passing:

Dönerek uçdu Beka sahnasına ruhul Emin
Rahmet ü mağfiretin sağarını eyleye nuş
Feyzine mazhar olup Hazret-i Mevlana'nın
Eylesin ruh-i revanı orada cuş u huruş

The soul of Emin has returned and flown to the realm of Eternity
May he drink from the cup of mercy and forgiveness!
Experiencing the sacred charisma of Mevlana,
May his living soul cry out and sing!

Halil Dikmen

Halil Dikmen (1906–64) represents a fundamentally different culture and career path to any of the *neyzen*s described above. He was neither an initiated Mevlevi, nor did he come from an Islamic clerical background. He never became a professional musician, and his public performances were extremely few. He was not a composer. His more public professional fame was mainly confined to his work as a painter, a teacher of fine arts, and a curator and arts administrator. For all of the above reasons the Turkish secondary musical sources – including the *Türk Musiksi Ansiklopedisi* – generally contain nothing about him. Nevertheless, he was universally acclaimed as perhaps the greatest *neyzen* of his generation. Through his outstanding student Niyazi Sayın (b. 1927), and the miniature painter and *neyzen* Ahmed Yakupoğlu (1920–2016), he may be said to be the stylistic 'grandfather' of almost all of the leading *neyzen*s in Turkey today. We are thus very much indebted to Beşir Ayvazoğlu (2007), who appears to have been the first writer in Turkey to research and publish a coherent narrative of Dikmen's musical life, as well as his broader artistic life. All this despite the fact that Halil Dikmen was such a well-known figure in the cultural life of Istanbul that his friend Ahmet Hamdi Tanpınar included a vignette of him as 'The Painter Cemil' in the very same 1949 novel, *Huzur*, in which his Mevlevi teacher Emin Dede makes an appearance. Dikmen was also a friend of the Mevlevi scholar Abdülbaki Gölpınarli, who used his tableau of a Mevlevi *sema* as the cover for his seminal *Mevlana'dan Sonra Mevlevilik* (1983), referred to so often in the present work. Part of this lack of self-promotion may be rooted in his residual manifestation of Mevlevi culture, for example, as described by Ayvazoğlu: 'He never put himself forward; because what he had learned from his teacher Emin Dede was not only the *tekke* style on the *ney*. He also acquired the Mevlevi delicacy and the Sufistic morality, and it was upon these that he built his personality' (Ayvazoğlu 2007: 62).

Halil Dikmen was born in the Fatih neighbourhood of old Istanbul, into a bureaucratic family. His father Mehmet Haşim Bey used to invite Levon Hanciyan, the well-known Armenian singer, to teach him music at his home. Halil's sister, Halide, related various anecdotes about these sessions. The *neyzen* Ihsan Aziz Bey (1884–1935), a student of the Beşiktaş sheikh Hüseyin Fahrettin Dede, used to come to the house as well, and before long he was giving lessons to the very young Halil. But it was clear to his parents that the young man also had a talent for visual art. So in 1923, after his elementary education, he was brought by his uncle, an officer in the Military Office, to the Fine Arts School (Sanayi-i Nefise Mektebi). He did very well in his painting, but he also found the time to study *ney* with Emin Dede.

By 1925, while still a student himself, he was able to teach art at the Kasımpaşa Elementary School. And in 1927, after winning first prize in a student painting contest, he was among a group of students chosen to continue their studies in Paris. This was Halil's first exposure to serious collections of European painting from various historical eras, and at first he was captivated by the Italian Renaissance and Baroque. Nevertheless he continued his practice on the *ney*, and by 1929 he was able to give a successful lecture demonstration at the Guimet Museum.

When Dikmen finally returned to Turkey, it was a very different place than the country he had left in 1927. The Mevlevihanes had already been closed before he left, but now, in 1932, Ottoman music was banned from the radio as well. To add to Dikmen's disillusionment, his first position was teaching art in a high school in the Central Anatolian city of Kayseri. But after a few dull years in Kayseri, Dikmen so impressed Ahmet Kudsi Tecer, then minister of Education in Sivas, that in 1936, he successfully applied for a position at the prestigious Galatasaray Lisesi in European Istanbul. Once there, he was so well thought of as a teacher, both for his knowledge and for his respect toward his students, that his professional path went only upward. Only one year later Dikmen was appointed director of the new State Museum of Painting and Sculpture at the Fine Arts Academy in Istanbul. How a thirty-year-old painter whose longest previous position was in a high school in Kayseri could possibly have reached this status is mysterious. In the absence of any other explanation, we may have to accept the version told by his sister, Halide Dikmen, namely, that at a meeting at the Academy of Fine Arts in which Halil was present, Kemal Atatürk – then in the last year of his life – demanded that a Museum of Painting and Sculpture be created within the Academy. Somehow he was so impressed with Halil, whom he had only met that day, that he simply appointed him to the position of director of the new museum (Ayvazoğlu 2007: 72). Thus, the thirty-year-old Dikmen was now working with the well-known French painter Leopold Levy (1882–1966) and the Turkish painter Cemal Tollu (1899–1968).

For the next twenty-five years Halil Dikmen's highly successful career was as a painter who integrated a variety of Cubist and more traditional styles, and as an administrator and teacher. He was of course known to the musical world, but he rarely performed in public or even on the radio, once Turkish music was reinstated there. In 1942 his invitation to a musical jury in Ankara by Mesut Cemil, who then directed the radio, led to a small but very well-appreciated concert, and then to an appearance on Istanbul Radio. Dikmen also taught a number of students, of whom the most illustrious is Niyazi Sayın. Thus, in a very real sense Halil Dikmen actively united the cultures of Ottoman and Republican Turkey on the highest level, and with the highest official support. His friend Ahmet Hamdi Tanpınar once told him, 'Halil, you cannot possibly know the importance of the work that you are accomplishing. Through this you are rebuilding Turkey from its foundations!' (Ayvazoğlu 2007: 75).

Neyzen Tevfik Kolaylı

Neyzen Tevfik (1879–1953) represents a total contrast with Halil Dikmen. While for Dikmen, training as a *neyzen* was part of his own private artistic cultivation amid a broad education that integrated Europe and Turkey, Tevfik Kolayli became so much identified with his instrument that he was often simply referred to as 'Neyzen'. And while Dikmen avoided both concerts and recordings but generously taught many private students on the *ney*, Tevfik's performance style is known through his recordings rather than through any students. Tevfik's life is so unexpected and improbable that he seems almost like an atavistic reincarnation of a wandering *qalandar* from the Middle Ages. But of course he was not that, but rather, an extreme personality reacting to the tensions within late Ottoman and early Republican society.

Tevfik was born in Bodrum to a high school teacher working in Urla. As a child, he was already fascinated by the *ney*. He also showed an interest in poetry at an early age. But in 1893, at age 14, he had his first epileptic seizure, which required treatment; the disease would plague him intermittently throughout his life. He left his high school in Izmir before graduation. At the same time, he studied *ney* with Neyzenbaşı Cemal Bey at the Izmir Mevlevihane. He published his first poem in the journal *Muktebes* coming out of Izmir in 1898. Shortly thereafter he went to Istanbul, where he further developed his *ney* playing at the Yenikapı Mevlevihane. He also was introduced to the well-known poet Mehmet Akif Ersoy (1873–1936), and through Ersoy, he was invited to many social events, where he played the *ney*. By 1900 he was able to record a *ney taksim* for his first 78 rpm disc for Odeon ('His Master's Voice'). At the same time Tevfik's poetry tended toward satire (*hiciv*) directed against social ills and injustices and often against the government itself. By 1902 this led to his brief imprisonment. Immediately afterwards he left Turkey for Cyprus. He played for and won the favour of the British governor in Larnaca. After several months there, he left for Egypt. After playing for a time in the Özbekiyye Café in Cairo, he and Manisalı Izzi Dede set up their own café, called the Neyzen. But in 1905 a satire that he published in the poet Eşref's journal *Daccal* earned him a death sentence from Istanbul. He remained in the safety of Cairo, where he found a wealthy Turkish patron, Yahya Bey. But a satire against the Egyptian Khedive, the ruler of Egypt, earned him one-and-a-half-months imprisonment there. His release coincided with the Second Constitutional government in the Empire, and he returned to Istanbul in 1908. Once there, he again was in the company of leading musicians and poets. He played regularly in the Yakub Café in Şehzadebaşı/Fatih. There he came to the attention of Refik Bey, then the Minister of Justice, who helped to involve him in a public concert at the Tepebaşı Tiyatrosu, along with such figures as Tanburi Cemil Bey, Kanuni Arif Bey, Udi Nevres, and Santuri Edhem.

With the outbreak of war in 1914, Tevfik was drafted, despite his history of epilepsy. He collaborated in setting up a *mehter* ensemble in Eskişehir, which also played to great acclaim in Istanbul, including for Enver Pasha and for Sultan Mehmed Reşad V. The immediate post-war years were also productive for Tevfik. In 1919 he published *Hiç* (Nothing), his first collection of mainly satirical poems, and he continued to record 78s for the Odeon and Columbia companies – his output would total 11 sides, all of them *taksims*. Tevfik was even invited to Bucharest to perform with piano accompaniment. But in the following year he spent time in the Haydarpaşa Hospital. When he was released, he followed an even more Bohemian life, playing *ney* in taverns and beer halls throughout Istanbul. He stayed in many homes, and even on the street. He was already impulsively giving away his money, a tendency that became more pronounced in later years. In 1923 he spent several months at the home of his brother Şefik. Nevertheless, his fame and popularity continued to grow, and the next year, he was ready to publish another book of poetry, *Azab-i Mukaddes* (The Sacred Suffering).

In 1926, a member of parliament, Süreyya Bey, who was a nephew of Tevfik's old friend and patron Şair Eşref (1846–1912), had him invited to a party being given for Kemal Atatürk in Balıkesir, where he was the principal musical entertainment. His performance was so affecting that afterwards Atatürk held Tevfik's hand to his breast and told him admiringly, 'What a great and powerful soul you have!'

These next years were even more productive for Neyzen Tevfik. In 1927 he was invited to perform on Istanbul Radio with Mesud Cemil and the *kemençe* virtuoso Ruşen Ferid Kam. He continued to record *taksims* for Odeon and Columbia and, in 1928, through the intervention of Avni Bey, an official in the Istanbul Municipality, he performed both classical and Izmir-region *Zeybek* melodies for Kurt Striegler (1886–1958), director of the Dresden Opera, when he visited Istanbul. In an interview for the local press, Striegler expressed himself at length about the performance, saying in part, 'In my life I have met many powerful artists. I looked closely at Neyzen Tevfik as he played his *ney.* In order to appeal to me with this Eastern art, he was ready to give up his soul. He wished that his soul would set fire to his ney and would fly away, departing as a flaming melody' (Akdoğu 1991: 47).

Shortly thereafter Tevfik made the acquaintance of the mayor of Istanbul, who was so impressed with him that he was appointed to the Municipal Conservatory, for which he received a monthly salary, though he appeared rarely at the Conservatory. Nevertheless, Tevfik continued to live almost without money, frequently sleeping in the streets. His alcoholism seemed to get worse. Finally, in 1936 he published a satirical poem against the classical Turkish musicians on the radio. To some extent he may have remained indirectly under the protection of Kemal Atatürk, but after Atatürk's death in 1938 the reaction against Tevfik among musicians became stronger. When Hüseyin Sadettin Arel assumed leadership of the Conservatory in 1943, he ended Tevfik's 'employment'. Nevertheless, three years later he was invited to perform another large concert in Istanbul, which was a great success, much written up in the press. In 1951 he appeared for the first and only time in a film, *Onu Affettim* (I Forgave Him), also to great acclaim. By the following year, however, his drinking had evidently shortened his breath, making it difficult to play the larger *Mansur ney.* Despite all this, among Istanbul's general public, Tevfik remained a much beloved figure. On 6 May 1952 Neyzen Tevfik's seventy-third birthday was celebrated as a Jubilee at the Municipal Theatre at Tepebaşı. The following year, Tevfik became partially paralysed, and by the autumn he contracted bronchitis, which proved fatal.

Thousands came to his funeral at the Kartal Cemetery, at which both Mevlevi and Bektashi ceremonies were performed. And the same day the Dresden Radio performed a piece that Kurt Striegler had composed for him. Although without students, Tevfik's fame and influence continues through his commercial recordings, his poetry and the colourful anecdotes told about his life.

PART II

MUSIC OF THE MEVLEVIS

6

THE POSITION OF MUSIC WITHIN THE MEVLEVIYE

Was there a Mevlevi Musical Discourse?

Before turning to an analysis of the musical forms comprising the *ayin* – the subject of chapters 7, 8, and 9 – it is worth considering Mevlevi discourse about music in a more general sense with the aim of elucidating its focus and perspective, and what this discourse has to say about the position of music within the Mevleviye. As explained in chapter 3, from Ahmed Sipahsalar in the later thirteenth century to Divane Mehmed Çelebi, in the beginning of the sixteenth century, Mevlevi discourse about the *mukabele* ceremony took the form of a series of metaphors on the nature of reality and existence. In these writings, music as such has no independent function apart from the *sema*. From the fifteenth until the later eighteenth centuries, Mevlevi authors also produced a literature of an entirely different nature about *'ilm al-musiqah* (T. *ilmül musiki*) – the 'science of music'. This Arabic term was universally employed to refer to the integrated structure of modes, rhythmic cycles, compositional forms and improvisations, that characterised the learned music tradition of urban cultural centres in medieval and early modern Islamicate lands. Thus, we must distinguish between two distinct branches of a Mevlevi discourse that, each in its own way, address music. A Mevlevi writer who was at once a sheikh and a practising musician, like Kutb-i Nayi Osman Dede (d. 1730), could embrace both of these branches.

On the other hand, a sheikh like Divane Mehmed, who was not a practising musician, confined his writing to the mystical realm. For most Mevlevi writers, the science of music constituted an autonomous area that did not need to refer to specific Mevlevi ritual practices for its legitimation.

Another factor to consider in approaching Mevlevi discourse on music is that while the bulk of the surviving *ayin* repertoire had been created, mainly after the sixteenth century, in Istanbul and, to a lesser extent, in Edirne, the combination of mystical, kinetic, and musical elements that comprise the *mukabele* ceremony had first been established in Anatolia – in Konya, Karahisar and other centres of Mevlevi activity. A brief review of the early Mevleviye in these Anatolian centres thus provides a useful prologue to the fuller account I offer in this and subsequent chapters of Mevlevi developments in Istanbul.

Despite the frequent wars and population displacements in Anatolia through much of the fourteenth century, an era marked by the decline of Mongol suzerainty, the transmission of both literature and the science of music continued into the following century. The fifteenth-century poet Ayni, quoted in the Introduction, was evidently surrounded by a high musical culture within the Karaman capital city, Konya. One of the most sophisticated theoretical works of the period was the Persian-language *Risale-i Musiki* of a Mevlevi dervish, Yusuf ibn Nizameddin of Kırşehir, written in 1411. While the Persian original has been lost, another Mevlevi dervish, Hızr ben Muhammad, created a Turkish translation in 1469, which survives in several copies (Doğrusöz 2012). Kırşehir is the province just to the east of Konya and was very much within its cultural orbit. As with later musical treatises written by Mevlevis, none of the terms specific to the Mevleviye are mentioned – *devir*, *sema*, *mukabele*, and so on. Mevlevi musicians evidently viewed themselves first and foremost as masters of the science of music.

Just as Kırşehirli's original text was written in Persian, what little we can know about the sophisticated courtly repertoire that exemplified the science of music in the fifteenth century suggests a style best described as Persianate.[1]

---

[1] In *The Venture of Islam*, Marshall Hodgson defined Persianate as consisting of 'cultural traditions, carried in Persian or reflecting Persian inspiration'. (Hodgson, vol. 2, 1974: 293).

Fifteenth-century evidence demonstrates a close connection between several Anatolian cultural centres – Mardin and Diyarbekir in the east, Konya and Tokat in the centre, Aydin in the west – and the dominant Persianate musical repertoires whose epicentre then was the Timurid realm in the east of Greater Iran. Sultan Yakub of Germiyan (d. 1429), an Anatolian *beylik* centred in Kütahya, was reputed to have been a composer and an inventor of musical instruments. A century later, the Ottoman Prince Korkut (1467–1513), while governor of Amasya, in north-central Anatolia, acquired a substantial reputation as a musician and composer. Cantemir transcribed one of his *peşrev*s, in *devr-i kebir*, which Wright accepted as a truly archaic item (1988). Later Ottoman sources attribute to him only instrumental *peşrev*s and *sema'i*s. The inclusion of Anatolia (Rum) within the wider Persianate musical world remained a convention of cultural geography until the middle of the seventeenth century. Thus the Indo-Persian musician Baqiya Nayini (d. 1640) was able to write in his musical treatise 'The Murmur of Unity' (*Zamzama-e Vahdat*), 'Know that what has been the conventional [practice] among musicians of Iran, Turkistan and Anatolia, in the past and present, includes nothing more than six *āvāze*s (hybrid modes), twelve *maqām*s (primary modes), twenty-four *sho'be*s (derivative modes), and forty-eight *gushe*s' (trans. Pourjavady).

Courtly musical genres of an avowedly Turkic nature with distinctive rhythmic cycles and sophisticated *gazel* lyrics in Turkish apparently did not develop anywhere in fifteenth-century Anatolia. Several sources mention folkloric genres with Turkish texts, described by the terms *küğ* and *koşuk*, but these were not the music of the court, just as related folkloric genres had not been current at the Timurid court in Herat (Feldman 1996: 41–2). Anatolian folk music would continue to show connections with Turkic Central Asia. This can be discerned in much of the vocal repertoire documented in the mid-seventeenth century by Ali Ufuki Bey, in parts of the orally transmitted Ottoman vocal repertoire, and in the *ilahi*s of the Sunni *tarikat*s. But during the fifteenth century, these Turkic practices were not primarily the business of the cognoscenti of the science of music. The prominence of the Turkic long-necked lute *tanbur* in this period, however, is quite striking, as evidenced by Ayni's poem quoted in the Introduction. The probable persistence of certain early Turkic musical features in the Mevlevi *ayin* is a separate matter, which I approach in chapter 9.

Despite the slow appearance of analytical approaches to musical description in Mevlevi treatises, all of the treatises from Kırşehirli Yusuf (1411) to Çengi Yusuf Dede (c. 1650) and Abdülbaki Nasir (1796) share one characteristic: they are concerned with the science of music. Though none of these treatises refer in detail to the music of the *mukabele*, it is understood that one and the same musical system existed in the *mukabele* and in the music of the Ottoman Court. In Ottoman Turkish, the use of the word 'science' (*'ilm*) in connection with music goes back at least as far as Seydi, in the fifteenth century, who specified that the sciences were written down, with the sole exception of music (Seydi, 2004). An alternative for *'ilmül musiki* in Ottoman was *'ilmül edvar*, the science of cycles. The background of this term refers to the near universal practice among medieval musicologists in the Islamic world of using drawings of circles to indicate both the complex rhythmic cycles that characterised the artistic music of all periods, and, separately, to indicate the relationships of modes, subordinate modal entities, and individual pitches. The underlying symbolism was expressed in a short *mesnevi* describing court musicians, written by the poet Ibrahim Cevri (1595–1654):

Ta ki devr eyleye nüh dayire-i çenber-i çarh
Ta ki icra oluna 'ilm-i usul ü edvar

So that the nine circles of the heavenly chain may revolve,
So that the science of rhythm and cycles may be performed.

The terms *'ilmül musiki* (*'ilm al-musiqah*) and *'ilmül edvar* both include the Arabic word *'ilm:* 'science'. *'Ilmül Musiki*, the 'science of music', was part of the title of Prince Cantemir's book *Kitab-i 'Ilmül Musiki ala Vechil Hurufati* (The Book of the Science of Music according to the Alphabetic Notation). Cantemir, a polyglot, wrote in Latin as well as in Ottoman Turkish, and it is revealing that in his *Historia incrementorum atque decrementorum Aulae Othomanicae* (History of the Growth and Decay of the Ottoman Empire), Cantemir refers not to the science of music but to music as an art, or *ars musicae*. An English translation of this work, published in 1734, uses the charming 'art of musick'. In describing music in these distinctive ways, Cantemir was following, on the one hand, a Western tradition of musical discourse rooted in what the Greeks call *technei* – skill and artistry – and on the other hand, a tradition rooted in the Golden Age of Islam, also inspired by Greek thought, which approached music as a mathematical science. These two traditions are united in the English terms 'art music' and 'classical music', and in the French *musique savante*, that is, a learned musical tradition with an explicit theoretical basis. For Mevlevi writers, however, the science of music did not imply an exclusive focus on theoretical, rather than practical, aspects of music. Even in the early fifteenth century, Kırşehirli Yusuf's *Risale-i Musiki* addressed both the modal *makam* system and an elaborate system of rhythmic cycles (*usul*), but these were by no means only theoretical. As Wright has shown for the Timurid and Safavid musical theorists (2017: 31–68), these rhythmic cycles were in constant flux, as would be expected from a system employed in compositions that had been created and transmitted orally. Nor should we forget that Cantemir, for all his originality, was the student of the major Mevlevi composer Buhurizade Mustafa Itri (d. 1712). A reasonable inference is that at least some of Itri's ideas about the science of music ought to have been preserved and developed in Cantemir's treatise.

Going back to Cantemir (chapter 10: 97), only rural folklore (such as *deyiş* and *ırlayış*) was considered not to represent the science of music. Thus the decision of Mevlevi writers on music in the seventeenth and eighteenth centuries to focus on the most general aspects of music theory suggests that they viewed all tonal and rhythmic creations as having a fundamental basis within the science of music. A similar spirit of inclusiveness characterised Mevlevi musicians themselves, who had spent centuries perfecting a distinctive musical genre to be performed exclusively in the *mukabele*, yet insisted on the legitimacy of performing and composing musical genres with an avowedly secular purpose. Eighteenth-century Mevlevi writers in Istanbul shared this point of view with Mevlevi musicologists writing in Konya and elsewhere in the fifteenth century. Indeed, with the exception of Abdülbaki Dede's documentation of the Suzidilara Ayini, all Mevlevi experiments with notation focused on the secular instrumental repertoire.

One of the earliest Mevlevi writings from Istanbul, however, had a totally different purpose. This is the *Tenzihiyye fi Şe'nil Mevleviye* (Demonstration of the Purity of the Mevlevi Practices) by Ismail Rusuhi Ankaravi (d. 1631), written in Arabic somewhat before 1623. The author had been appointed sheikh of the Galata Mevlevihane in 1610. Ankaravi was neither a *neyzen* nor a composer, but rather an extremely learned scholar of both Sufistic and Islamic legal and traditionalist literature. Galata had recently been returned to the Mevleviye after over a generation of Halveti control. Tensions between the Ottoman government, the ulema, and the Janissary Corps – which had supported the Bektashiye – were high in this period. The Çelebi in Konya evidently felt that the initial Mevlevi sheikh of Galata, Sırrı Abdi Dede, was too sympathetic to the esoteric *batini* tendencies within Sufism, which also characterised the Bektashiye. Ismail Rusuhi Ankaravi had previously been initiated into the Bayrami *tarikat*, a blend of Halveti and Naqshibandi, founded in Ankara by Hacı Bayram Veli (d. 1429), and had later been trained as a Mevlevi in Konya. Hence Ankaravi was seen as an ideal candidate to 'purify' the Mevlevi *tarikat* in Galata.

Ankaravi apparently penned his *Tenzihiyye* in response to criticisms of the Sufis by a preacher and physician attached to the Court. His choice of the Arabic language was ideal for a clerical (ulema) readership. His book quotes many traditionalist and legalistic sources – all of them in Arabic – that address legal and moral aspects of music, dance and *samā'*. Although Ankaravi's *Tenzihiyye* has been published in modern Turkish translation as *Mevlevilik ve Musiki* (Akdoğan 2009), the treatise addresses neither music as an art nor the Mevlevi practice of music or *sema* in any detail. Rather, it is both a scholarly and a polemical work, best understood within the political atmosphere of its time.

A generation later, around 1650, a little book of music theory was produced by Çengi Yusuf Dede (d. 1669), who was then a *neyzen* in Beşiktaş and later the sheikh of the Mevlevihane. His biography is included in chapter 5, on *neyzens*. Recently edited and published by Recep Uslu (2015), this *Risale-i Edvar* is important as an early attempt to summarise the *makams* and *terkibs* in use in the first half of the seventeenth century; it is thus contemporary with the notations of Ali Ufuki Bey (Bobowski). As a harpist (*çengi*), Yusuf Dede also composed secular pieces, and Es'ad Efendi cites his *murabba beste* in *makam* Rast, *usul devr-i revan*. In his tiny treatise, after first introducing the *çeng*, he describes the secondary modal entities (*ağaze, terkib*), and then the rhythmic cycles (*usul*). He never mentions any compositional form, whether secular or Mevlevi. But before presenting his chart of *usuls* he writes, 'Our Saint Hazreti Mevlana (may his secret be blessed), by continually whirling with this love, invited us to the World of True Meaning'.

The next significant Mevlevi musical treatise was written almost a half century after the death of Yusuf Dede by Kutb-i Nayi Osman Dede (1652–1730), who became the sheikh of Galata and wrote the versified Persian musical treatise *Rabt-i Ta'birat-i Musiki*, which dates from c. 1718. In this treatise, Osman Dede, whose career is outlined in chapter 5, primarily presents a detailed account of the modal entities in use in his time while saying nothing about rhythmic cycles nor about any compositional forms. His short versified introductions do speak about the spiritual significance of sound and of the *sema*, but without invoking any details of the Mevlevi *ayin*. For example, about the *sema* he writes:

12. *Her melek meshghul shod ba dars-e khish*
     Her chi ra memur nā pest āmad nā pish
     Every angel is busy with his own lesson
     He moves neither down nor up from what he was commanded

13. *Chun semā' ra kard tezyin ān janāb*
     Ba kevākib ba melāika u āfitāb
     For the stars, the angels and the sun
     All glorify the sight of the Lord

About sound itself:

14. *Nutq u harf u savt bāyad sem'ra*
     Tā ki yābad qalb te'sir-e sadā
     Speech, syllable, and voice reach the hearing
     So that the heart will register the affect of sound
     (Akdoğu 1991: 10)

Thus, the purpose of music is in its affective quality (*te'sir*). Later Osman Dede mentions the Prophet Idris and the philosopher Pythagoras (Fisagor) in this connection. Before introducing the modal entities – which form the substance of the work – Osman Dede briefly mentions *hikme-i tesnif* ('the wisdom of composition') and then *ika'* (rhythm). But he never attempts to demonstrate or analyse any connection between these abstract principles and actual compositions.

These verses call to mind several of the couplets quoted in chapter 4, on the *ney* in Mevlevi music. The many ingenious images within these whole poems or couplets focus on the *ney* as a kind of metonym standing in for moral, spiritual and musical concepts. No doubt within the oral tradition of the Mevleviye, poetry with such imagery was employed in a variety of creative ways to teach aspects of music relevant to the spiritual development of the dervishes. In a sense these verses are almost like Zen *koans* used as an aid for meditation. Partly for this reason, it would be fruitless to attempt to extract a Mevlevi 'philosophy of music' from the theoretical texts alone, which had a more technical purpose quite separate from the larger spiritual significance of musical practice among the Mevlevi. One might imagine that Osman Dede felt the need to preface his musical treatise with more purely allegorical and spiritual verses about the celestial *sema* and sound before commencing his primary task: an accurate enumeration of the modal entities as they were then understood.

While Osman Dede's treatise was dedicated to the leading figures of the Court, such as Nevşehirli Damat Ibrahim Paşa (1717–30), its discourse is an internal Mevlevi one. And, indeed, it was preserved only among Mevlevis. Although it was written over a decade later than Prince Cantemir's 'Preface to the Science of Music' (*Dibaçe-i 'Ilm-i Musiki*), it does not attempt to analyse any concept, whether of mode, rhythmic cycle, or composition, even at the elementary level of Cantemir's *Preface*. Osman Dede had created a system of musical notation, with which he notated only *peşrev*s and *sema'i*s, but nothing from the Mevlevi repertoire.

In the middle of the eighteenth century a Mevlevi dervish named Mustafa Kevseri compiled a collection using Cantemir's notational system. Like the previous two notated collections, it contains only *peşrev*s and *sema'i*s. There is no treatise attached. Long unavailable, it has recently been published by Uğur Ekinci (2015) through the OMAR organisation at Istanbul University.

It is only at the very end of the eighteenth century, with Abdülbaki Nasir Dede's *Tetkik ü Tahkik* of 1796 (Topkapı Sarayı Emanet Hazinesi) that a Mevlevi theoretical work shows an interest in critical analysis in addition to musical notation. Abdülbaki Nasir Dede's discussion of *usul* shows an awareness of the profound changes in tempo and rhythmic structure that had occurred over the last half century. And for the first time, an Ottoman author attempts to classify all existing modal entities according to their period of origin, altogether presenting nine historical periods (Tura 2006: 21). Even though the chronology of these historical periods is left rather vague, this attempt to envisage an internal process of change and development was a novelty within Ottoman musical culture. Nevertheless, even this work does not approach issues of musical genre. In his other work, *Tahririye* (Süleymaniye Nafiz Paşa), Abdülbaki Nasir Dede used an original system of Islamic musical notation that differs from both Osman Dede's and Cantemir's, to write down a Mevlevi *ayin* (in *makam* Suzidilara) composed by his patron, Sultan Selim III (Uslu and Doğrusöz 2009). An interlinear transcription of this *ayin* together with its performed version at the beginning of the twentieth century is given in the Darülelhan *Mevlevi Ayinleri* (vol. 10).

Another piece of evidence for the status of music among the Mevleviye is the simple fact that among the possible qualifications to become a *postnişin* (the resident sheikh of a Mevlevihane of any size), skills such as musical performance and composition as well as poetry, calligraphy, and religious scholarship could all be considered. Kutb-i Nayi Osman Dede offers perhaps a unique example of a *postnişin* who embodied all of these skills and types of knowledge. The aforementioned Yusuf Dede, *postnişin* at Beşiktaş was also known for his poetry, but he was primarily a master musician. As mentioned in chapter 5, many *neyzens* ended up not only as *neyzenbaşı* of one or more Mevlevihanes, but not infrequently as the sheikh. The lesson to be drawn from these cases is that musical skill was regarded as not lesser than any of the other arts and sciences, and that all of them could contribute to the qualifications for spiritual leadership within the Mevleviye.

Mevlevi Musicians and Poets in Seventeenth-century Ottoman Culture

I now turn from the role of music within the Mevlevi Order to the role of the Mevlevi Order in the creation and dissemination of music. This larger process is reflected in the creation of the musical repertoire for the *mukabele*, which seems to have its beginning – at least in its surviving form – in the period extending from the later sixteenth century to the start of the seventeenth century. This creative and pedagogic process continued until the end of the Ottoman Empire in the early twentieth century.

Commenting on the prominent role of Mevlevis in the *Atrabül Asar* (The Most Entrancing Compositions), the early eighteenth-century biographical dictionary of musicians written by the Şeyhülislam Es'ad Efendi, Cem Behar noted the 'key role played by Mevlevis in the development and the transmission of the secular *fasıl* repertoire to later generations . . .' (2010: 190). To comprehend this phenomenon in all of its ramifications, one must first understand the situation of music both in Ottoman Turkey and in Safavid Iran. Furthermore, some of the Mevlevi involvement in Ottoman culture was also evident in literary trends in poetry, and it will be helpful to characterise where this intersection of the arts occurred. This is a large topic, to be sure, but an appreciation of at least its outlines is essential to an understanding of the role of the Mevlevis in Ottoman culture.

Unsurprisingly, the political history of the Ottoman Empire has been far better researched than Ottoman high culture or Ottoman sciences. Since the early 1990s, Ottoman historians have engaged in lively debate concerning the periodisation of Ottoman imperial history and the internal structure of the state in each era. A great deal of this research, especially that of Rifa'at Abou-El-Haj, questions earlier views about Ottoman 'decline' and attempts to look closely at the actual social and political processes at work. Baki Tezcan's many articles and his monograph *The Second Ottoman Empire* (2010) lay out the social and political map of this long period most clearly. In the cultural realm, these perspectives have been taken up especially by Harun Küçük for the history of science. Meanwhile, attempts at a broader cultural and political synthesis are all but absent, and the connections between politics and literature in the seventeenth century have only begun to be uncovered.

In general, however, we can accept Tezcan's conclusion that in the seventeenth and early eighteenth centuries, 'The sociopolitical progress in upward mobility and the limitation of royal authority, on the one hand, and the setbacks in the military and scientific fields, on the other, were closely related' (2010: 240). To these 'setbacks' we must also add the decline in the role of the Court as a patron of either music or poetry, especially in most of the first half of the seventeenth century. At the same time, important initiatives were taken both in music and in poetry, but usually outside, or on the margins, of the imperial court. Given this relative vacuum the Mevlevi Dervishes – and, to a lesser extent, Halveti Dervishes – were able to step in and help to effect major transformations in the musical and poetic arts. The novelist and literary historian Ahmet Hamdi Tanpınar (1901–62) created a shorthand for characterising the history of Ottoman poetry in the sixteenth century as the 'Palace Era' (*Saray Devri*), and in the mid-seventeenth century as the 'Sufi Era' (*Tasavvuf Devri*).[2]

Mevlevis had indeed been present in Istanbul since shortly after the Conquest in 1453. More than a century later, the *Surname* of Murad III (1582) documented some Mevlevi *neyzen*s playing with secular flautists and other instrumentalists in the open-air performances at the Atmeydanı. But it was only in 1491 that the Mevlevis acquired their own meeting place in the new capital – the Galata Mevlevihane – and this was removed from their hands in 1533. The Yenikapı Mevlevihane was completed in 1597, Galata was returned to the Mevlevis in 1610, and the Beşiktaş and Kasımpaşa Mevlevihanes were both built in 1622. There were also functioning Mevlevihanes in Gelibolu and in Edirne, in Thrace. The latter dated back to 1439, toward the end of the long period during which Edirne had been the Ottoman capital (1369–1453). To create the Edirne Mevlevihane, Sultan Murad II apparently converted the Muradiye Mosque that he had built previously. This Mevlevihane was considered to be an *asitane*, in which both training of dervishes and performance of the *mukabele* could take place. While Edirne continued to function as a major Mevlevi centre, the sudden availability of four large Mevlevihanes in Istanbul within a twenty-five-year period (1597–1622), could not but augment the influence of the Mevlevis within the Ottoman capital. In a sense, then, the deeper penetration of the Mevlevis into the culture of Istanbul may be said to have begun in the early decades of the seventeenth century.

The 'Classical Age' for Ottoman poetry – from the middle of the fifteenth to the later sixteenth century – was not a classical age for Ottoman music. Even while paying rather scant attention to music, the major sixteenth-century sultans Selim I and Süleyman I were major patrons of poetry. Süleyman was himself a respectable poet. Literary biographical dictionaries, which have been edited and studied by many recent Turkish scholars, give us a glimpse

---

[2] Turan Alptekin, *Bir Kültür Bir İnsan: Ahmet Hamdi Tanpınar ve Edebiyatımıza Bakışlar* (Istanbul, 1975: 58).

into the world of the poets. In the English language the major scholar and translator was Walter Andrews (d. 2020), a long-time faculty member at the University of Washington, in collaboration with his former student Mehmet Kalpaklı, a professor at Bilkent University, Ankara. Their annotated anthology *Ottoman Lyric Poetry* (1997) and broad-ranging *The Age of Beloveds* (2005) offer superb introductions to the aesthetics of the court poetry of the Ottoman Classical Age. Within Turkey, most academic studies of Ottoman poetry have dealt with this broad era, when the Empire and its system of patronage for poets was at its zenith. However, there has long been an alternative academic school more concerned with the poetic movements that came along in the mid-seventeenth century to challenge the hegemony of the 'official' Ottoman literary style.[3] Several movements coalesced in the creation of the new poetic style, known in both Persian and Turkish as the 'fresh speech' (*taze-gui*). Since the nineteenth century it has more often been referred to as the 'Indian Style' (*sabk-i Hindi*), due to the major influence of Persian poets writing in Mughal India. In a 2018 article, I noted the contrast between the Classical and the new poetic styles:

> In the generation following the death of Süleyman the Magnificent in 1566, the poets of the higher bureaucracy and the upper clergy were determined to preserve this aesthetic, but by the first decades of the following century, a significant number of poets began to experiment with the literary revolution going on in India under the Mughal emperors . . . The marginality of the Indian Style within the current canon of Ottoman literature is in part the result of a longstanding fissure within Ottoman literary culture, by which many of the literati separated themselves from the court following the end of the great days of court patronage during the classical Ottoman age. Whereas scholarly discussions of Ottoman culture usually see the court as the initiator of the Ottoman cultural synthesis, here the new style, or 'fresh speech' was

---

[3] The earliest scholar within this alternative school was Ali Nihat Tarlan (1898–1978), the first graduate student of Fuad Köprülü, at Istanbul University, followed by his students, including Haluk Ipekten, and then several other Turkish literary scholars, such as Tahir Üzgör, Hüseyin Ayan, and Mahmut Kaplan. I convened a conference on part of this topic, with Andrews, Kalpaklı and Paul Losensky, at the University of Pennsylvania in 1996. The proceedings are published in *The Turkish Studies Association Bulletin*, 21 (Fall 1997).

not encouraged by the court and was being introduced by an intelligentsia outside of it. (Feldman 2018: 4–5)

These new poetic techniques emerged in India, partly as an internal Persian development, and partly in response to the translation of much Sanskrit literature into Persian under the encouragement of the Mughal emperors Akbar, Jahangir, and Shah Jahan.[4] This movement was quickly taken up, in Turkish, by poets who usually had an affiliation with the Mevleviye, or sometimes the Halvetiye, as well as by poets without such a connection. The appearance of this Indo-Persian poetry opened up new vistas for poets in Istanbul and Edirne, and set a new standard with which they could compete. The Mevlevi sheikh Neşati's friend in Edirne, the poet and biographical *tezkire*-writer Güfti (d. 1677), went so far as to say:

Rotten luck has made me into
a *rind* sitting in the shadow of the land of Turkey
If only a heart-sick one like me
could have been bound to the flourishing locks of India!
If only I had been a *rind* in the land of passion –
a fire-worshipping *rind* of Hind!
(Feldman 2018: 29–30)

Neşati must have shared some of Güfti's enthusiasm, as among his writings is an 'Explanation of the Difficult Verses in Urfi' (*Şarh-i Müşkilat-i Örfi*) – referring to the court poet Jamal al-Din Urfi, who was born in Shiraz in 1556 and died in Lahore in 1590. Neşati also wrote a grammar of the Persian language (*Kavaid-i Fürs*) for his students. In the same vein, the great Ottoman poet Na'ili (d. 1666) wrote:

The writings of my pen
turned Rum into Lahore.
(Feldman 1997: 45)

[4] This process is documented in Audrey Truschke, *Culture of Encounters: Sanskrit at the Mughal Court*, Columbia University Press, 2016.

An intriguing link between poetry and music is the fact that Na'ili seems to have been a teacher of Hafiz Post (d. 1694), a major composer of both courtly song and Halveti *ilahi*s. His Anthology (*Mecmua*) forms one of the earliest documents of the new repertoire that came to dominate Ottoman court music after the middle of the seventeenth century. Hafiz Post – along with Koca Osman – was in turn the teacher of Buhurizade Mustafa Itri (d. 1712), a Mevlevi *muhibb*, who became perhaps the leading composer of the later seventeenth century. Apart from his numerous courtly compositions, Itri composed the famous Hymn to the Prophet (*Naat-i Peygamberi*), and an *ayin* in *makam* Segah. Itri's *kar* in *makam* Neva (with Persian lyrics by Hafiz Shirazi) remains one of the great classics of the earlier Ottoman repertoire. Itri seems to have been the recipient of substantial patronage from the Ottoman court and even more so from the Crimean Khan Selim Giray. Itri was also known as a poet, although his *divan* has not survived. No doubt some of the lyrics to his compositions are his own (Feldman 2012). In all of these cases, within this generation the highly influential interaction of musicians and poets of the Mevlevi and Halveti *tarikat*s is evident, within both the secular and the mystical spheres.

One of the founders of this 'fresh' or 'Indian' movement within Turkish literature was the poet and calligrapher Ibrahim Cevri (1595–1654). Cevri had attended the mystical discourses of Ismail Rusuhi Ankaravi in the Galata Mevlevihane, and became Ankaravi's *muhibb*. He was also a close confidante of Sarı Abdullah, the commentator on Rumi's *Mesnevi*. Cevri studied calligraphy at the Yenikapı Mevlevihane, becoming a master of the *ta'lik* and *nasta'lik* scripts with which he made many copies of the *Mesnevi*, some of which are still extant. While Cevri was not himself a *dede* or a Mevlevi poet per se, his poetry had a strong influence on the most renowned poets in Istanbul and Edirne, both within the Mevlevi and Halveti *tarikat*s and in other circles (See Ayan 1981; Feldman 1997 and 2018). Several Mevlevi sources mention Cevri, and they also confirm that his house became the centre of a poetic group that included other Mevlevis, such as Dervish Arami, as well as the high bureaucrat and Mevlevi *muhibb* Mezaki, and the court official Vecdi. According to Esrar Dede, these meetings went on regularly for many years. They were evidently not the kind of traditional *meclis* (gathering) documented by such Ottoman Classical Age sources as Aşık Paşa, which featured lighter verses sung to quasi-folkloric music accompanied by the consumption of alcoholic beverages. But they were not spiritual seances either, as Cevri was neither a *dede* nor sheikh of the Order, nor was any sheikh present.

It is no accident that Cevri – a poet and calligrapher with a strong Mevlevi background and involvement – would take the initiative in opening and continuing a lively literary discourse. We can read about Cevri's humorous temperament, which must have been reflected in some of the discussions at his *meclis* sessions, in his *gazel* with the monorhyme *satalum* – 'let us sell'. In one of its verses he says:

> Let's draw the veil of hypocrisy
> over the face of spiritual signification;
> Appearing different from how it is,
> Let's sell a picture to the world!
>   (Feldman 1997: 57)

Cevri also left a remarkable 'Description of the Singers of the Court of the Sultan' (*Ta'rif-i Hanendegan-i Saray-i Padişahi*), in which a Mevlevi connection plays an important role. The poem contains 53 couplets, and judging by its personae, it would appear to have been composed before the death of Sultan Murad IV in 1640 (Ayan 1981: 110–13). The first musician whom Cevri treats is the chief singer of the court, Hanende Ali Ağa, who receives one of the longest descriptions:

> One of them is Hanende Ali Ağa; at every moment
> With his breath he revives the dead!
> When he commences to passionately sing a *taksim* of two couplets,
> He demonstrates the *makam*s according to the Theory of Music.
> In complete harmony he sings *naqsh*, *savt*, *'amel* and *kar*,
> He reveals his magical power while he demonstrates their movements.
> He had studied the science of music with Dervish Ömer;
> We stand in profound admiration both to the teacher and to his student!

Despite Cevri's high praise, seventeenth-century sources do not mention Hanende Ali Ağa, whose title would imply a *devşirme* background at the

Court. He was evidently a master-performer but not a composer. His teacher, Tokatlı Dervish Ömer (c. 1545–1630), was one of the key musicians of this period, and is referred to both by Es'ad Efendi and Evliya Çelebi, who had been his student. Dervish Ömer's theoretical knowledge of the science of music was linked with a specific artistic repertoire that he was able to perform and teach on a professional level at the Court as well as transmit onward. The leading *neyzen* in the Imperial orchestra was 'Yusuf-i Derviş' – evidently the aforementioned Çengi Yusuf Dede, who was also the *neyzen* and later, sheikh, of the Beşiktaş Mevlevihane and the author of the *Risale-i Edvar*. Cevri lavishes eloquent praise upon his playing (Ayan, 1981: 112):

> Another one was Dervish Yusuf who with his *ney*
> vivifies the spirit of Mevlana.
> Through the aid of Mevlana he finds the breath of the soul,
> With his every breath he alludes to a pure spiritual blessing.
> While his *ney* reveals the secrets of the heart
> Like the Mevlevis he causes the whole creation to whirl.
> If the sound of his *ney* were to enter the universe of spirits
> The souls of Sanayi and Attar would start to dance!

This final literary touch, mentioning two of the iconic authors of Persian Sufi poetry – both of whom had been influential on Rumi – is probably a gesture to Dervish Yusuf's stature not only as a musician but as a poet and the author of a *nazire*, a poetic 'response' to Rumi's *Mesnevi*.

The Mevleviye and Musical History in Anatolia and Iran

The remarkable career of the Anatolian Dervish Ömer at the Ottoman court brings up the issue of the musical life of the Mevleviye in Anatolia. While the Mevlevihane of Tokat was only built in 1638, the nearby Çorum Mevlevi-hane was one of the oldest in Anatolia, going back to the time of Arif Çelebi (d. 1329). It is crucial not to view the musical life of Anatolia through the prism of Istanbul from the early eighteenth century to the present, when most of the rest of Anatolia and Thrace became the *taşra* – the 'outside'. Even in the writings of Evliya Çelebi (1611–82), several Anatolian cities could boast of a sophisticated musical life, or at least of certain individuals with a high level of musical knowledge. The opening section of this chapter mentions links that had connected the art music of Karamanid and early Ottoman Anatolia with Greater Iran. But as the Ottoman Empire became increasingly centred in the capital, Istanbul, and subsequently, in the nearer and more distant Balkan provinces, it was mainly the Mevleviye that upheld the science of music in Anatolia, and that could continue to contribute high-level practitioners to the Ottoman capital.

Ömer was both a Gülşeni and a Mevlevi dervish, and served as *zakirbaşı* of the Gülşeni *tekke* in Istanbul.[5] At the same time, he composed *peşrev*s, which were notated both by his contemporary Ali Ufuki Bey and later, by Cantemir. He had been the *hanendebaşı* (lead singer) at the court of Murad IV, who appreciated him to the extent of calling him 'father' (*peder*). He was also described as 'Tokatlı', indicating that he had been born in that Central Anatolian city. Yet he is one of the very earliest of the high-level musicians documented in the musical life of Istanbul during the first half of the seventeenth century. His connection to an Anatolian branch of the Mevleviye is potentially significant. It is only in the case of his student, Ali Ağa, that Cevri takes the trouble to indicate what his repertoire had been. And this repertoire consists of the *naqsh*, *savt*, *amel*, and *kar* – all of them Persianate musical genres featuring complex musical movements with medium and long rhythmic cycles and texts mainly in Persian. These were the composed musical genres of the Timurid period and thereafter. As I will discuss in the following chapter, they still had a role in early eighteenth century Istanbul.

As noted by Babur for the court of the Timurid ruler Husayn Bayqara (ruled 1469–1506) in Herat, the principal city of Khorasan, musical genres for the court were restricted. And, indeed, they represented the same group of genres that Tokatlı Dervish Ömer would teach to Hanende Ali Ağa in Istanbul a century later. For instrumental music in Herat there was also *peşrev*, which was not mentioned by Cevri. The distinctive Ottoman novelty in Cevri's *Description* is the improvised vocal *taksim* on the *ney* (discussed in chapter 4). The lyrical texts for compositions were in Persian; but we cannot be certain in which languages *taksim*s were sung.

---

[5] On the founder of the Gülşeniye, see Side Emre, *Ibrahim-i Gulshani and the Khalwati-Gulshani Order* (Leyden: Brill 2017).

At the end of Cevri's list of musicians in his *Description of the Singers of the Court of the Sultan*, he adds Çöğürçi Muhammed (*beyt*s 40–4), who evidently performed an *aşık* repertoire related loosely to the Anatolian and Central Asian epic *Koroğli* (*beyt* 44). According to Cevri's detailed description of the music of the court in his time, the courtly composed genres were generally in Persian, except for some of the *nakış* and folkloric items in Turkish. Thus, while a 'classicising' Turkish-language genre was emerging from within the Ottoman vocal form *murabba*, it seems not to have been a fully accepted part of the courtly repertoire in this period. Since a number of such Turkish *murabba* songs were documented by Ali Ufuki Bey (Behar 2008; Haug 2019) around a decade later, they were certainly known by some court musicians. But it is striking that Cevri, who was a major poet in the Turkish language, did not choose to include them as forming a significant part of the repertoire of any major court musician during the 1630s.

After the Conquest of Constantinople in 1453, Mehmet the Conqueror had attempted to attract major musicians from Anatolia to his court in the new capital. We have the names of some of these men, such as Konyalı Çengi Hüseyin, Tokatlı Valihi, Aydınlı Şems-i Rumi, Şems-i Hisari, and Mardinli Hüseyin (Uslu 2007). But Constantinople could not remake itself overnight into a centre of the Islamicate *'Ilm al-Musiqah*. Had the succeeding Ottoman sultans of the later fifteenth and sixteenth centuries wished to develop the existing musical infrastructure of Anatolia, and especially its Mevlevi component, by inviting or moving it to Istanbul, much greater continuity of secular musical practice might have occurred. But that does not appear to be what happened.

As the 'classic' Ottoman Empire developed with its capital in Istanbul, the science of music became increasingly rooted in the Imperial Palace and its servants. The documentation of Palace musicians in 1525 – five years after the accession of Sultan Süleyman – mentions forty names. Ten of these are Iranians and the remainder, mainly of *devşirme* origin, emerged from the Palace School (see Uzunçarşılı 1977: 84–7 and the discussion in Feldman 1996: 64–72). Other sources mention slaves of various origin and the slave-women of the harem. Characteristically, under Süleyman, the chief musician and music teacher at the Court was not a musically learned Anatolian, like Dervish Ömer, but rather, Hasan Can Çelebi (1490–1567), a müezzin who had been captured as a youth by Selim I in Tabriz, in 1514

(Öztuna 1969: 253). Hasan Can also composed *peşrev*s, which appear in the Ali Ufuki and Cantemir Collections.

By the mid-sixteenth century and thereafter, there is no longer evidence for the influx of learned musicians from the Anatolian cities, as there had been under Mehmed II nearly a century earlier. What movement there was came almost exclusively through Mevlevi channels. And by the later sixteenth century, Anatolia was experiencing serious social and economic dislocations. Within Istanbul and Edirne, social stratification taking place in this period wouldn't have allowed much space for a learned repertoire of the *Ilmül Musiki* outside of the Palace. The official *mehter* ensemble became a strong musical institution, which preserved a wide knowledge of *makam*s and *usul*s. These *mehter* musicians became all the more influential as the musical gap with Anatolia widened.

The 'Science of Music' in Iran and Istanbul and the Role of Mevlevi Musicians

The increasing restriction of higher level musical knowledge and instruction to the confines of the Ottoman Palace without the wider participation of learned musicians from Anatolia posed inherent dangers to musical creativity and continuity. These dangers were only amplified by the relative indifference, and, at times, hostility, of the ruling Ottoman sultans toward the art of music, which lasted for more than half of the sixteenth century. Another major factor was the downturn in support for artistic music in Iran – an abiding source of musical talent for the Ottoman court. This downward turn began shortly after the Safavid conquest of Iran in 1501, and its forcible conversion to Shiite Islam early in the sixteenth century. By 1533, the second Safavid Shah, Tahmasp, went so far as to prohibit music and order the execution of several leading performers (Pourjavady 2005: 62). Some Iranian musicians emigrated to India, while several of the provincial Iranian courts (in Khorasan and the South Caucasus), defying the capital, sheltered musicians and preserved elements of the older repertoire. Other musicians were captured or sought refuge with the Ottomans. Since the Ottoman Palace had become dependent on Iranian specialists, this negative Safavid development could only weaken the position of music in Istanbul. A generation later, in the literary *tezkire* of Aşık Çelebi, completed in 1565, the kind of *meclis* meetings he describes feature Turkish *gazel*s as well as, most commonly, the middlebrow and folkloric genres of Turkish music, including the *türkü*, which remains to this day the most common term for a folk song (Şenel 2015: 195–209). None of the high-status learned genres, with Persian lyrics and complex rhythms, such as the *amel* or *kar*, make an appearance. There are references to the *naqsh* (*nakış*), a middlebrow genre that uses shorter *usul*s and either Turkish or Persian texts. Thus, for Aşık Çelebi, music had become mainly a form of entertainment that, along with dancing and alcohol, was part of an evening also featuring the recitation of poetry.

In his *History of the Growth and Decay of the Ottoman Empire*, Cantemir focused on the one early seventeenth-century musician who had founded a musical lineage, of which he himself was a part. 'The art of musick almost forgot, not only reviv'd, but was rendered more perfect by Osman Efendi, a noble Constantinopolitan' (Cantemir 1734, I. 15–52). In his treatise, Cantemir mentions five of Osman's eminent students: Hafız Kömür, Buhurcuoğlu (Itri), Memiş Ağa, Küçük Müezzin, and Tesbihçi Emir. Hafız Post (d. 1694) was yet another major student of Osman's. Cantemir himself had studied with Osman's student Buhurcuoglu or – as he is generally known – Buhurizade Mustafa Itri, whom he quotes in his *Book of the Science of Music*. Evliya Çelebi and Esad Efendi are equally enthusiastic about Osman, whom the latter calls Koca Osman – the 'Elder' Osman – perhaps to distinguish him from Kutb-i Nayi Osman Dede, although this is by no means clear. His neighbourhood of Istanbul was Kasımpaşa, so he is often referred to as 'Kasımpaşalı Osman'. For Evliya 'he was a perfect master, a venerable *imam*, who resembled an angel in the heavens'.[6]

For the art of music to be 'almost forgot' are strong words indeed. And they must reflect how the musical situation in the previous generation appeared to Cantemir's musical teachers. Elsewhere I write at some length about Koca Osman (2015).[7] He himself was a *mütefferika*, and thus a part

---

[6] Evliya Çelebi Seyahatnamesi, I, Istanbul, 1996, p. 302, quoted in Cem Behar, *Şeyhülislam'ın Müziği: 18 Yüzyılda Osmanli/Türk Musikisi ve Şeyhülislam Es'ad Efendi'nin Atrabü'l-Asar'i*. Istanbul: Yapı Kredi, 2010, p.125.

[7] 'The Musical "Renaissance" of Late Seventeenth Century Ottoman Turkey: Reflections on the Musical Materials of Ali Ufki Bey (c. 1610–75), Hafız Post (d. 1694) and the "Maraghi" Repertoire', in *Writing the History of 'Ottoman Music'*, ed. Martin Greve, Würzberg: Ergon, 2015, pp. 87–138.

of the military aristocracy, rather than a court musician. Apart from Itri and Memiş Ağa, the students whom Cantemir lists are all mosque singers (*hafiz*es and müezzins). Tesbihçi Emir was a maker of prayer-beads. Itri was a Mevlevi *muhibb* and prominent in the musical life of the Mevleviye. Osman's musical teachers are not named in any source. Was it only a coincidence that a new Mevlevihane had been opened in his neighbourhood of Kasımpaşa in 1622, or did this sudden proximity to the Mevlevis perhaps influence his musical direction?

Although Cantemir has generous words about the Mevlevi Dervishes in general, he does not note any Mevlevi connection with Koca Osman. And his own relationship to Kutb-i Nayi Osman Dede (d. 1730) in particular may have complicated his assessment of the musical activities of the Mevleviye. While Cantemir notated a couple of Osman Dede's *peşrev*s, the fact that this Mevlevi sheikh and *neyzen* had created a musical notation almost identical to Cantemir's own is never alluded to. But it is also true that Osman Dede presented his treatise to the Court over a decade after Cantemir had left Istanbul, in 1711. In Cantemir's *History* – written in Russia – he claims that the notation was his own 'invention', and that musical notation had been 'unknown among the Turks'. And despite the high praise given to the Mevlevi Dervish Ömer by both Cevri and Evliya Çelebi, he does not figure into Cantemir's recent history of music in the Ottoman capital; nor does Cantemir mention the musical treatise of Çengi Yusuf Dede from roughly fifty years prior to his own. All in all, Cantemir's account of the musical situation in the immediately preceding generations, while extremely valuable, is incomplete, and needs to be supplemented by other sources.

As I have shown, an overview of the Mevleviye, and of Mevlevi musicians' position in seventeenth- and eighteenth-century Istanbul can be synthesised from sources that include Cevri, Evliya Çelebi, Yusuf Dede, Ali Ufuki Bey, Hafiz Post, Osman Dede, Es'ad Efendi, and, of course, Prince Cantemir. This overview, supplemented by what can be gleaned from documents chronicling the antecedent tradition of Persianate music at the sixteenth century Ottoman court, and in fifteenth century Anatolia, might take the form described in the following paragraphs.

At once a musical practice and music theory, a so-called science of music of a predominantly Persianate character had flourished widely throughout much of Anatolia during the fifteenth century. The musical model for both practice and theory was mainly the Timurid court in Khorasan. Mehmed the Conqueror (1432–81) attempted to import this tradition physically to the new Ottoman capital. But two major factors worked against this strategy: the increasing reliance of the Ottoman Palace upon its own unfree service through the *devşirme* for music, and the rise to prominence of either free or unfree Iranian music teachers. Another factor was a broad decline in knowledge of the science of music in Anatolian cities, probably as part of larger social dislocations. As Popescu-Judetz and, later, Doğrusöz, have shown, the production of original books of music theory in Anatolia seems to have come to an end with Seydi's *El-Matla* in 1504 (Doğrusöz 2015: 79).

The sixteenth-century Ottoman sultans evinced little enthusiasm for music of any kind. Contemporaneously, the Safavid government in Iran began to actively persecute music and musicians, thus lowering both the status and the availability of qualified masters of the science of music for the Ottomans. By the early seventeenth century, several different musical tendencies were emerging. One of these elevated formerly folkloric genres such as *türkü* and *varsağı* into both entertainment and 'listening' music. In particular the genre known as *murabba* became the locus of active experimentation and development. All of these genres demanded Turkish, rather than Persian or Arabic, lyrics that might be either of a bardic (*aşık*) nature or drawn from Turkish-language 'divan' poetry.

The most stable element in the performance and creation of the science of music was undoubtedly the *mehterhane* – the official military ensemble consisting of janissaries. The *mehterhane* preserved in its musical repertoire both sophisticated modal (*makam*) and rhythmic (*usul*) structures. The early seventeenth century witnessed the emergence of what could be described as crossover musicians, who came from the *mehterhane* but played indoor instruments. The most prominent example from this period was Solakzade (d. 1658), who performed on the *mıskal* panpipes, composed *peşrevs*, wrote poetry, and combined so many skills that he became a boon companion (*nedim*) of Sultan Murad IV. No doubt it was through musicians such as Solakzade that the *peşrev* became so broadly accepted among urban musicians. Cantemir himself notated more *peşrevs* by Solakzade than by any other composer, and he is mentioned prominently by Evliya Çelebi.

Also in the first half of the seventeenth century, in addition to the cross-over *mehter* musicians, three other social groups outside of Court service entered the breech to preserve and disseminate the science of music: clerical (*ulema*) musicians, who bridged the gap between purely religious (mosque) music and secular art music; secular aristocrat musicians; and Mevlevi and other Sufi musicians. In the following generation, Muslims (and some non-Muslims) of more humble social backgrounds also entered this musical scene. It was the combination of these four social groups in Istanbul that set the stage for later developments.

Higher Islamic clergy (*ulema*) and *müezzins* had already been involved in musical art, and seem to have been active in perfecting the art of improvised vocal *taksim*, which rapidly took on an instrumental expression as well. By the beginning of the eighteenth century, the Şeyhülislam Es'ad Efendi documented members of this clerical group as composers working within the science of music. Apart from new formal experimentation, there was an interest in learning and preserving what was still available from the antecedent Persianate tradition. This was the repertoire that Cevri associated with Tokatlı Dervish Ömer, and that Cantemir refers to both in his *Treatise* and in his *History*. By the middle of the seventeenth century, the repertoire attributed to the fifteenth-century Iranian theorist and composer Abd al-Qader (Abdülkadir) Meraghi (d. 1435) seems to have appeared in Istanbul as a kind of pious pseudographia, although input from pieces created at the same time in Iran is also a possibility (Feldman 2015: 130–4).

Despite an evident decline in numbers during the first half of the seventeenth century, the *mutriban* of the Mevlevi Asitane in Konya maintained their musical standards so that they were able to teach the great *neyzen* and harpist Yusuf Dede (d. 1669). Apparently the Mevlevihane of Edirne continued its musical life from before the Conquest of Constantinople. But with the creation of the new Mevlevihanes in Istanbul – Yenikapı in 1597, Beşiktaş and Kasımpaşa in 1622, and the return of Galata to Mevlevi use in 1610 – the Mevlevis entered a new era of visibility within the musical life of the capital. As they were not dependent on a role in the Palace Service, and were open to instructing any and all qualified musical students, their effect on the musical life of Istanbul could only grow. Once we reach the 'long eighteenth century' – from the last third of the seventeenth century until the early decades of the nineteenth – several new patterns emerge, whose beginnings were marked by Amcazade Hüseyin Efendi (1644–1702), a member of the Köprülü lineage, becoming both a Grand Vizier and a Mevlevi follower. Throughout the long eighteenth century, the connections of the Mevlevis in the capital with members of the Ottoman elite became even stronger than they had been in the previous century.

Another major pattern was the entry of non-Muslims into the highest levels of Ottoman music. Among the earliest of these was the Greek Tanburi Angelos, who is praised by Evliya Çelebi and later served as the *tanbur* teacher of Prince Cantemir. Evliya also singles out the Jews Tanburi Karakaş and Mıskali Yako. The first half of the eighteenth century witnessed the spectacular career of the Armenian Tanburi Harutin, who spent the years 1736–42 travelling with the Ottoman Embassy to Iran and then to India with Nader Shah. He later returned to Istanbul and composed a book of music theory in Armeno-Turkish (Taghmizian 1968; Popescu-Judetz 2002). The prominence of these non-Muslims marks a striking departure from the previous century. In Cevri's 'Description of the Singers at the Court of the Sultan', from the 1630s, for example, no non-Muslims are mentioned.

This new appearance of non-Muslims in the music of the court was the product of the greater social mobility of the time in general, and also of the enhanced status of members of Greek and Armenian elites. The former group, known as Phanariots, were given formal authority over the Danubian Principalities after the War of 1711 and the defection of Prince Cantemir to Russia. Armenians came to dominate the banking system. From this period onward, Greek, Jewish, and Armenian musicians were able to reach the highest levels as both performers and composers of Ottoman court music. But exactly how they were able to gain access to in-depth knowledge of the science of music is not well-documented. In the middle of the century, perhaps the most influential of these non-Muslims was Zaharya Hanende (d. 1780?), whose vocal compositions in the *beste* and *ağır sema'i* genres were still considered classics by Ismail Dede Efendi in the following century. Also in the middle of the eighteenth century, Kemani Corci ('Yorgi', d. 1775?) introduced the Western violin into the music of the Court, and was also a major composer. Corci, as 'Georges', was mentioned prominently by the Frenchmen Fonton and de Blainville (Feldman 1996: 129). His contemporary was the Jewish Haham

Musi (Moshe) Faro (d. 1770), the leading *tanbur* player at the court of Mahmud I (1730–51). By the end of the century, the outstanding *tanbur* player was yet another Jew, Tanburi Isak Fresko (d. 1814). Isak was a teacher of Sultan Selim III, along with the Mevlevi Musahhib Seyyid Ahmed (1728–94), who had been prominent in the previous reign of Abdülhamid I (1774–89).

As a matter of principle, the Şeyhülislam Es'ad Efendi excludes all non-Muslim musicians from his *Atrabül Asar.* He also fails to cite the Sufi compositions of Mevlevi and other dervish musicians whom he does mention. By contrast, Cantemir mentions his teachers, including the Jew 'Chelebico', and the Greek Tanburi Angelos. He transcribed *peşrev*s by Angelos, by the unknown 'Ermeni Murad', and by Yahudi Harun, also known as Aaron Hamon (d. before c. 1725?), who was a major composer of the artistic Hebrew liturgical (and paraliturgical) repertoire known as the Maftirim among Sephardi Jews living in Edirne, Istanbul, Izmir, and Salonika. The few existing sources suggest that this repertoire had its beginning with a composer named 'Avtaliyon', who lived in Edirne, evidently in the early seventeenth century, but whose precise dates are unknown. As Seroussi has shown (2001: 81–93), while Avtaliyon had been a student of the great paraliturgical hymn writer Israel Najara (1555–1625), the two existed in different musical worlds. Najara's songs reflect a popular and, at times, Janissary repertoire, but Avtaliyon is fully informed of the Persianate art repertoire and the newer Turkish genres. Later patterns show the Edirne Mevlevihane as the major source for the courtly repertoire that became the Hebrew Maftirim. In Avtaliyon's generation, it would be difficult to imagine him learning this repertoire other than from a set of Mevlevi teachers – a pattern repeated by other Jewish composers who created the Maftirim. Yet whether their teachers had been Mevlevi or secular, these Jewish composers invariably drew their compositional genres from the courtly *fasıl* –including the *peşrev* – and never from the central vocal genres of the Mevlevi *ayin*. Thus, the Maftirim must be viewed as a 'classicising' Hebrew liturgical repertoire, rather than as a mystical repertoire based on a Sufi model.

In general, the long eighteenth century demonstrates an interaction of Ottoman Greek and Muslim musicians both on a social and structural level. No other non-Muslim musical element had as profound an effect on Ottoman court music as did Byzantine music. This influence appears already in Itri's Na'at-i Peygamberi, as well as in the *terennüm* section of his Neva Kar. Interestingly, apart from Itri's Na'at, it does not seem to have touched the basic musical structure of the *ayin*. However Byzantine musical 'theses' are evident in the *beste* compositions of the leading mid-eighteenth-century Ottoman composer, the Greek Zaharya Hanende. And in the second half of the eighteenth century, the career of Petros Peloponnesios (1740–78), an innovative and influential composer of the artistic genres of Byzantine church music, as well as Ottoman court music, illustrates the Ottoman – Neo-Byzantine interaction in full force. Petros was also known to play both the *ney* and the *tanbur*. Greek sources mention his intimate association with the dervishes of the Galata Mevlevihane. This association was evidently so close and collegiate that, on his death from the plague in 1778, the dervishes of the Galata Mevlevihane obtained permission from the Orthodox Patriarch to perform a Mevlevi ceremony after the Christian funeral. They even placed a *ney* in Petros's hand in his coffin, so that he could 'play for the angels in Heaven' (Apostopoulos 2005: 42–3). No doubt Petros was a highly unusual and flamboyant character, but his biography suggests how earlier church composers and music theorists like Panayiotis Challatzoghlou (d. 1748) and Zaharya Hanende might have been initiated into *Ilm al-Musiqah*. Ottoman-Neo-Byzantine musical interaction seems to have transformed many aspects of Ottoman court music, from musical intonation to the connection of melody and *usul* cycles, and largely defines secular Ottoman musical expression in the long eighteenth century – a topic that still awaits serious and sustained musicological research.

Once biographical sources become more plentiful during the nineteenth century, the central role of the Mevlevis as teachers of non-Muslim musicians becomes clearer. In the earlier nineteenth century, Ismail Dede Efendi (d. 1846) was the teacher of the Armenian Nikogos (1836–85), who went on to become a major Ottoman composer. Dede taught him Mevlevi as well as secular compositions, so that Nikogos was known as an expert on the music of the *mukabele*. In the case of the Armenian jeweller and court musician Oskiyam (1780–1870), he had learned (and later transmitted) the *tanbur* technique from the Jewish Tanburi Isak, while he mastered the *ney* from Deli Ismail Dede (1808–60) of Galata. Oskiyam then taught the distinctive *tanbur* technique he had learned from Isak to the Sheikh Abdülhalim Efendi

(1826–96), who taught it to Mesut Cemil (1902–63). Thus the Armenian Oskiyam was responsible for transmitting the traditional Ottoman *tanbur* technique both to a Sufi sheikh, and then, indirectly, to the leading Turkish *tanbur* players of the following three generations – Tanburi Cemil Bey (d. 1916), his son Mesut Cemil, and his student Tanburi Necdet Yaşar (1930–2017).

When the Swedish traveller Karsten Niebuhr visited Istanbul late in the eighteenth century, he determined that the Mevlevis were 'esteemed the best musicians among the Turks' (Niebuhr 1792, quoted in Feldman 1996: 96). They also had played a critical role in disseminating knowledge of the science of music in all its forms to the leading non-Muslim musicians. And, as ought to be clear, their crucial influence can be traced into our own time.

7

THE MUSICAL STRUCTURE OF THE *AYIN*

The Music of the *Ayin* as Part of an Oral Transmission

The musical structure of the *ayin* was introduced in chapter 3, 'Development and Cultural Affinities of the Mevlevi Ayin', as a point of departure for investigating kinetic elements of the *sema* and their relationship to the mystical symbolism, artistic form, and functional goals of the *mukabele* ceremony. This discussion continues here, but with a shift of focus to musical structure itself, based on a close analysis of sections of several *ayins*. Such a focus on rhythmic structure and melodic relationships within several *ayins* is a necessary basis for any future analysis of a complete *ayin*. It will also be useful to compare the musical structure of the *ayin* to that of the Ottoman *fasıl*, the suite-like courtly musical form. First, however, I offer a few general observations about how Ottoman musicians, including Mevlevis, have contextualised the *ayin* and its development in the historiography of Ottoman music.

References to a long, centuries-old historical past figure frequently in indigenous, and even in some modern, musicological discussions of prestigious repertoires glossed as 'classical' in Near Eastern and Asian musical cultures. As Hodgson had noted in his perceptive *Venture of Islam* (1974), legitimation through the past was typical of cultures in what he called the 'agrarianate' stage of development. Local beliefs about the antiquity of a musical repertoire under such cultural conditions may or may not draw on evidence from actual history. In some parts of Asia, repertoires of undoubtedly ancient provenance do exist, for example, the Gagaku of Japan and the *qin* tradition of China, but great antiquity may also be claimed for quite modern repertoires, such as the *dastgah* system of Iranian traditional art music. Even relatively old and conservative repertoires such as the *nauba* of Morocco and Algeria, which probably originated in the seventeenth century, have acquired a popular aura of much greater antiquity extending back to the high culture of medieval Muslim Spain, over half a millennium earlier.

During much of the Ottoman period, belief in the antiquity of significant parts of the courtly repertoire was strong. Thus Ottoman musicians of the later seventeenth century believed that they possessed the compositions of the Iranian Abd al-Qader (Abdülkadir) Meraghi, who died in 1435 (Feldman 2015). Many Turkish musicians still share this belief today. Some Ottoman musicians even believed they possessed pieces composed by the philosopher Plato (Eflatun). Research by Owen Wright (1992) has demonstrated that belief in the antiquity and continuity of the secular Ottoman repertoire grew particularly in periods when musical continuity was weak, as in the later sixteenth century, leading to the loss of most of the earlier repertoire. During another period of crisis and cultural loss at the end of the nineteenth century, Ottoman musicians such as Ismail Hakki Bey (1865–1927) actively fabricated items they claimed had been composed by the medieval Islamic philosophers al-Farabi and Ibn-Sina, or indeed, by Mevlana's son, Sultan Veled. Ismail Hakkı Bey attributed the Acem Peşrevi in the modern *devr-i kebir usul* in 28/4, which was possibly his own composition, to Sultan Veled, despite the fact that the *peşrev* genre only came into use more than two centuries after Sultan Veled's death, in 1312.[1]

The Mevlevi dervishes did not entirely share the prevalent Ottoman attitude toward the repertoire of the past. On the contrary, they seem to have adopted a pragmatic and historical point of view, only attributing to composers pieces for which the attribution could be documented. Furthermore, they refrained from inventing or completing repertoire items that had been entirely or partially forgotten during the process of oral transmission. The existing Mevlevi repertoire shows evidence of modernisation, but also of conservatism

---

[1] This argument is presented in my article 'Cultural Authenticity and Authority', *Asian Music*, 1990.

and faithfulness in transmission that is far greater than in the secular Ottoman repertoire. Indeed, a strong and reliable chain of transmission exists from the earliest notated *ayin* in the period of Selim III (1789–1808) through the time of Ismail Dede Efendi (1778–1846) and down to the present. Though only one complete *ayin* is extant from before the last third of the seventeenth century, the existing Mevlevi repertoire includes a number of individual *ayin* compositions that were transmitted orally. These compositions are significant, but their musical details should not be taken as absolute. Thus, while I discuss stylistic features of certain *ayin*s created between the second half of the sixteenth and second half of the seventeenth centuries, these features must be understood as representing merely a consensus among later musicians about how to interpret music of the past that came to them through oral transmission.[2]

In all, fifteen *ayin*s survive from the period prior to Ismail Dede Efendi:

1. Pençgah (unattributed)
2. Dügah (unattributed)   '*beste-i kadimler*' ('ancient compositions')
3. Hüseyni (unattributed)

---

4. Beyati: Mustafa Dede (d. 1683)
5. Segah: Buhurizade Mustafa Itri (d. 1712)
6. Rast: Osman Dede (d. 1730)
7. Uşşak: Osman Dede
8. Çargah: Osman Dede
9. Hicaz: Osman Dede
   [Gap of fifty-odd years in the surviving *ayin* repertoire]
10. Irak: Abdürrahman Şeyda Dede (d. 1804)
11. Hicaz: Musahip Seyyid Ahmed (d. 1794)
12. Nihavend: Seyyid Ahmed
13. Suzidilara: Selim III (d. 1808) *earliest notated *ayin**
14. Acem-Bûselîk: Abdülbaki Nasir Dede (d. 1804)
15. Hicaz: Abdürrahman Künhi Dede (d. 1831)

---

[2] In 'Structure and Evolution of the Mevlevi Ayin: the Case of the Third Selam' (2001), I pointed out some of these stylistic features in relation to the *devr-i kebir* section of the Third Selam in a number of pre-nineteenth century *ayin* compositions.

The first three *ayin*s are known collectively as the *beste-i kadimler*, or 'ancient compositions'. The three *beste-i kadimler* are in the *makam*s Pençgah, Hüseyni, and Dügah (the ancient Dügah is equivalent to the modern Uşşak combined with Hüseyni). Of these, only the first is complete, with all four of its sections (*selam*) intact. The Dügah Ayini has two and a half sections – it lacks most of the third and all of the fourth *selam* – while the Hüseyni Ayini has only one section: the first *selam*. It is highly significant that the Mevlevi tradition did not fabricate attributions to composers for the 'ancient' *ayin* compositions. Evidently, later Mevlevi musicians were able to tolerate the existence of unattributed compositions and allow them to remain fragmentary, without the addition of appropriate second, third and fourth sections.

The earliest known composer of *ayin*s was Köçek Mustafa Dede (d. 1683), whose Beyati Ayin is listed above as no. 4. This *ayin*, and the subsequent compositions on the list up through no. 12, are known only through oral transmission, though, as evident in the list, they are attributed to well-known musical figures of the seventeenth and eighteenth centuries, such as Buhurizade Itri (d. 1712) and Osman Dede (d. 1730).

The last group of *ayin*s (nos. 10–15) were all created during the reign of Sultan Selim III (1789–1808). These include the earliest notated Mevlevi *ayin*, in *makam* Suzidilara, composed in 1794 by Selim III himself. The fifty-year gap from Osman Dede to Selim's reign is difficult to explain. The ban on *ayin* performance had already ended in 1684. By the early eighteenth century, all five Mevlevihanes in Istanbul, as well as in Üsküdar and Gelibolu, were functioning. The reign of Sultan Mahmud I (1730–54) was musically rich, and marked by the entrance of major non-Muslim composers to the court, including Tanburi Haham Musi, Zaharya Hanende, and Kemani Corci. The middle of the eighteenth century was a period of musical innovation in secular Ottoman music, and perhaps the *ayin* compositions of this era were deemed too idiosyncratic for later taste. This, however, is only a hypothesis, and other explanations are certainly possible.

Musical Structure of the Ayin Compared with the Ottoman *Fasıl*

The attitude toward composition manifested in the *ayin* differed from that manifested in the courtly *fasıl* (Turkish: 'season' or 'section') in several crucial ways. A distinctive feature of the Mevlevi *ayin* is the attribution of each *ayin* to a single composer. Since the four *selam*s of the *ayin* were considered to comprise a single piece, it was understood that one composer would compose all four *selam*s, and that he would pursue a consistent compositional direction from beginning to end. Indeed, from the Beyati Ayini of Köçek Mustafa Dede onward, every *ayin* in the repertoire is the work of only one musician. The composition of the four *selam*s of an *ayin* by one individual meant that the *ayin* became the largest arena in which a Turkish composer could channel his skill.

Recent research by Behar (2008), along with my own work (2015), shows that, following the decline of the older Persianate court repertoire, in Ottoman Turkish the term *fasıl* gradually shifted its meaning from a group of compositions in the same *makam* to a cycle of pieces with a fixed compositional structure and order of performance. This change seems to have taken place only after the middle of the seventeenth century. Both Bobowski (Ali Ufuki Bey) in 1650 and Evliya Çelebi used the earlier meaning, while the newer usage is standard for Prince Cantemir, for example, as in the final chapter of his book on the science of music, 'The Fasıl and the Performance of Music According to Genre' (*Fasıl u Icra-i Musiki ala Vech-i Nev*), completed c. 1700.

The unitary composition of the *ayin* contrasts with the convention for the courtly *fasıl* in that, while a secular composer might compose all the component genres in the *fasıl*, later performers were not obliged to perform the original *fasıl* composition in toto, and might substitute movements from other *fasıl*s in the same *makam*. That is to say, many complete *fasıl*s were apparently performed during the lifetime of the composer, but with the passage of time, often only certain items would be remembered. Thus, the *mecmua* sources do not usually group *fasıl*s by composer but rather, by *makam*. A performer of a later generation might choose which items from the past he wished to sing. And if a given piece was not learned by any major performer for a generation or more, it might well be forgotten.

On the other hand, even in the later seventeenth and eighteenth centuries, it was understood that certain earlier 'classic' compositions in the Persianate *amal* and *kar* genres could have a place within an Ottoman composer's *fasıl*. Also, during the eighteenth and nineteenth centuries a small series of recent *şarkı* songs – either anonymous or by various composers – might be introduced in the later part of a *fasıl*, according to the taste of the audience. As noted by

Wright (2019: 178–9), during the sixteenth century courtly musical repertoires 'were not adequately sustained' either in Iran or in Turkey. Chapter 6 posits that the Ottoman *fasıl* was a relatively recent musical development, not attested prior to the last third of the seventeenth century. Cevri's description of music at the court of Murad IV in the 1630s, quoted in chapter 6, shows no evidence for the Ottoman *fasıl*. Thus, the *fasıl* apparently emerged in Istanbul and Edirne in the generation preceding that of Cantemir.

Multipart suites consisting of a series of vocal pieces in which longer and slower rhythmic cycles occur toward the beginning while shorter and faster cycles occur toward the end are common in Middle Eastern and Central Asian urban musical culture, and the Ottoman *fasıl* concert generally accords with this principle. Following Cantemir, a typical courtly *fasıl* of the later seventeenth and early eighteenth century would have the following structure:

1. instrumental *taksim*
2. 1 or 2 *peşrev*s
3. vocal *taksim* (in either Turkish or Persian)
4. *beste* in a long or medium *usul* (in Turkish)
5. *naqsh* (Turk. *nakış*) (in Persian or Turkish)
6. *kar* (in Persian)
7. *sema'i* (in Turkish)
8. instrumental (*saz*) *sema'i* in 6/8 or possibly in 10/8
9. vocal *taksim* (in either Turkish or Persian)

By the later eighteenth century this structure was more typically the one listed below, and mainly with texts in Turkish:

1. instrumental *taksim*
2. *peşrev*
3. vocal *taksim*
4. first *beste* (in compound *usul zincir*) or a *kar*
5. second *beste* (in another long *usul*)
6. *ağır sema'i* (in 10/8 or 10/14)
7. small suite (*takım*) of *şarkı*s in short *usul*s
8. *yürük sema'i* (in 6/8)
9. instrumental (*saz*) *sema'i* (in 10/8)
10. vocal *taksim* (optional)

As it developed in the long eighteenth century (c. 1680–1810), the vocal core of the *fasıl* commenced with a *beste* in *usul zincir*, a compound of five *usul*s, in 16/4 + 20/4 + 24/4 + 28/4 + 32/4. These might be followed by a *kar* and/or *nakış* sung in Persian and using moderately long *usul*s, e.g., 32/4 or 16/4. Then the middle of the *fasıl* would feature the *sema'i*, usually in both its slower (*ağır*) *usul*, in 10/4 or 10/8, and its quicker (*yürük*) form, in 6/8. There might be a *şarkı* or two in short *usul*s such as 14/8 or 9/8. The whole of the vocal *fasıl* was framed by an instrumental *peşrev*, usually in one of the long *usul*s, at the beginning, and an instrumental (*saz*) *sema'i*, in 10/8 and 6/8, at the end. During the earlier eighteenth century, the vocal cycle was preceded by both vocal and instrumental *taksim*s. It closed with a vocal *taksim*, which seems to have been termed '*gazel*' by the later nineteenth century, after its poetic Turkish text.

The *fasıl* tended to express a mixture of elegance, subdued passion, and wittiness over a foundation that could be perceived as leisurely. These concepts accord well with the emphasis on *rahat* (Arabic: 'rest', 'relaxation') that Harun Küçük conceptualises as a perception of time, a state of being, and a moral disposition: 'In the eighteenth century, when stability, peace, and prosperity were entirely new to most in Istanbul, leisure, or the lack thereof, seemed to be on people's minds because there seemed to be so little of it. It was almost as if people had entirely forgotten about it during the tumultuous seventeenth century' (Küçük 2019).

The performance practice as well as the compositional techniques of the *fasıl* items emphasised this goal. The repetition of textual syllables in long *terennüm* sections – particularly in the long *usul*s of the *beste* – gave way to a very gradual acceleration in the shorter *usul*s of the *ağır sema'i*, in 10/4 or 10/8, and *yürük sema'i*, in 6/8. But despite the shortening of the *usul* cycles, the initial pulse of the music in the *fasıl* underwent little change. Nothing could disturb the overall otium, the deep *rahat* of the listener. Much of the aesthetic pleasure of this music was connected with an interaction of rhythmic cycle, modality, modulation, and musical gesture. Particularly in the *beste*s, these gestures tended to overwhelm the *usul* basis of each composition. Indeed, the melodic phrase as part of a musical gesture not infrequently extended beyond the formal boundaries of an *usul* cycle (Feldman 2017).

Rhythmic Cycle and Poetic Metre

The relationship of rhythmic cycle to poetic metre has been brought up often in Turkish musicological writing within the past thirty-odd years, but this topic appears in absolutely none of the Ottoman musicological texts, where *usul* is treated as an entity completely independent from poetic *vezn* (Arabic: 'measure'), hence the long and short syllables of the poetic metrical system known as *aruz*. Cantemir had used the term *vezn* as a way of indicating tempo for his transcriptions of instrumental music, which, of course, had no poetic text at all. It is worth repeating that neither the secular *fasıl* nor the Mevlevi *ayin* shows any determining influence of poetic metre on musical composition. Bülent Aksoy has treated this question from several angles in his important article from 2008, 'Was the Music of the Fasıl a Music of Divan Poetry?' (Fasıl Musikisi Divan Edebiyatının Musikisi Mıdır?). He even points to an article by Sadettin Arel from 1950 in which Arel demonstrates that the use of prosodic mnemonic syllables in earlier Persian music had no relevance to Ottoman musical composition. The same conclusion appears in Wright's recent discussions of Safavid-era Persian theorists (2017a, 2017b). By contrast, Genichi Tsuge (1970) had shown that the structure of the *avaz* core of modern Persian art music is indeed based on poetic metres. But in Iran, the classical *usuls* – recently so well documented by Wright and Pourjavady – had been forgotten by the end of the eighteenth century, and early in the nineteenth century a new system was created in which *usul* had no place (Lucas 2019). The modern Shashmaqom of Bukhara, a repertoire that Uzbeks and Tajiks both claim as central to their musical heritage, appears to display a confluence of the *aruz* metrics and some of the older *usul* patterns.[3]

Within the *fasıl*, it is true that in all compositions using short *usuls*, care must be taken not to align a short syllable with an extended musical note. But an early-nineteenth-century *şarkı* with a syllabic, as opposed to *aruz*-based, *aşık* minstrel text, could be set over a 'medium' *usul* (*evsat*) in 26/8 (Feldman 2017: 164–5). Clearly the *aruz* metre determined nothing, as there was none

---

[3] The issue of poetic metrics and *usul* is brought up in Otanazar Matyakubov, *Maqomot* (Tashkent 2004: 177–84), and more briefly in Summits and Levin (2016: 323–33).

in this piece. Even more telling, in the Mevlevi repertoire, the famous open-ing lines from Rumi's *Masnavi* describing the reed-flute (quoted in chapter 4), appear in the beginning of the Third Selam in the Pençgah Ayini in *usul devr-i kebir*, yet were used much later by Ismail Dede Efendi in *usul devr-i revan* as the lyric for the First Selam of his Ferahfeza Ayini. While it is true that both of these *usuls* are based on fourteen-beat patterns, their tempo (14/4 and 14/8) and the way they interact with melody are quite different. Here, then, one and the same poem is set to music in two different *usuls*. The same phenomenon can be observed in the Third Selam in Beyati by Köçek Mustafa Dede and the Third Selam in Acem-Buselik by Abdülbaki Naşir Dede, ana-lysed below. And in chapter 8, I show certain melodic and gestural patterns within particular First Selam compositions that, while not contradicting the *aruz* metrics, were certainly not determined by them.

As explained in the following section and in the next chapter, the entire metro-rhythmic conception of a musical suite or cycle differs in the Mevlevi *ayin* and the courtly *fasıl*. Both the early and almost all later Mevlevi *ayins* begin with the First Selam (*selam-i evvel*) in a rather quick 14/8 *usul* (*devr-i revan*, or 'flowing' rhythm). The Second Selam (*selam-i sani*) is always in a stately nine quarter-beat *usul* (*evfer*) at a somewhat slower tempo (9/4). The Third Selam (*selam-i salis*) displays two contrasting rhythmic structures. The opening section uses *devr-i kebir* (of the seventeenth and mid-eighteenth century) in fourteen quarter notes (14/4). *Ayins* from the earlier eighteenth century retain the older form of this *usul* while those from the later part of the century and thereafter use the newer form, which is twice the length and considerably slower, better understood as 28/4 (Feldman 2001). The second part of this *selam* displays a marked contrast with the entrance of the much shorter and faster *semai* rhythm in 6/8. This rhythm and some of the melodic structures seem to refer to an older body of Turkish-language Sufi hymns that were more Central Asian in inspiration, and were not part of the Halveti-Kadiri *zikr* complex. The Fourth Selam (*selam-i rabi'*) returns to the 9/4 rhythm of the Second Selam.

Modulation

Movement between modal entities had already characterised the art music of the Islamic world in medieval times. As the older Persianate art music of the Ottoman court declined in the second half of the sixteenth century, modulation became much less common within compositions (Feldman 1996: 291–2). This is the situation in much of the repertoire documented by Ali Ufuki Bey, and most of the older *peşrev* repertoire notated by Cantemir. Modulation evidently became more frequent in the performance-generated *taksim* genre (1996: 293). There had also been instrumental *peşrev*s and vocal *kar* compositions that featured multiple modulations: the *küll-i külliyat* (compendium) *peşrev* and the *kar-i natik* ('speaking *kar*'). Cantemir specifically links a highly developed, modulating *taksim* with the *küll-i külliyat peşrev* (1700: 7, 63). Cantemir was the first early-modern Ottoman theorist to attempt to address this issue. But as a pioneer, his terminology was limited. He used the term *şedd* to describe 'transposition' of the same modal entity to a new pitch level. Beyond that, however, he has only the rather dramatic concept of 'musical agreement and aversion', which is the title of his Chapter 7: *Hiss-i Ünsiyyet zidd-'Arbedet-i Musiki*. The goal of such composition or improvisation (*taksim*) is that 'the agreement of *makam*s is that which should mix together the notes, *makam*s and *terkib*s of music without showing any conflict or contradictions' (7: 56). The attention Cantemir lavishes upon this concept is a testament to its key role in the musical renascence that had already begun in Turkey during the later seventeenth century.

Twentieth-century Turkish musicians developed the word *geçki* (transition) for what we would term 'modulation'. It is fundamental to all Turkish music, and particularly to the higher, courtly-derived *fasıl* genres. As mentioned earlier, it is enshrined in the *miyan* (middle) principle by which the third line of a vocal composition will either move the modality to a new pitch, or, more commonly, to a new *makam* altogether.

It is striking that, beginning with the anonymous *ayin* in *makam* Pençgah, all Mevlevi compositions feature modulations even more widely than does the courtly *fasıl*. In his brief but very sound analysis of modulation in both *fasıl* and *ayin*, Karl Signell noted that since the First Selam – the longest section of the *ayin* – consisted of several musical 'strophes' (*bend*), modulation in the *ayin* always went much beyond the single large modulation in the single *miyan* of a secular composition. Signell used the expression 'multiple *miyans*' to describe the principle of modulation in the First Selam of the Mevlevi *ayin* (1977: 118). Speaking about the Beyati Ayin, he wrote that '. . . a rich panoply of makams would be encountered in one continuous musical sequence' (Signell 1977: 118–20). Although we do not possess this or any of the other early *ayin*s in their original form, it is very likely that their strong emphasis on the practice of modal shifting was a legacy of earlier Persianate art music that was better preserved among the Mevlevis than it was among urban musicians in Istanbul during the sixteenth century. And from that starting point, it had longer continuity as a musical practice among the Mevlevis than among the musicians of the Ottoman court. Curiously, while it is not unlikely that Mevlevi sheikhs, *neyzen*s, and other composers attributed a spiritual meaning to modulation as a sort of musical journey or transformation, none of the Mevlevi musical theorists from either the pre-Ottoman or the Ottoman era addressed it in written discourse. Rather, it was that keen musical and cultural observer, Ahmed Hamdi Tanpınar, who articulated it best. In the following passage from his novel *Huzur*, he speaks about the Ferahfeza Ayini (1839) of Ismail Dede Efendi:

> Dede expressed the development characteristic of Turkish music, which consists of small appearances of the *makam*s, modulations, and wandering among the final tones in such a fashion that the *ayin* has become a symbol of his personality. Sometimes this searching, this disappearing, and self-awareness is in the highest degree human, and Dede's inspiration says: 'If you do not appear, there's no harm, I am carrying you within me!'; sometimes, however, one is overcome by a despair which is as hard as matter. (Tanpınar 1949: 320–1, trans. Feldman)

Mevlevi composers did not value repetition as a means of inducing a trance-like state. On the contrary, as the Mevlevi compositional tradition developed – perhaps at its highest point with Ismail Dede Efendi – the melodic line changes ceaselessly, wandering into new and unexpected paths. The music of the *ayin* expresses the journey of the soul, with all its many states and moods, from despair to exaltation.

Both the music of the court and of the Mevlevi ceremony were essentially based on metrical compositions. In courtly circles the composer was called a *bestekar* (or *sahib-i beste*), a Persian term that replaced the Arabic *musannif,* which had been in use in Timurid times (Feldman 1996: 39–44). A crucial issue was the ordering of the compositional forms into a strictly regulated cycle of contrasting rhythmic structures. In the chapter cited above, Cantemir employed the term *nev* (type or genre) to distinguish the constituent elements of the *fasıl*. But each genre had a separate name and somewhat distinct function. While they were only performed as a group within the 'fasıl of the vocalist' (*fasıl-i hanende*), the instrumental sections could be performed as the 'fasıl of the instrumentalist' (*fasıl-i sazende*), and the *şarkı* could become the nucleus of another, less formal *fasıl*, together with vocal and instrumental *taksims*.

All of the available evidence demonstrates the tighter organisation of the Mevlevi *ayin* around the work of a single composer than is the case in the existing secular *fasıls*. The material presented in this chapter and the previous chapter shows the sharp break in transmission in the music of the court during the sixteenth century. Yet this seems to have been the period during which the Mevlevis were developing their organisation of the *mukabele* as a 'mystical' suite. The three anonymous Mevlevi *beste-i kadimler* would appear to have been created approximately one century prior to the Ottoman courtly *fasıl*. As will become clear, they demonstrate a sophisticated compositional style that developed incrementally over the following centuries. Given their social and economic independence, the Mevleviye were in an ideal position either to create or to perpetuate any musical structure they deemed appropriate for the *mukabele* ceremony.

The order of the entire *mukabele* as well as the individual *selams* reflects the aesthetic decisions of Mevlevis in several historical eras. These finally coalesced between the later seventeenth century, when Itri's Na'at was introduced, and the mid to late eighteenth century, when the instrumental *peşrev* of the Sultan Veled Devri was instituted in its current form. The musical analysis in this and following chapters isolates antecedent stages of the *ayin*'s evolution and then suggests overall principles of rhythmic organisation, particularly where auxiliary notated materials from as early as the middle of the seventeenth century may help elucidate general compositional principles. On the whole, these principles follow Owen Wright's fundamental discoveries concerning the historical evolution of the Ottoman musical repertoire (Wright 1988). I will offer a few suggestions about the possible chronological evolution of the *ayin*. These concern mainly rhythmic structures and some related issues with regard to sources. The few cases where older notations exist can also suggest probable methods through which earlier musical structures have been expanded over the centuries of oral transmission – discussed in more detail in chapter 8.

Musical Techniques within a Mystical and Artistic Compositional Form

As I showed in chapter 3, the *mukabele* as a whole consists of six distinct musical genres.

- *Na'at:* a rubato composed piece
- *Baş-taksim:* a performance-generated piece in flowing rhythm played on the *ney*
- *Peşrev:* a metrical instrumental piece
- *Ayin:* a cyclical composition composed in four sections (*selam*) showing a fixed relation of metrical structures in each section
- *Son peşrev* (final *peşrev*): a shorter instrumental *peşrev*
- *Son yürük sema'i* (final *yürük sema'i*): an instrumental piece in 6/8

Before discussing (in this chapter and also chapters 8 and 9) the compositional forms used in the *ayin*, let me first say a few words about the two non-metrical genres that appear in every *mukabele* performance regardless of the nominal *makam* of the composed *ayin*, namely, the *Na'at-i Peygamberi* and the *baş-taksim*.

The Na'at-i Peygamberi

The Mevlevi *na'at* or *Na'at-i Peygamberi* (Eulogy of the Prophet) is part of a broader family of Ottoman musical genres comprising the *durak, temcid-munacat,* and *mi'raciye*. In the seventeenth century, the form *tesbih* seems to have been part of this group as well. The *na'at* in use in the *mukabele* today was composed by Buhurizade Mustafa Itri (d. 1712) in *makam* Rast. Itri's *na'at* is a multi-section composition featuring several modulations to other *makams*. In the *mecmua* anthologies, the *usul* for Itri's *na'at* is given as *Turki-zarb* in 18/4. However, *Turki-zarb* is among the most obscure *usuls* in Ottoman music – no other item in this *usul* survives – and Prince Cantemir, in his treatise of c. 1700, does not even bother to give its structure. The reason was apparently that it was used only in vocal music, while Cantemir was more concerned with notating instrumental pieces, and that already in his time, singers did not adhere strictly to *Turki-zarb*'s structure. Cantemir states: 'Be aware that vocalists are not bound by the length of the second *düm* beat in the *usul Turki-zarb*, so that they may extend it as long as they please'. Thus, whatever Itri's original intention in his *na'at*, the performance tradition has only a loose relationship to a hypothetical *usul* of *Turki-zarb*.

It appears that the custom of performing the *na'at* at the beginning of the *mukabele* was added by the Çelebi in Konya toward the beginning of the eighteenth century, i.e., during the lifetime of Itri. This gesture toward orthodox Sunni piety may well have been a response to hostility from orthodox quarters, which had led to the prohibition of the *mukabele* during the previous generation (1666–84). Other *na'at*s had been sung in the past, but today only Itri's is remembered. Although the name *na'at* is known in other Islamic cultures, the Mevlevi *na'at*, like all the other related genres mentioned above, is distinctive to Ottoman culture and does not resemble the structure of any of the non-Ottoman forms.

What is distinctive about these Sufi rubato-like genres is their relation to rhythm. All of them vary between rubato and flowing rhythm, and avoid close adherence to *usul* rhythmic cycles. While Itri's *na'at* was apparently composed in the rather amorphous *Turki-zarb usul*, the more numerous *durak*s had no connection to *usul* at all. Nevertheless, they are completely precomposed, and each performance of them is almost exactly the same. Individual performers develop personal variants that differ only in their ornamentation and overall pulse. This entire musical family came into existence during the seventeenth century, and the extant early masterpieces of *durak* are attributed to such composers as Hafiz Post (d. 1694), Ali Şirügani (d. 1714), Itri (d. 1712), Yusuf Çelebi (d. 1728), and Osman Dede (d. 1730). During the nineteenth century, Mevlevi composers such as Zekai Dede (d. 1896) and secular composers such as Haci Arif Bey (d. 1885) composed notable examples of the *durak* genre. Transmitting such complex compositions that do not admit fixed rhythmic cycles is extremely difficult, and requires frequent practice and performance. After the closing of the *tekke*s in 1925, the hundreds of pieces in these genres quickly shrank to something approaching forty. Today the functioning number is closer to twenty.

Since Cantemir's treatise in the early eighteenth century, Ottoman music theory has divided all music into two categories: genres composed in rhythmic cycles (*usul*) and vocal and instrumental performance without *usul*. The latter is held to be performance-generated, or 'improvised', and given such terms as *taksim*, *gazel*, and *kaside*. Since earlier Ottoman music theory never dealt with any kind of religious or Sufi music, it was not difficult to ignore the existence of a large body of music that did not conform to this general rule. That is, these genres were completely pre-composed and did not allow for significant improvisation, yet they were not bound to any rhythmic cycle. Their existence would prove to be problematic during the twentieth century, when Turkish musicologists such as Dr Subhi Ezgi and Sadrettin Arel rejected the idea of composed items that lacked an *usul* structure. Consequently, they invented an *usul* for the *durak* and proceeded to distort the existing *durak*s to conform to their hypothetical *usul*. Ezgi's 'transcriptions', published in 1935, are therefore inventions, and are in conflict with the traditional performance practice of the masters of the genre. Arel went on to compose numerous *durak*s in his invented metrical structure, not a single one of which is performed today (see Behar 2001).

Traditionally the *na'at*s, *durak*s, and other such genres were taught by master musicians who specialised in these genres alone. In addition to their distinctive musical structures, they also had to be performed with a special vocal style known as *durak tavrı* (the *durak* style). This style emphasised a particular nasal intonation that focused on long held notes sung to a constant pulse. *Durak tavrı* differed significantly from the Qur'anic *tecvit*, which featured a higher pitch and much faster transitions between notes. In the nineteenth century, Behlül Efendi (1830–95) and Hacı Nafiz Bey (1849–98) were considered the masters of *durak* style and repertoire, and those few singers who performed the *durak* and *na'at* in the twentieth century learned from their students. The difference between the performance style of the *durak* or *na'at* and the Qur'anic *tecvit* is so great that most Sufi *tekke*s had different specialists for each. For example, during the 1970s and 1980s, in the Halveti-Cerrahi *tekke* of Karagümrük, the Qur'an and related Sufi genres, such as the *kaside*, were sung by the professional *hafiz* (Qur'anic chanter) Kemal Tezergil while *durak*s were sung only by Kemal Baba, a *zakir* who specialised in the *durak*. In recent years, the great reciter Hafiz Kani Karaca (1930–2004) mastered both styles, and was famous for his singing of Itri's Na'at-i Peygamberi at the Mevlevi ceremonies as well as for his Qur'anic recitation there and elsewhere.

It is culturally significant that the *durak* style shares many basic features of vocal production with the style employed by cantors (*psaltes*) of the Patriarchal Church of the capital as well as by Jewish cantors in the larger Ottoman synagogues, where the Maftirim repertoire had been performed in the past. Over the last three centuries, an evidently high degree of mutual influence among dervishes, Jewish cantors, and Greek Orthodox *psaltes* produced what might be termed a common 'mystical voice'. This vocal production differs significantly from that of the *hafiz*, whose style had more influence on the performance of secular Ottoman court music, where professional vocalists had often also been mosque cantors (Feldman 1996: 80–4). A deeper discussion of this issue would require the study of relevant recordings using sophisticated analytical techniques.

Itri's Na'at, in the form in which it was transmitted orally, displays many rhythmic phrases that resemble the *theses* of Neo-Byzantine chant, particularly in the 'artistic' *kontakion* genre. Itri's generation was the first in which non-Muslim musicians attained some prominence performing and composing secular Ottoman music. As mentioned in chapter 6, Itri's notable student, Prince Cantemir, had studied the *tanbur* with the Greek Tanburi Angelos, several of whose *peşrev*s he transcribed. Itri himself was a near contemporary of the noted church composer Petros Bereketis (1680–1715). The slim biographical material about the latter does not mention any contact with Mevlevi *tekke*s or dervishes, but it is striking that the Ottoman term *bereket* (abundance) was added honorifically to Petros's name. Both this title, and certain musical features within his compositions, are often taken as indications of the beginnings of mutual influence between Ottoman music and Greek church music.

The Baş-taksim

The *baş-taksim* (head *taksim*) introduces the nominal *makam* of the *ayin* and does not relate to the mode, or even the pitch, of the previous *na'at*, which is always in Rast. The *baş-taksim* is usually majestic and of considerable length. Unlike secular *taksim*s, even when played on the *ney*, the *baş-taksim* does not attempt to compress extensive modal material and modulation into a short space, but rather develops at a leisurely pace, also taking into account the conditions of the dervishes at the time. In general, it is also significant that the pulse of the *baş-taksim* is often nearly identical to the *na'at* and to the whole *na'at-durak* family, attesting to a long interrelationship of these genres. Most *baş-taksim*s feature a slow ascending movement. Considering that the *ayin*s are pitched low, requiring the use of the largest of the *ney*s, this low pitch imparts an additional gravitas. A second *taksim* is played at the end of the *ayin*. Depending on the *makam* employed, this *taksim* may often have a descending motion, and develop faster than the *baş-taksim*. It is also common for the accompanying *ney*s to hold drones (*dem*) for parts of this *taksim* as the *neyzen* reaches new tonal centres.

Devr-i Kebir: Origins and Issues of Historical Change

Of the features that distinguish the music of the Mevlevi *ayin* from the Ottoman courtly *fasıl* listed earlier in this chapter and in chapter 3, several concern rhythmic structure – a key element of the skeletal structure of the music. It is thus appropriate to examine another group of *usul* rhythmic cycles that together make up the greater part of the rhythmic structure of the entire *ayin-i şerif* repertoire. Two *usul* rhythmic cycles predominate in this repertoire: *devr-i revan*, in the First Selam, and *devr-i kebir*, at the opening of the Third Selam. A few other rhythmic cycles appear as rare exceptions. For example, *düyek* (in 8/4) is used by Sultan Selim III (First Selam of Suzidilara Ayini), Ismail Dede (Saba-Buselik and Şevkutarab Ayins), and Osman Dede (Third Selam of Hicaz Ayini). Osman Dede also uses *frenkçin* (in 12/2) for his Rast Ayini. Both *devr-i revan* and *devr-i kebir usul*s are based on a seven-beat nucleus that is expanded into fourteen beats. *Devr-i kebir* underwent further expansion over the course of the eighteenth century, as discussed below. It is clear from both Ali Ufuki's Western notation and from Cantemir's Ottoman-Islamic notation that the only essential difference between these two *usul*s in the seventeenth century was tempo. *Devr-i revan* was phrased as 14/8 (in our terms) while *devr-i kebir* was 14/4. After Cantemir's time it could also be phrased yet slower, as 14/2.

Despite somewhat different stylistic usages within diverse musical genres, the *usul devr-i revan* seems to have maintained its basic structure from the seventeenth century down to the present. The other fourteen-beat *usul* used in the *ayin*, *devr-i kebir*, has a more complex history. As Owen Wright notes, it appears in Ottoman sources from the seventeenth century, without being mentioned in Persian sources (2017a: 33). In the Mevlevi *ayin-i şerif*, it has two manifestations: one as the rhythmic cycle of the *peşrev* accompanying the Sultan Veled Devri procession (described in chapter 3), and the other at the beginning of the Third Selam, as a vocal form. For both Ali Ufuki and for Cantemir (and Kevseri), *devr-i kebir*, in its historically earlier form, was an extremely productive *usul* for the *peşrev* genre.

The vast majority of *peşrev*s in the Sultan Veled Devri in modern sources employ some form of *usul devr-i kebir*. In twentieth-century Turkish publications in Western notation, including the early Darülelhan series *Mevlevi Ayinleri*, *peşrev*s in *devr-i kebir* are written in 28/4, or occasionally, in 14/2. Beginning with Popescu-Judetz and Ciortea (1973) and the present author, most researchers working with either the Ali Ufuki or Cantemir manuscripts transcribe this *usul* as 14/4. The resulting difference in the length of the *usul* cycle implies a slower tempo for the modern examples, along with considerable melodic elaboration. This is the case even where a modern *peşrev* is claimed to be a version of a seventeenth-century 'original'. Not infrequently the differences are so significant as to suggest a new composition. The vast stylistic discrepancy between compositions in *devr-i kebir* that appear in seventeenth-century notated sources and the use of *devr-i kebir* in the Mevlevi *mukabele* from the eighteenth century to the twentieth century prompted Owen Wright to create an extensive analysis of the *usul*'s transformation, published in a 106–page article, 'Aspects of historical change in the Turkish classical repertoire' (Wright 1988), which I summarise below. It is of interest that Rauf Yekta Bey had anticipated Wright's discovery in a footnote to his edition of volume two of the *Mevlevi Ayinleri*, published in 1934. But the great Mevlevi musicologist passed away the following year, and his observations were not taken further by any musicologist in Turkey over the following half century. Therefore we must view Wright's contribution as a major and scientifically sound development of Yekta's fundamental observation. In 1934 Yekta had observed: 'As can be understood from the *peşrev*s written 250 years ago in the Cantemir notation – the era when these *peşrev*s were composed in the quick metre called *vezn-i kebir* – the *devr-i kebir usul* was written in the oldest form comprised of 14 beats, as I have written it' (1934: 285; translated in Feldman 2001: 53).

Wright's own painstaking analysis of *peşrev*s notated by Cantemir and Bobowski, together with their nineteenth- or early twentieth-century 'versions', posits that during a period of over three centuries, the tempos of *peşrev*s had decreased by a ratio of 5 to 1, while the melodies of the *peşrev*s continued to develop around a skeleton of the original composition. Wright termed these two processes 'rhythmic retardation' and 'melodic elaboration'. Any attempt to view the evolution of the Ottoman repertoire must take this thesis into account. Wright hypothesised that these changes must have taken place through a gradual and incremental process.

More recently, Wright's hypothesis about the incremental nature of this development has been critiqued by Jacob Olley (2017 and 2018), who uses evidence from the nineteenth-century Hamparsum-notated manuscripts. These suggest that several approaches to the expression of *usul* may have existed simultaneously, even within a single piece, and that the final process of general rhythmic 'retardation', which affected the entire *peşrev* repertoire, may have occurred much more rapidly, especially toward the last third of the eighteenth century. Cantemir himself had shown an awareness both of differing tempos in the same *peşrev* genre, and even within sections of the same piece. In his 'Book of the Science of Music' he explains his use of three 'metres' (*vezin*) to express different tempos and levels of melodic density, as follows: 'The reason for this is that in some *terkibs* [sections] the metre of the *usul* is taken very slowly (*aheste aheste alınur*) . . .' (Cantemir c. 1700: 1, 15; in Feldman 1996: 333 and 2015: 105). In line with Olley's recent research, I noted in the Festschrift for Professor Wright, that 'different social strata, even within the literate Ottoman urban society, may have favoured different evolutionary phases of the rhythmic and modal systems even within the same generation' (Feldman 2018: 75).

I turn now to the appearance of *devr-i kebir* in the *peşrev* and then in the Third Selam. From the outset we may note that the processional using the *peşrev* most probably was adopted at some point after the second half of the eighteenth century, in a generation when the tempo of *devr-i kebir* was accepted to be slow enough, and the melodic line long enough, to be appropriate for a formal procession. And as explained in chapter 3 (in Inançer's detailed description from 1994), this procession involves turning and bowing in a highly ritualised manner, which would be physically impossible, or at the least, uncomfortable, at the brisk tempo of what Yekta called 'the quick metre of *devr-i kebir*'. And indeed, when we examine the detailed description of the *ayin-i şerif* written by Sieur du Loir in 1639 (quoted in chapter 3), there simply is no procession. As soon as the opening 'hymns' are over, the *kudüm* is beaten, and the dervishes rise to begin their whirling: 'The one who is closest to the sheikh goes to him and stands, he bows to the ground and greets the sheikh with his head, and then begins to whirl with such speed that the eye cannot follow it'. At present, the accessible documentation of the *ayin* from Mevlevi sources has not yet turned up a clear reference to the creation of this 'tradition', subsequently attributed to the venerable Sultan Veled, who lived at a period in which the composed *mukabele* as such had not yet been created, nor had the *peşrev* as a musical genre yet been invented.

In order to contrast the musical styles of *peşrev* in *devr-i kebir* from the later seventeenth to the later eighteenth century, we can compare two *peşrev*s in *makam* Nihavend composed roughly a century apart. The first was composed by 'Dervish Mustafa' (probably Köçek Mustafa Dede, d. 1683) and notated by Prince Cantemir. The second was composed by Tanburi Musahip Seyyid Ahmed (d. 1794) and notated by Zekaizade Ahmet Irsoy in 1936. As an intermediary stage, it is useful to view a *peşrev* composed by Cantemir himself. But for this, we will need to switch to *makam* Pençgah, since Cantemir did not compose a *peşrev* in Nihavend *devr-i kebir*.

Cantemir transcribed this piece in his *vezn-i kebir*, the 'large metre', indicating that it was meant to be performed at a relatively quick tempo and had

Fig. 7.1 Scale of Makam Nihavend.

Ex. 7.1 Nihavend *devr-i kebir*, Dervish Mustafa (Cantemir no. 116); *serhane and mülazime terkib* A.

relatively few note-changes per measure, generally between 10 and 16 per 14/4 cycle. This *peşrev* is created almost entirely from antecedent-consequent pairs of phrases. Its *serhane* is an ABA¹C structure in two cycles of *devr-i kebir*. Its ritornello (*mülazime*) consists of three sections (*terkib*) of one cycle each, of which I show the first. Hence this *peşrev* is an extremely symmetrical composition. Moreover, it offers little evidence of any of the compositional techniques on display in Mustafa Dede's *ayin* in *makam* Beyati, provided in ex. 7.4 (p. 187).

Here, now, is Cantemir's *peşrev* in *makam* Pençgah, which I referred to above as an 'intermediary stage' of *peşrev* composition. The compound *makam* Pençgah combines the scales of Nişabur and Rast:

Fig. 7.2 Scales of Makams Nişabur, Rast, and Pençgah.

Ex. 7.2 Pençgah *devr-i kebir* 'Huri', Cantemir (no. 321); 'Huri' (Cantemir no. 321); *serhane* and *mülazime terkib* A.

Prince Cantemir (1673–1723) was born a decade before the death of Mustafa Dede, and was evidently the most innovative Ottoman composer of his generation. Cantemir's innovativeness was fostered by his Greek *tanbur* teacher Angelos, about whom little is known apart from the compositions notated by his princely pupil, and an enthusiastic mention by Evliya Çelebi. This one *peşrev* in Pençgah by the Prince illustrates major conceptual changes in compositional style.

Cantemir notated his *peşrev* in his 'smallest of the small' metre. His note-changes are generally around 20 per cycle, which is considerably higher than in the previous example. He also uses more attacks on repeated pitches. No doubt this resulted in a somewhat slower overall tempo. But beyond these features, the compositional technique is utterly different. He unifies his *serhane* by repeating the opening six-note phrase in the second *usul* cycle. But he does not work this repetition into a true antecedent-consequent relationship. The remainder of the second *usul* cycle bears little resemblance to the first one, and even features a note alteration, in which the C# is changed to the note C (*çargah*) in the middle of the second *usul* cycle. The *mülazime* is equally inventive, skipping to the upper octave of the *makam*, and starting the second *usul* cycle with an ascending sequence from the note C-sharp. Thus, in the 40–50 years separating these two *peşrev*s, much musical innovation was taking place.

The last *peşrev* in this series is the only one which, in all probability, had been composed for use within the Mevlevi *mukabele*. Its composer, Musahip Seyyid Ahmed Ağa (1728–94), represented an amalgam of the courtly and the Mevlevi musician. Seyyid Ahmed Ağa was the son of the major court musician and musical theorist Kemani Hızır Ağa (d. 1760), who had been a musician for Sultan Mahmud I (1730–54). Kemani Hızır Ağa was educated in the Enderun School at court, and wrote the treatise *Tefhimül Makamat fi Tevlidül Nağamat* (The Comprehension of the Makams in the Generation of Melodies), dated to 1749. Later Seyyid Ahmed studied at Yenikapı Mevlevihanesi and became the *kudümzenbaşı* at Galata. He is known also as 'Tanburi', indicating his mastery of that instrument, which makes him one of the relatively few Mevlevi composers who was not a *neyzen*. He invented the *makam* Ferahfeza, which would be used prominently in the next generation, especially by Ismail Dede Efendi, who composed an *ayin* in this *makam* in 1839. Seyyid Ahmed himself composed three Mevlevi *ayin*s – in Hicaz,

Nihavend, and Saba, of which only the first two survive. And he was also a composer of courtly vocal music and *peşrev*s.

Seyyid Ahmed was a major composer for Sultan Abdülhamid I (1774–89). When Sultan Selim came to the throne, in 1789, Seyyid Ahmed was elevated to the rank of 'companion', hence his title Musahib (Musahip). Seyyid Ahmed Ağa was also a friend of the Sultan's spiritual mentor, the poet Sheikh Galib of Galata (1758–96), who composed this *tarih* (chronogram) on his death: *Musahip oldu hamuşan ahbap*: 'The Companion has become one of the Friends among the Departed'.

In the *Mevlevi Ayinleri* series, Ahmed Irsoy writes about Seyyid Ahmed, 'He has many superb *peşrev*s in various *makam*s. Each one of them is worthy of becoming a model of emulation' (1936: 483). One could ask to what extent processional *peşrev*s served as an integral part of any particular *ayin*. After the middle of the eighteenth century, in cases where the composer of the substance of the *ayin* was the same as the composer of the preceding *peşrev*, we may assume that there was a musical connection. This would seem to be the case for Musahip Seyyid Ahmed, Ismail Dede Efendi, and many other later Mevlevi composers. However, this does not seem to be the case with the *ayin*s of Osman Dede (d. 1730). In his time, the processional Mevlevi *peşrev* did not exist, and he evidently composed his *peşrev*s for purely secular contexts. As Wright has shown (1988), the extant notations for these secular *peşrev*s published in early and later twentieth-century Turkish sources show only the slimmest connection with anything that Osman Dede might have composed. In the case of Osman Dede, the likelihood of a 'faithful' transmission is also rendered slimmer by the fact that the Sultan Veled Devri – to the accompaniment of the *peşrev* – did not yet exist in his lifetime.

Cantemir's notations of the *peşrev*s of Osman Dede furnish some of the only examples of *peşrev*s by Mevlevi composers from his own generation. Wright's thorough analyses reveal that the existing instrumental items attributed to Osman Dede might perhaps have been modernised into unrecognisability. Or they might be apocryphal items altogether, similar to the famous Sazkar Havi Peşrevi, attributed to Prince Cantemir in modern sources. There is no trace of such a piece in Cantemir's notated Collection, and he also specifically rejected the usefulness of this modal category. Moreover, this very elegant *peşrev* shows every feature of an item of the early nineteenth, rather than of the early eighteenth century.

On the other hand, even where a *peşrev* of a nineteenth- or twentieth-century Mevlevi composer, for example, the Pençgah *peşrev* by Salih Dede or the Beyati *peşrev* by Emin Dede, was accepted for use in the corresponding more antique *ayin*, the composer may well have adapted his inspiration to the existing *ayin-i şerif*. That is to say, while neither of these modern Mevlevi composers uses archaic compositional techniques for the *peşrev*, melodic and modal material from the corresponding more antique *ayin* may nevertheless appear in their *peşrev*s.

With this general background, we can turn to the Nihavend *devri-kebir peşrev* by Musahip Seyyid Ahmet (**website**, ex. 7.3: Nihavend Peşrev in *devr-i kebir*, Musaihp Seyyid Ahmed, [Irsoy 1936], *serhane*). It is likely that Seyyid Ahmed (d. 1794) was among the first generation of Mevlevi musicians to compose their own *peşrev* for the Sultan Veled Devri, which would have preceded their own composition for the *ayin*.

The *peşrev* in ex. 7.3 was published first in the *Darülelhan Külliyati* (no. 104) by Rauf Yekta Bey, and then again in volume 10 of the *Mevlevi Ayinleri* series, where, in a slightly variant version, it appears as the *peşrev* preceding the Mevlevi Ayin in Nihavend by Musahip Seyyid Ahmed.

In both editions the *usul* is written as 14/2. The number of note-changes per cycle of *devr-i kebir* average 20, which puts it in the same range as Cantemir's Pençgah *peşrev*. But evidently its function as the music for the Sultan Veled Devri would suggest a somewhat slower tempo. Both of these versions were published a little more than a century after the death of the composer. Nevertheless, the fact that this *peşrev* was composed as part of a *mukabele* at a time when the *peşrev* genre was no doubt already in use for the opening procession would suggest that any changes in *usul* or tempo that occurred in the process of oral transmission were probably not of a fundamental nature.

As for the Nihavend *peşrev* of Seyyid Ahmed, both *usul* and note-changes seem consistent with a composition from the second half of the eighteenth century. The use of melodic progression is likewise conservative, although it is likely that certain movements may have been developed to some extent in the course of oral transmission. The Darülelhan edition indicates the basic drum beats underlying the *devr-i kebir usul*. However, the manner in which the *peşrev* was written in both of the Western notated editions creates a problem in understanding the underlying relation of *usul* and melody. With the transcription in *Mevlevi Ayinleri* as a basis, I indicate the *devr-i kebir usul* as a construction of 6+8+6+8. Ex. 7.3 (**website**) presents the first two sections of the *serhane*, marked as *a* and *b*. The melody is continuous within each *devir* (rhythmic cycle) of 14/2. The antecedent-consequent structure of the earliest *peşrev* is completely absent, without even a suggestion, as in Cantemir's Pençgah *peşrevi*. Whether this new and far more sophisticated use of melody and *usul* originated with the Mevlevi *ayin*, or whether it was also being developed by purely secular composers, is unknowable on the basis of evidence now available. Only further research into the middle and later eighteenth-century *peşrev* repertoires may enlighten us. But it is likely that a multifaceted musician like Musahip Seyyid Ahmed – a *kudümzenbaşı*, court *tanbur* player, theorist, and composer in all the major genres – would have had a central role in furthering this musical experimentation.

Ex. 7.3 [**website**] Nihavend Peşrev in *devr-i kebir*, Musahip Seyyid Ahmed, *serhane*.

Let us now turn from the *peşrev* to the use of *devr-i kebir* within the vocal *ayin* itself. To compare the older and newer usage *of usul devr-i kebir* in the Third Selam of the *ayin*, I take two compositions somewhat more than one century apart. The first is from the Beyati Ayini of Köçek Mustafa Dede (d. 1683) and the second, from the Acem-Buselik Ayini of Abdülbaki Nasır Dede (1765–1820). Here is the Persian text from the Beyati Ayini:

Nagehan anbar feşan amed saba (beli yar-i men aman)
Buy-e müşkü zafaran amed saba (beli yar-i men dost)
Gül şukufta ender in sahn-i çemen
Sad neva-yi bülbülan amed saba
Şams-i Tebrizi sabah al-aşkı güft
'Aşıkan-ra can-ü can amed saba.

Aruz: fa'ilatun fa'ilatun fa'ilun

The morning breeze suddenly appeared,
diffusing a scent of amber.
It came with the smell of musk and saffron!
The rose blossomed in this spreading meadow.

The morning breeze came with the tunes of a hundred nightingales.
Said Shams-e Tabrizi – the dawn of love:
'For the lovers comes the morning breeze, as the soul of the soul!'

This section of the Beyati Ayin has modulated into *makam* Hüseyni:

Fig. 7.3 Scale of Makam Hüseyni.

Ex 7.4a Third Selam, Beyati Ayini, Mustafa Dede (d. 1683), 1979 edition.

Ex 7.4b Third Selam, Beyati Ayini, Mustafa Dede (d. 1683), 1931 edition.

Comparing the editions of Yekta and Irsoy (1931) and Heper (1979), we can observe several differences in the presentation of the *usul* although the melody is essentially identical. The 1979 edition goes back to the older Turkish practice of Western notation in dividing the *usul* into equal measures of 4/4. The time signature is 28/4. Here the entire rhythmic cycle is broken up into measures of 4/4. This practice had become more or less standard in the writing, and, especially, in the publishing, of Ottoman music in staff notation ever since the official introduction of staff notation by Donizetti Pasha, in 1828, for use in the new Muzika-i Hümayun band that had replaced the abolished Janissary ensemble. Giuseppe Donizetti Pasha (1788–1856), the older brother of the well-known opera composer, was a most interesting character, and he did make some effort to master the Turkish *makam* system. But it is doubtful that he exerted the same effort with the system of rhythmic cycles. While the practice of breaking up the long *usuls* into notated measures of 4/4 had been a custom for almost two centuries in Turkey, Rauf Yekta Bey and his associates avoided it in notating *usul devr-i kebir* in the Third Selam.

In Heper's 1979 edition, the pages that explain the *usuls* of the *ayin* show the syncopated *velvele* pattern of drum-beats used in the Third Selam. Interestingly, the following page, which gives the *usuls* with metronome markings, presents *devr-i kebir* as 14/4, with the quarter note as 56. Turning to the 1931 edition of the Beyati Third Selam (ex. 7.4b), we see the same 14/4 signature. In addition, Rauf Yekta marks the entire 14/4 cycle as one measure, and supplies the basic drum beats below the line. In example 7.4b, I use Yekta's version as the basis for dividing the melody according to the *usul*. The first cycle of *devr-i kebir* is essentially one seamless melodic line, beginning on the finalis *a*, resting on the fifth *e*, and concluding on the *d*. Within this broad melody there is a pause right after beat number 7 of the 14, where the melody rests on *e*. However, this caesura on beat 7 divides the word '*anbar*' into two syllables (written as '*a-ni-ber-i*' in the text underlay), with '*an*' ending on beat 7 and '*bar*' beginning on beat 8. Likewise, the close of the first *devir* of 14 splits the word '*amed*' on the first syllable 'a – '. Rather unexpectedly, the syllable '-*med*' starts the second *devir* while the second syllable of the word '*saba*' is stretched from beat 4 to beat 7 – half of the *devir*, thus: '*Nagehan an – bar feşan a – med saba*'. Beat 8 – the second half of *devr-i kebir*, begins with a non-textual *terrenüm*.

Perhaps even more surprisingly, this *terennüm* (*beli yar-i men aman*) begins a continuous descending melody which then continues as an ascending melody in the following cycle with the second poetic line '*Buy-e müşkü zaferan amed saba*'. However, the melodic line breaks right in the middle of the *devir*, reposing on finalis *a* with the syllable '*kü*'. Then a non-textual '*ah*' is inserted for the first three beats of the seven-beat section, followed by the word '*zaferan*' and the first syllable '*a* – ' which ends the *devir* on the note *f*. This is not a closing or a reposing point of the *makam* at all, and the melody flows seamlessly into the next *devir* with the syllable '*-med*'.

The second syllable of the word '*sa-ba*' now forms a caesura on the note *c*, while the remainder of the *terennüm* '*beli yar-i men dost*' closes the *devir* on the note *e*, the fifth degree, which is where the initial *devir* had first reposed. The resulting compositional structure is highly asymmetrical. Part of the first poetic *mısra* (hemistich) indeed forms a closed unit of 14 beats in the first *devir* of the *usul*. But the second half of the *mısra* flows into a *terennüm* and then into the second *mısra* at the opening of the third *devir*. Broadly speaking, these four *devir*s of the *usul* can be grouped into a melody for the first *devir*, and then one very long melody extending over three full *devir*s, a total of 42 quarters. And this long melodic line seems to take little account of the poetic structure, as parts of the lyrics are split across cycles, and the poetic *mısra* itself can be interrupted by non-textual syllables ('*ah!*'). Both of the two *mısra*s are followed by verbal *terennüm* sections. The whole melodic section consisting of four units of 14/4 ends with the non-textual exclamation '*dost!*' (Friend). Then the exact same structure is repeated for each of the three poetic *mısra*s. As I show in greater detail in the following chapter, this rhythmic complexity has nothing to do with the extremely regular and predictable poetic metre (*aruz*) of the lyrics.

After the relentless complexity of the *devr-i kebir* opening of the Third Selam, the ensuing hymn 'Ey ki Hezar Aferin' in the *sema'i usul* in 6/8, and then the entire conclusion of the *selam*, which continues in *sema'i*, must be perceived as a deep musical catharsis. This compositional structure has no parallel within any genre of the Ottoman courtly repertoire.

Let us now turn to the use of *devr-i kebir* in the Third Selam of a major *ayin* composition from somewhat over one century later: the Acem-Buselik Ayini of Abdülbaki Nasır Dede (ex. 7.5). Abdülbaki Nasır Dede (1765–1820), mentioned in chapters 5 and 6, was the sheikh of Yenikapı, following the tenure of his older brother, Ali Nutki Dede (d. 1804). His primary musical activity was as a theorist, with two major musicological works and a new system of notation to his credit. He also created new *makam*s and a complex long *usul*. His younger brother Abdürrahim Künhi Dede (d. 1831) was also a composer, and had been the teacher of Musahip Seyyid Ahmed. Nasır Dede composed three *ayin*s, of which only the one in Acem-Buselik survives. Following the assassination of his patron Sultan Selim III, in 1808, he does not seem to have created any new compositions. His sole surviving *ayin* displays a new approach to the organisation of melody, rhythmic cycle, and poetry in the Third Selam. Given his scholarly predilections, it is not surprising that the poem he chose for this section of the *ayin* is replete with Qur'anic allusions.

Aşıkan laf ez tebarek rabbünel a'la zened
Sadıkan lebbeyki vayhullahı ma'evha zened
La cerem ez aşıkan ü sadıkan ez suzidil
Darbına ber tabl-ı subbhanellezi esra' zened

The speech of the lovers is always the praise of our Most Exalted Lord.
The faithful say 'I am here' for whatever inspiration the Lord designs.
It is no fault for the lovers and the faithful, if with each beat of the drum of the
Most Highly Praised, they speak at once from their heart's pain.

In the *Mevlevi Ayinleri* edition (volume 10), the editors, under the direction of Zekaizade Ahmed Irsoy, wrote the *devr-i kebir* of the Third Selam in a continuous measure of 28 quarter notes, under the signature of 28/4. Among the surviving *ayin*s, it is only with this composition of Nasır Dede that the new conception of the *usul* is fully expressed in the Third Selam.[4] Even the Third Selam of the Nihavend Ayini of Musahip Seyyid Ahmed (which appears on pp. 474–5 of the same volume) is written as one measure of 14/2, although compared with the Beyati Third Selam of Mustafa Dede, its melodic density is higher. The tempo marking for both the Acem-Buselik and the Nihavend Third Selam is identical – 56 per quarter note.

[4] Feldman 2001: 47.

Fig 7.4 Scales of Makams Acem and Buselik.

Ex. 7.5 Third Selam, Acem-Buselik Ayini, Abdülbaki Nasir Dede.

Unlike the Beyati Third Selam, here the entire composition is arranged in a variant of the AABA standard form in the courtly *fasıl*. That is, in any genre in the *fasıl* (*beste, ağır sema'i, yürük sema'i*), the first, second, and fourth poetic lines are set to one melody (known as the *zemin*), while the third line has a different melody (*miyanhane or miyan*). Unlike in the *beste*, there is no *terennüm*, but only the exclamation '*heyi*' at the end of lines 1, 2, and 3. There are no repetitions or interruptions for textual or non-textual *terennüm* syllables or words. The melody within the *devr-i kebir usul* is divided into two units of 14 quarters (14 x 2 = 28), with the half-cycles perfectly symmetrical. The first poetic *mısra* is stretched over one cycle of *devr-i kebir* (28/4). In the transcription, the *redif* monorhyme *zened* ('they say') appears on the fourth line, on the note *a*, which is the finalis, and it is the beginning of the eight-quarter unit that closes the cycle. The line ends with a skip to the note *d* with the exclamation '*heyi*'.

Following the internal structure of the *usul*, in the first line the first beat begins on the note *d* (*neva*) and returns there on the sixth beat. The following eight-beat phrase then ends on *d*. Hence, the first *mısra*, '*Aşıkan laf ez tebarek rabbünel a'la zened*' is broken up into four musical lines of 14/4 each:

1. *Aşıkan laf*
2. *ez tebarek* (*i*)
3. *rabbünela*
4. *-la zened*

Despite a general agreement of the *zemin-miyan* structure illustrated in the preceding examples with the genres of the courtly *fasıl*, none of these genres, even the lengthy *murabba beste*, attempted to achieve a similar effect. A comparison of the *murabba beste* with the Third Selam in the Beyati Ayini of Mustafa Dede shows that the extremely long melodic line within several cycles of *usul* in this Third Selam represented musical sophistication of another type. As for the Third Selam of Nasır Dede's Acem-Buselik Ayini, detailed comparison with the *murabba beste* of the *fasıl* would show some similarities but also many stylistic differences from the vision on display in Nasır Dede's groundbreaking composition. Only this section of the *ayin* introduced such an expansive synthesis. It had been preceded by the driving tempo of the shorter *usul devr-i revan* for the First Selam and the more moderate *evfer* (9/4) in the Second Selam, and it would be followed by the ecstatic *sema'i usul* in 6/8 for the remainder of the Third Selam. Surveying the entire structure of this Third Selam, we can see a broad expansion, a musical vision displaying a very slow and gradual presentation of the key pitches of the *makam*, with its modulation, and an internal alignment of the *usul* with the syllables of the poem. Composing over a century after Mustafa Dede, Nasır Dede created a broad expanse with a grand symmetry that for performers and listeners alike demanded simultaneous detachment and immersion.

8

MUSIC, POETRY, AND COMPOSITION IN THE *AYIN*

Devr-i Revan and the First Selam

As the longest individual section of the *ayin*, the First Selam offers an extended demonstration of the techniques and the vision of the *ayin*'s composer. It also signals the start of the 'whirling' of the *semazen*s. The three 'ancient compositions' for the *mukabele*, as well as Mustafa Dede's Beyati Ayini, all commence with the First Selam in *usul devr-i revan*. This practice was evidently a tradition that, with very few exceptions (noted in chapter 3), was maintained by later Mevlevi composers. The prominence of *devr-i revan* in the Mevlevi compositional tradition merits further exploration of this *usul*'s history and evolving cultural context.

In the seventeenth century, Ali Ufuki/Bobowski had devised a relatively clear method for specifying the numerical structure of individual *usul*s, as had his fellow foreign-born Ottoman musician Cantemir in the early eighteenth century. Their Iranian contemporaries, however, did not devise any similarly transparent system to indicate an *usul*'s numerical structure. Thus Owen Wright, in two recent articles comparing Safavid and Ottoman sources, aims to interpret how Safavid authors intended their descriptions to be understood (Wright 2017a, 2017b). In an analysis of the Safavid Amir Khan Gurji's text from 1697, Wright addresses the *usul* '*revani*' (Pers. 'flowing'): 'The obvious term of comparison here is the Ottoman *devr-i revan*, pointing therefore to a total of either seven time units, which is what Ali Ufuki's notation suggests, or fourteen, as specified by Cantemir . . .' (Wright 2017b: 53). In Ali Ufuki's two manuscripts, we can read his *devr-i revan* as a seven-beat cycle:

Fig. 8.1 Devr-i Revan, Bobowski, Turc 292.

On the other hand, Cantemir explains this *usul* as having fourteen beats:

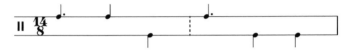

Fig. 8.2 Devr-i Revan, Cantemir.

A century earlier, the Safavid writer Mir Sadr al Din Muhammad (d. 1599) mentions a single *usul*, which he refers to both as *dowr-e revān* and *samā'i-ye revān*. Although this author occasionally supplies a few remarks about the social context of the *usuls* he describes, in this case he offers no information.[1] But the term 'samā'i-ye revān' may well suggest some sort of Sufistic context. A metaphor used by the poet Sa'eb (1590–1676), while hardly conclusive, is also suggestive of such a context. Sa'eb himself was not a Sufi but a court poet. He was born in Tabriz and lived with his family in Isfahan before spending seven years in India, where he was befriended by the Mughal governor of Kabul. He returned to Iran in 1632 and eventually became the poet laureate of the Safavid Shah Abbas II while continuing to lead a life outside of the court in Isfahan. Thus his life's journey took him from Azerbaijan (indeed from the birthplace of Shams Tabrizi three centuries earlier) to Kabul and to India proper. In one of his *ghazals*, Sa'eb writes:

Gardūn ba zowq-e nāla'e mā mikonad samā'
In asiye bagard z tab'-e revān-e mā

---

[1] I thank Amir Hosein Pourjavady for allowing me to read his doctoral dissertation while still in progress. See Amir Hosein Pourjavady, 'Music Making in Iran: Developments between the Sixteenth and Late Nineteenth Centuries' (CUNY Graduate Center, 2019), chapter 4 ('Rhythm'), p. 184.

The heavens perform their mystic dance
to the pleasure of my wailing tune;
Our flowing nature turns this celestial mill!
    (Abbasi 1946, *ghazal* no. 778, p. 266)

Sa'eb uses the literal meaning of *revān* as 'flowing' to express his inner nature. *Tab'-e revān* (flowing nature) was not a fixed idiom in Persian poetry. That it appears together with *samā'* and *nāla* (wailing) can only suggest a musical accompaniment to the *samā'* 'dance', where the Heavens turn like dervishes to a 'flowing' melody. Read more literally, they may turn to the *usul* named *revān* (or *revāni*). Without this allusion to a real-life context, these images would be rather obscure. Putting together his literary reference to *revān* and *samā'* with the somewhat earlier reference by Sadr al Din to the *usul samā'i-ye revān*, it would seem that the association of the *samā'* with an *usul* named *revān* or *revāni* must have been widely understood in the Persian-speaking world, and particularly, in Iran proper.

Wright's reconstruction of the time-values behind Amir Khan Gurji's presentation of the *usul revāni* (2017b: 52) confirms a fourteen-beat structure, at least by the later seventeenth century. This fourteen-beat rhythmic structure was evidently held in common in sixteenth to seventeenth-century Persian music and in seventeenth-century Ottoman music of several genres. However, unlike the case of the Ottoman *usul sema'i*, discussed in chapter 9, *usul revāni* lacks abundant links with later folkloric and popular Sufistic musical genres that extend from Anatolia to Central Asia. Thus, when the three anonymous 'beste-i kadim' *ayin*s were composed, probably between the later sixteenth and early seventeenth centuries, and when Mustafa Dede composed his Beyati Ayin later in the seventeenth century, *devr-i revan* was already established as the predominant *usul* for the First Selam of the Mevlevi *ayin*. That said, surviving written and notated Ottoman sources from the seventeenth to early eighteenth centuries preserve it in a variety of secular genres rather than as a rhythmic element of the Mevlevi *ayin*.

In the twentieth century, a rhythmic pattern in seven beats, broken up as 3+2+2 exists in the traditional folk music of a wide geographical swath extending from Afghanistan and Iranian Khorasan in the east through Anatolia and into Greece. The prominence of usul *devr-i revan* in secular music notwithstanding, Mevlevi practice and contemporaneous Iranian terminology both suggest that by the sixteenth century, this *usul* was well established among

Sufi groups. That Mir Sadr al-Din, a learned writer in mid-sixteenth-century Isfahan, acknowledged the existence of *devr-i revan*, with its Sufistically-tinged name, suggests that it must have been used in some variety of *samā'* ceremony several generations earlier. It would not be too far-fetched to imagine a figure like the wide-ranging Divane Mehmed Çelebi, discussed in chapter 3, returning from one of his journeys to the East with melodies and rhythms that the Mevlevi *mutriban* in Konya and Karahisar could introduce into the pre-composed *devir*s of the *mukabele*. While this is only speculation, we do need to account for the consensus among the Mevleviye by the sixteenth century that *usul devr-i revan* was appropriate as the dominant rhythmic cycle for the entire First Selam, which both begins the whirling ceremony and is also usually its longest section.

Ali Ufuki, as an 'outsider' turned 'insider', did include a large repertoire of Sufi hymns of various genres among his notations, among which was the 'Ey ki hezar aferin' hymn that opens the *sema'i* section of the Third Selam (see chapter 9). But in general, non-Mevlevi sources do not allude to these Sufistic compositions. In Ali Ufuki's Paris Manuscript, *devr-i revan* is divided equally between instrumental and vocal items, with four of each. The *usul devr-i kebir* (14/4) skews toward the instrumental category, generally *peşrev*s (five), in addition to three vocal items (Haug 2017: 99).

In the early eighteenth century, Es'ad Efendi mentions secular vocal items that use *devr-i revan*, including *nakış* and *murabba beste*s. For example, under the composer 'Hafız Kömür, *murabba ve makam-i Saba'da usul-i Devr-i revan'da*,' Es'ad Efendi also includes the aforementioned *murabba beste* in *makam* Rast by Çengi Yusuf Dede (Behar 2010: 239). But Es'ad Efendi also lists several other pieces in *devr-i revan* without specifying the genre, e.g., '*Imam-i Sultani Ibrahim Efendi, makam-i Hüseyni'de*' (2010: 224) and '*Odabaşızade Efendi, makam-i Nevruz-i Acem'de*' (230).

According to Es'ad Efendi's contemporary Prince Cantemir, *devr-i revan* was one of the favoured *usul*s for the urban popular genre *şarkı*, the other being the ubiquitous *sofyan*, in 2/4. Since Cantemir notated only instrumental pieces, the musical examples in his Collection, which is appended to his 'Book of the Science of Music', include no *şarkı*s. Instead, there is a preponderance of *peşrev*s in *devr-i kebir*, with a few in *devr-i revan*.

As examples of early secular and Mevlevi usage of the *devr-i revan usul*, let us compare the relationship of rhythm and melody in three items: Rast Peşrevi, *devr-i revan* 'Kadim' (Cantemir no. 170); Rast Makamında Nakış (Acemler); and the Pençgah Ayini, First Selam. Of the three, only the Rast *peşrev* represents an early notated document, from Cantemir's own hand. Cantemir wrote the word *kadim* (ancient) at the end of the title in place of a composer, though it is difficult to establish how 'ancient' the piece might be. Possibly the earliest item in his Collection is the *peşrev* in *devr-i kebir* attributed to the Ottoman Prince Korkut (1467–1513). As Wright demonstrated (1988: 78), this item shows a relationship between melody and *usul* that seems to predate the other pieces in the Collection, which includes only a few names of sixteenth-century *mehter* composers. For the most part, Cantemir's 'ancient' stratum derives from composers of the first half of the seventeenth century, in particular the group of foreign musicians brought to Istanbul by Sultan Murad IV in the 1630s, who are named collectively the 'Persians' (Acemler). Part of the repertoire of these 'Persians' included *peşrevs* by the 'Indians' (Hindiler), who were probably other Persian musicians working in the Mughal court. Ottoman oral tradition preserved several vocal items attributed to these foreign-born experts, also known collectively as the 'Acemler'. The Nakış in ex. 8.2 is one of these pieces. In general, these pieces are less elaborate but structurally similar to the pseudographic repertoire attributed to Abdul Kadir Meraghi (d. 1435), which I, and also Wright, assign to the early to middle seventeenth century – two centuries later than their putative composer.[2]

All three items shown below (exs 8.1, 8.2, and 8.3) are based on the Rast makam, a major-like mode here pitched on finalis *g*, with its initial tetrachord moving upward to the secondary tonal centre a fifth higher, on *d* (*re*). Though Pençgah *makam* is a compound (*mürekkeb*) mode based on both Rast and Nişabur (previously discussed in relation to Cantemir's *devri- kebir peşrev* 'Huri', in chapter 7, ex. 7.2), in the First Selam of the anonymous Pençgah *ayin*, the modality is still that of the basic Rast *makam*, and thus fully compatible with the two secular pieces in Rast that appear in examples 8.1 and 8.2.

Comparing the fundamental rhythmic structure of the *peşrev* in ex. 8.1 with that of the *nakış* in ex. 8.2, we see an identical partitioning of the 14 eighth note values that make up one *usul* cycle, or *devir*. This partitioning

---

[2] For a discussion of the seventeenth-century historical context for the creation of the 'Maraghi' repertoire, see 'Pseudographia and the "Maraghi" Repertoire in Iran and Turkey' (Feldman 2015: 130–4).

Ex. 8.1 Rast Peşrevi Devr-i Revan Kadim, *serhane* and *mülazime* a.

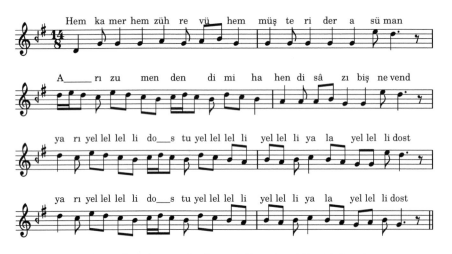

Ex. 8.2 Rast Makamında Nakış Acemler (Zemin) (from Darülelhan Külliyati).

begins with a unit of 3/8 expressed as a quarter note followed by an eighth note, which forms the initial part of a unit of 7/8. The 7/8 unit is immediately repeated to fill out one cycle of the 14/8 usul: 7/8 + 7/8 = 14/8. This rhythmic pattern dominates several *peşrevs* in *devr-i revan*, including Eyyubi Mehmed's Arazbar and Cantemir's own Buselik (no. 335). It has a modern analogue in the rhythmic partitioning of melodies for the *kalamatiano syrto* in Greek folklore. Both Rast Peşrevi and Rast Nakış are constructed from an antecedent-consequent structure. In the *peşrev* this structure takes the form of ABA¹C. In the *nakış* (Persian: *naqsh*) it is formulated as AA¹BA²BC, thus with considerably more internal elaboration. The elaboration in the *nakış*, however, does not disguise its fundamental ABAC structure. The first half of the *nakış* (shown in ex. 8.2) presents a *zemin* with a rather artless Persian text, followed by a *terennüm*.

> *Hem kamer hem zühre vü hem müşteri der asman*
> *Arzu mendeni mihadendi sazi bişneved*

> The moon, Venus and Mars are in the Heavens
> I want to hear the sound of instruments!

The first hemistich (*mısra*) stretches exactly over the first two measures of *devr-i revan*, reposing on *d*, while the second *mısra* begins on *d*, descends in a sequence for one measure, and then leaps back up to *d* for the fourth measure.

The *peşrev* opens with a leap from finalis to dominant (G to d) via passing note *e*. This is followed by a descent back to *G*, and then a gradual rise via *B* and *C* up to *d*, before creating a cadential phrase resolving on *G* in cycle four. It begins a descending sequence in section (*terkib*) a of the *mülazime* ritornello.

The *nakış* initially is centred around *G*, with a leap from the lower fourth (*D*) and small cadence using the third above the finalis. Thus, the closing notes of measure 2 of the *zemin*, with their sudden movement *G-e-d*, seem to echo the opening measure of the *peşrev*. The descending sequence that constitutes the *terennüm* (staves 3 and 4) seems like a more elaborated version of the *mülazime* of the *peşrev*. While the vocal *nakış is* significantly different from the instrumental *peşrev*, both as item and as genre, one can sense commonalities of compositional thinking which suggest that these pieces are contemporaries. Thus, Cantemir's notated document from c. 1700, which represents an item created perhaps a century earlier, offers a rare confirmation of the Ottoman oral tradition notated at the beginning of the twentieth century.

Let us now turn to the opening of the First Selam of the 'ancient' Pençgah Ayini, which appears in Rauf Yekta Bey's *Mevlevi Ayinleri*, volume 1, and is reproduced in ex. 8.3 (**website**). Its striking theme from Rumi's *Divan-e Shams-e Tabrizi* indeed concerns the *samâ*:

> *Şehbaz-ı cenab-ı Zülcelalest sema'*
> *Ferraş-ı kulub-ü ehl-i halest sema'*
> *Der mezheb-i münkiran haramest sema'*
> *Der mezheb-i aşıkan halalest sema'*

The *samā'* is the royal falcon at the side of the Lord of Glory
The *samā'* cleans the hearts for the people of ecstasy
The *samā'* is forbidden to the sect of deniers
The *samā'* is permitted to the sect of the lovers.

Ex. 8.3 [website] Pençgah Ayini, Selam I, first hemistich.

As Ex. 8.3 makes clear, in the first hemistich of Pençgah Ayini, Selam I, rhythmic partitioning within *devr-i revan* is quite similar to that in the *peşrev* and the *nakış*, featuring two parallel units of 7/8 with the opening 3/8 section divided as quarter and eighth note. But the actual melodic period construction is quite distinctive. There is no antecedent-consequent structure. The opening poetic *mısra* is stretched over three full *devir*s (cycles) of 14/8, but even then it does not resolve on the finalis. Rather, the word *'sema'* is stretched from the end of the third *devir* into the first half (7/8) of the fourth *devir*, but it ends only on a half cadence on the note *D*. Then, in the middle of the measure, the *terennüm* enters with the exclamation 'hey!' and continues for another two and a half measures (*'hey hey ra'na-i men can-i men vay!'*), but concludes on the fifth degree (*d*), before the second *mısra* begins with the words *'Ferraş-ı kulub'*, set to a repetition of the entire melody.

Thus, the first hemistich is sung to a continuous melody of three and a half *devir*s, lasting for the equivalent of 49 eighth notes. The following *terennüm* is sung for another two and a half *devir*s, equivalent to 35 eighth notes. This section of the *selam* employs only the basic pitches of the *makam* Rast with not even a hint of a modulation, or even of the full complexity of the compound mode Pençgah. Compositional sophistication lies in the development of the melodic line over the rhythmic cycle. Thus, although *devr-i revan* is considered a 'short' *usul*, and indeed, it had been in use for many different secular vocal genres as well as the instrumental *peşrev*, none of the other genres composed in this general historical period display such complexity.

Given the realities of oral transmission and conscious re-composition over many generations, there is no sense in claiming that the version of the First Selam of Pençgah Ayini notated by Rauf Yekta Bey represents an original version of such an 'ancient' composition. Nevertheless, the nature of the complexity of even this opening section of the First Selam suggests a manner of musical thinking appropriate for the artistic, functional, and mystical purpose of the *mukabele*.

Analysis of the First Selam: a Comparison of the Dügah and Beyati Ayins

The Dügah Ayini is one of the three 'ancient' and anonymous *ayin* compositions, which also include Pençgah and Hüseyni. The Dügah Ayini is relatively intact, missing only the *sema'i* sections following the hymn 'Ey ki Hezar Aferin' in the Third Selam. The Pençgah Ayini is completely intact, while the Hüseyni Ayini has preserved only its First Selam.

'Dügah' is no longer used as a term to designate the modal entity in this *ayin*. It is, however, currently used as a name for the note conventionally written in Turkey as *A* and usually performed as *E*. As such it is the *finalis* of a great many *makam*s, of which Cantemir mentions Uşşak, Neva, Hüseyni, Muhayyer, and Gerdaniye, among others. He described *dügah* as 'the gateway and the measure of music'. But it would appear that at the turn of the eighteenth century there was some disagreement among musicians about how to define the *makam* named Dügah. To Cantemir it was a superfluous name that simply concealed the *makam* Uşşak. This is a minor-like *makam*, reaching from *A* to *a*, with the neutral second step *B* (*segah*), a dominant on the fourth degree *d* (*neva*), and the minor sixth degree *f* (*acem*). Cantemir states, with some indignation, that even the blind could see that Dügah had no modal distinction from Uşşak (c. 1700: 26).

Nevertheless, forty-odd years later, Tanburi Küçük Artin (Harutin), a highly acclaimed court musician, whose Armeno-Turkish musical treatise was written during the reign of the musical Sultan Mahmud I (1730–54), does consider Dügah as a separate *makam*. Harutin enumerated the notes of *makam* Dügah with a raised sixth degree *f#* (*eviç*), thus bringing it closer to *makam* Hüseyni and giving it a character distinct from Uşşak (Popescu-Judetz 2002: 35). This is the modality we see in the anonymous Dügah Ayini. Something closer to modern usage of the name Dügah appears in Harutin (2002: 32) as 'Dügah-i Rumi' ('Anatolian Dügah' or 'Turkish Dügah'), which Cantemir does not mention at all. This form of Dügah – which is a compound *makam* related to *makam* Saba – became dominant

Fig. 8.3 Scale of Makam Uşşak.

only at the start of the nineteenth century, and thus is not relevant to the 'ancient' Dügah Ayini.

In 1796, Abdülbaki Nasır Dede also mentioned both *makam*s. The *makam* of the Ayin is termed 'Dügah-i Kadim' (Ancient Dügah), while Harutin's Dügah-i Rumi is simply 'Dügah' (Tura: 2006: 53).

Fig. 8.4 Comparison of Makams Dügah and Hüseyni, ca 1700.

Modally, the Dügah Ayini displays a melodic progression (*seyir*) closer to *makam* Uşşak, but with some features of both the scale and the progression (*seyir*) of Hüseyni, and hence conforms to Harutin's description.

This 'ancient' and anonymous *ayin* preserves a version of *makam* Dügah that in Cantemir's time was going out of fashion, and it is probably for this reason that he was not willing to accept it. In fact, the Dügah Ayini is one of the very rare surviving examples of this modal usage. Yilmaz Öztuna's *Türk Musikisi Ansiklopedisi* (vol. 1, 1969) follows Cantemir in denying that the 'ancient' Dügah was any different from *makam* Uşşak, and proceeds to describe the compound *makam* that, to Harutin, was 'Dügah-i Rumi', and which does have a considerable, but newer, repertoire. It is likely, then, that the version of *makam* Dügah in the Dügah Ayini had been composed several generations prior to the writing of Cantemir's treatise and even longer before the treatise by Harutin, thus confirming the Mevlevi oral tradition.

Let us look at the poetic text and then the musical structure of the First Selam, which is divided into musical units, usually called *bend* (strophe). The three *bend*s in the First Selam each consist of a different type of poetic material. In the following transcription and translation of the Persian (and Turkish) text, the letters A, B, and C to the left of each line of the *bend* refer to the function of the musical lines. Bend I has an A/B A/B structure, wherein the first and third poetic *mısra*s are set to melody A, while the second and fourth *mısra*s are set to melody B.

Dügah Ayini, First Selam

Bend I

A   *Aşkast tarik-ü rah-i Peygamber-i ma*
B   *Ma zade-i aşk u aşk mader-i ma*
A   *Ey mader-i ma nühüfte der çader-i ma*
B   *Pinhan şude der tabi'at-i kafer-i ma*

Love is the way and the path of our Prophet
We are the children of Love and Love is our mother
Oh mother of ours, concealed within our tent,
Hidden within our faithless natures.[3]

A   *Men bende-i Kur'anım eğer can darem*
B   *Men hak-i reh-i Muhammed-i muhterem*
A   *Ger nakl küned cüz in kes ez güftarem*
B   *Bizarem ez-u v'ez-in sühan bizarem*

So long as I have a soul I am the slave of the Qur'an
I am the dust on the way of Muhammed the Exalted
Should anyone repeat something different from my discourse
I reject him and I reject such speech.

Bend I uses lyrics from two *ruba'i*s of Rumi that form an elegant and meaningful pair of statements. In the first *ruba'i*, Rumi opines that though love is the essence of the teaching of the Prophet, we have hidden our mother Love away, and our perfidious nature renders us unworthy of her. In the following *ruba'i*, pride of place is taken by the Qur'an and the Prophet

[3] The text of the fourth line appears in the Darülelhan Ayinleri vol. 1 (p. 282 and 289) and in the other published Mevlevi sources. It differs from the better known Persian text, e.g., in the volume by Anvar and Twitty (2008): *pinhan shode az tabiat-e kafir-e ma* ('hidden from our faithless nature') (pp. 92–3).

Ex. 8.4 Dügah Ayini, Bend I, A and B.

Muhammad, who is now named. It is perhaps as if the anonymous Mevlevi composer were protecting himself from any possible misunderstanding that might arise from the seeming universalism of Rumi's message of Love, even though, in his first *ruba'i*, the poet states that 'Love is the way and the path of our Prophet'.

The rhythmic partition of the *devr-i revan* and construction of musical phrases in this *bend* differ markedly from both the 'ancient' Rast *peşrev* and the Rast *nakış* of the 'Persians', displayed in exs 8.1 and 8.2, respectively. In Bend I, the initial 3/8 of the fourteen-unit cycle in each of the first two *devirs* of the A section is indeed phrased as quarter + eighth note, and neither of these phrases forms part of a symmetrical unit echoed in the second 7/8 of the *devir*. Melody A, set to the first poetic *mısra*, is divided into two sections: the first section occupies one and a half *devirs* in the lower area of the *makam* (from F# to C) while the second section jumps to the middle range, on *d* and *e*. Together these two sections of melody fill three *devirs* of *devr-i revan*. The word *tarik* (way) is split between the first and second *devirs*. The fact that both melody A and melody B of Bend I require three cycles (*devir*) of the *usul*, negates any possible use of an antecedent-consequent structure.

In Bend I, the second *mısra* of the *ayin* uses melody B, which jumps from the dominant *d* to *g*, and then descends, using both *f#* and *f* in successive phrases. Together, the three *devirs* of melody B form one indivisible melodic 'sentence' in which words are routinely stretched over the beginning and end of cycles. After the opening of melody A in the lower range of the mode, the leap upward in melody B and its subsequent descending motion seems like a musical gesture. This gesture also emphasises the important shift in the text, from the Prophet to 'we', in: 'We are the children of Love and Love is our mother.' Melody B constitutes a unified melodic line of 42/8 (3x 14/8). The entire first *bend* repeats this A/B/A/B structure, based on units of three *devir*s of the *usul*.

In the Rast Nakış, the second 7/8 of the *devir* comprises a broader ante-cedent-consequent structure that dominates the first two *devir*s, followed by a partial descending sequence in *devir*s 3 and 4, and then a *terennüm* (*yel let lel li*) that fills another four *devir*s. Nothing comparable exists in Bend I of the *ayin*. The Rast Nakış in ex. 8.2 displays nothing of this stretching of poetic text over the *devir*s, preferring a bouncing, dance-like structure that fits the highly symmetrical balance of melody and rhythm.

Bend II

A	*Ba an ki midani mera hergiz nemihani mera*
B	*Hestem segi z-in asitan ez der çi miranı mera*
B	*(Hey) Aşık oldum bilmedim yar özgelerle yar imiş*
B	*(Hey) Allah Allah aşıka bunca cefalar imiş*

> Although you know me you never reach out to me
> I am a dog in this court, so why do you shun me?
> (Turkish)
> (Hey) I fell in love but I did not know that the Beloved was involved with others
> (Hey) Allah Allah! the lover undergoes such torture!

The poetic, linguistic, and musical structures shift somewhat in Bend II. The Persian verses (lines 1 & 2) do not have a clear literary source, and, according to the Darülelhan editors, they appear somewhat distorted (p. 290).[4] They are followed by two thoroughly folkloric lines in Turkish. Melody A, based in the middle range of Dügah, around *d* and *e*, extends for four *devir*s, and is followed by three exact repetitions of melody B, each extending over four *devir*s (ex. 8.5). Melody B reaches up to *g* before descending back to the middle range and finally closing on *finalis A*. The musical rhetoric of this

---

[4] I thank Professor Iraj Anvar, of Brown University, for successfully interpreting the Persian text.

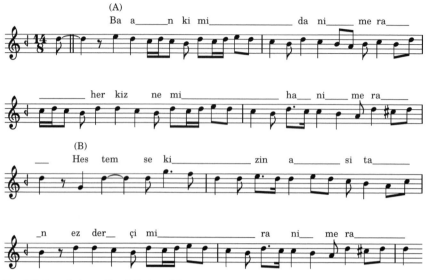

Ex. 8.5 Dügah Ayini, Bend II, A and B.

bend generally resembles melody B of Bend I. Unlike the elevated poetry of Bend I, however, these verses set a more mundane tone.

Bend III

A (Ey) Bivefa yar inçinin bi-rahm u seng-i dil mebaş
A (Ey) Derdimendani tüyim ez hal-i ma gafil mebaş
B Der çemen üftad 'ey' nale-yi bülbül (canım)
C Ta tu der ay-i (yarimen) der hayme-yi gül

Oh faithless beloved, don't be so merciless and hard-hearted!
I am the one who suffers for you; don't ignore my state!
The song of the nightingale spreads over the meadow
Until you enter into the rose's tent.

The length of the melodic sentences is now four *devir*s each (ex. 8.6). But melody A is almost a repetition of A from Bend I, with a prolongation of one *devir*. Melody B features a gentle modulation to *makam* Segah on the note *B*, at the beginning of its third *devir*. Melody C begins with a new melody that shifts from the lower to the middle range within the four-*devir* length. Melodically it is almost an exact repetition of melody A of Bend I. After repeating verbatim,

Ex. 8.6 Dügah Ayini, Bend III, A, B, and C.

it shifts to a *terennüm* with the words '*sultan-i men, hünkar-i men*' ('my sultan, my king') for four *devirs*. This *terennüm* is almost an exact reprise of the same melody A of Bend I.

Judged by the standards of later *ayin*s, or even of the Pençgah Ayini, the Dügah Ayini seems to work within a more restricted framework. Nevertheless, the expression of the poetic text unevenly over the three *devir*s in Bend I is elegant indeed. And the 'gestural' rhetoric in melody B is most expressive – all the more so when we consider the strength of the lines from Rumi's *rubaiyat* that the anonymous composer had chosen to open Bend I. Most of the musical ideas in the First Selam are expressed in Bend I, and are subsequently recycled in Bend II and Bend III after being stretched from three to four *devir*s. The main melodic shift occurs in the third line of Bend III, with its brief modulation to Segah.

In our own time, it is difficult to determine whether the relative melodic uniformity of Bends II and III – even with their shift from 3 *devir*s to 4 *devir*s – was a compositional strategy of the composer's era, or whether it was an attempt by later Mevlevi musicians to reconstruct a melodic form appropriate to the first *bend* – or perhaps an attempt to expand a preserved 'ancient' Bend I into a longer composition. In pondering these unanswerable questions, we might also recall that Prince Cantemir found the *makam* Dügah to be so obscure as to lack all substance. Considering this judgement from the early eighteenth century, it is all the more remarkable that later Mevlevis would have attempted to preserve this representative of an earlier modal entity and compositional style.

Beyati Ayini of Köçek Mustafa Dede, First Selam

The Beyati Ayini is the earliest surviving *ayin* attributed to a known composer, Köçek Mustafa Dede, of Edirne (d. 1683). Remarkably it retains great popularity to this day. During the earlier twentieth century, Emin Dede (d. 1945) even composed a new *peşrev* for its Sultan Veled Devri, which is still widely played. Like the Dügah Ayini, the Beyati Ayini presents issues of modal nomenclature that need to be addressed prior to an analysis of the music itself. The modern *makam* known as Beyati uses exactly the same scale as Uşşak (presented in Fig. 8.3) but has a different melodic progression (*seyir*). Rather than commencing below the finalis and gradually ascending, like Uşşak, Beyati commences on the fourth scale degree – *d* (*neva*) – and has a descending and ascending movement (*inici/çıkacı*). This is both the modern (nineteenth century) basic scale and the *seyir* found in Mustafa Dede's Beyati Ayini (see fig. 8.5).

To Cantemir, however, as in the seventeenth century, Beyati was a *makam* that used 'secondary' scale degrees – in this case, the note named *beyati*, equivalent to an e^b located somewhere between *d* and *e*. As late as 1796, Abdülbaki Nasır Dede agrees with this usage (Tura 2006: 58).

Evidently *makam* Beyati was somewhat fluid in the seventeenth century and well into the eighteenth century. Hence, c. 1740, Tanburi Harutin was able to present something like the 'modern' Beyati that was evidently in use by some musicians even then (Taghmizian 1968: 68). The existing notations that Cantemir presents reveal a melodic *seyir* that resembles the modern one, but with a frequent alternation of the fifth scale degree. Evidently some musicians considered the flattened fifth degree as an alteration of the normal fifth – *hüseyni*. Others – among them Cantemir – regarded the note *beyati*

Fig. 8.5 *Seyir* of modern Makam Beyati by Şefik Gürmeriç.

Fig. 8.6 Scale of 17th-century Makam Beyati.

(e^b) as fundamental to the identity of this *makam*. It is a moot point whether the modern modal usage that exists in the Beyati Ayini is the result of some 'modernisation', i.e., the elimination or alteration of phrases using the flattened fifth (*beyati*), or whether this variant of the *makam* had already existed in either Turkish or Persian usage during the lifetime of Mustafa Dede in the seventeenth century.

A good example of seventeenth-century usage of *makam* Beyati is the 'Persian' *peşrev* in *devr-i revan* presented in ex. 8.7. This composition also shows some similarities and many contrasts with the rhythmic and melodic

Ex. 8.7 Beyati Peşrevi Devr-i Revan Acemi, *serhane* A.

structure of the First Selam of Köçek Mustafa Dede's Beyati Ayini, which we will be looking at.

This *peşrev* begins with a section that touches briefly on the note *beyati* (e^b), but e♮ returns in the next *terkib* of the *serhane*. Thus, the piece as a whole furnishes evidence both for the more archaic and for the more modern forms of the *makam* Beyati. Rhythmically and compositionally it displays the sequences, symmetry, and 'sprightliness' that resemble the ancient Rast *peşrev*, the Persian *naqsh*, and other vocal items of that genre, such as the 'Meraghi' pseudographic repertoire. The fact that the Beyati *peşrev* is a notated document that exemplifies a musical style of the mid-seventeenth century strengthens Wright's supposition that the existing 'Persianate' Ottoman vocal repertoire did indeed originate in that century (1992). But the *peşrev*'s stylistic distance from the Dügah Ayini is considerable, and from the Beyati Ayini it is vast, as we will see below. Let us now turn to Mustafa Dede's Beyati Ayini.

Beyati Ayini, First Selam

Bend I

A *Şaha zi-kerem ber meni derviş niger*
(*hey hey sultan-i men day hey hey hünkar-i men vay*)

A *Ber hal-i meni haste-yi dil-riş niger*
(*hey hey sultan-i men. . . .*)

B *her çend neyem layik-i bahşayiş-i tü*
(*hey hey sultan-i men. . . . hey yar*)

A *Ber men me-niger ber kerem-i hiş niger*
(*hey hey sultan-i men . . . vay*)

Oh King, out of generosity, look at me the poor one!
Look at my condition, weak and sore of heart.

Though not worthy of Your forgiveness
Look not at me, but at Your own generosity!

[Transition]

B   *Ah hey ihsan meded vay vay*
    Oh, hey Generous one, help!
B   *Hey gufran meded vayi heyi yar*
    Hey All-Forgiving one, help!
    Yar yüreğim yar gör ki neler var (hey yar) [Turkish]
    Oh beloved, split my breast and see what is there!

Ex. 8.8 Beyati Selam I Bend I (A, B), from Yekta and Irsoy, *Mevlevi Ayinleri*, vol. 2

The First Bend of this Beyati Ayini has an expanded structure of three *devir*s of verse plus three *devir*s of *terennüm* for both the A melody and the B melody. This structure agrees with the structure of *bend*s in the First Selam of the Pençgah Ayini but differs from the structure of *bend*s in the First Selam of the Dügah and the Hüseyni Ayins, which are based on two *devir*s of verse plus two *devir*s *of terennüm*. However, from the very first *devir*, the composer has made decisions that differentiate his piece from any of the three earlier surviving *ayin*s.

All the *ayin* melodies in *devr-i revan*, like the Persian *peşrev* and the Persian *naqsh*, begin each *devir* with a quarter plus eighth-note unit. This often imparts a sprightly, bouncy quality to the rhythm. In the case of the *naqsh*, the antecedent-consequent structure adds a dance-like quality to the melody. While this tendency is certainly more subdued in the *ayin* compositions, Mustafa Dede has taken one step further in 'internalising' the rhythmic and melodic expression of the opening melody (A). He begins the first *devir* with a dotted quarter on the dominant *d*, and then closes the cycle in the same way. He continues the melodic movement centred on *d* in the first half of the second *devir*, and maintains the same narrow movement centred on the dominant even in the third *devir*. This alone imparts a meditative and inward quality, well in keeping with the plaintive text: 'Oh King, out of generosity, look at me, the poor one!' The composer also enlists metrics to emphasise his musical decisions. 'Şaha' (Oh King!) contains two long vowels, which helps to strengthen the rhetorical gesture of the held note on the dominant (*d*) and then the downward movement from *e* to *B*. In the following cycle he essentially repeats the dotted quarter note structure for the words *ber* and *men* (upon me). Although the *Darülelhan* edition supplies the vowel *i* to close each syllable ('*beri*' and '*meni*'), these are merely non-grammatical aids to sung articulation. Both *ber* and *men* are sung as if to one long syllable. These musical techniques allow the composer to close the first cycle as a unit, but then to extend it, as though expanding its musical rhetoric by repeating the word *men* in the middle of *devir* 2. He extends the word *derviş* into two cycles, and begins *devir* 3 with the syllable '-*vi*', recreating the opening of *devir* 1 almost exactly.

The following *terennüm* presents a contrast in both melodic movement and rhythmic partitioning. While the verse in the third *devir* concludes on *d*, the *terennüm* drops suddenly to the *finalis A* and to the sub-tonic *G*, before ascending all the way to *f*. Melody B – the *miyan* section – presents a bold contrast by essentially modulating to the upper range of *makam* Hüseyni, focusing on the upper *g* (*gerdaniye*), and with *f#* in place of *f*. The composer maintains this new modality for a three-*devir* continuous phrase, or musical sentence (*cümle*). He follows this with a *terennüm* that uses similar modality but is even longer, totalling four cycles. He then returns to the melody of A in the verse and *terennüm*. But after this point he inserts a section that apparently had no precedent in the earlier *ayin* compositions. Lacking any fixed terminology, I describe it simply as a 'transition'. It begins as a reprise of the *miyan* melody B in four *devir*s, using new words for a *terennüm*, as shown in ex. 8.8a (**website**).

Ex. 8.8a [**website**] Beyati Selam I Bend I (B); *terennüm* 'transition'.

The next four cycles use a folk-like Turkish verse:

> *Yar yüreğim yar gör ki neler var (hey yar)*
> Oh beloved, split my breast and see what is there!

Bend II

A	*Ya rab zi dü kevni bi-niyazem kerdan*
A	*V'ez efser-i fakr-i ser-efrazem kerdan*
B	*Ender haremet mahrem-i razem kerdan*
A	*An rah ki ne suy-i tüst bazem kerdan*

> Oh Lord, make me without need of this world and the next!
> Exalt me with the crown of spiritual poverty!
> Make me a confidant of the secrets in your Sanctuary!
> Turn me back from the road that leads not to you![5]

The following *bend* (II) uses another Persian *ruba'i* text, and the poetry of this *ruba'i* shows a subtle shift from the previous one. In Bend I the speaker was the poorest dervish, begging to be noticed by his Lord. Here the speaker seems to have already achieved some internal development, as his spiritual ambitions are rather vast. He wants to be without need in this world and in the next. Referring to the words of the Prophetic Hadith *alfaqri fakhri* ('poverty is

---

[5] The translation of this verse was inspired by Ibrahim Gamard's version on the website Dar-al-Masnavi.org, which belongs to the American Institute of Masnavi Studies.

Ex. 8.9 Beyati Ayini, Bend II (A, B).

my pride), he wishes to be exalted with the crown of spiritual poverty. By the *miyan* verses he wishes to be admitted as a confidant (*mahrem*) in the Inner Sanctuary (*haramet*). As extra spiritual security, he still needs to be sure not to take any path that fails to lead to Him.

The melodic construction of Bend II is based on a narrow Saba melody that is repeated with variations over almost the entire eight *devir*s of both the text and the *terennüm* of melody A (ex. 8.9 shows only the first *devir* of the *terennüm*). The *miyan* melody, beginning with the words '*ender haramet*' (in Your Sanctuary), quite unexpectedly leaps up to the pitch *gerdaniye* (*g*) and presents a melody based on a transposition of the Saba tetrachord on the fifth degree, the note *e* (*hüseyni*). The first two *devir* cycles vary the melody minimally, in the manner of *makam* Saba. Then, in the third *devir*, it descends all the way to the actual note *saba* (*d*). Even more surprisingly, the following single-cycle *terennüm* repeats the basic melody of the *terennüm* of A, which then leads into the identical melody as the beginning of the *hane* A.

Bend III

A   *Biya biya ki tü-yi can-ü can-ı sema'*

A¹   *Biya ki serv-i revani bebostan-i sema'*

B   *Biya ki çeşme-i hurşid zir-i saye-i tüst*
B[1]   *Hezar zühre tü dari ber asuman-i sema'*
      Come, come! for you are the soul of the soul of the *sema*!
      Come, for you are the flowing cypress in the garden of the *sema*!
      Come, for the eye of the sun lies beneath your shadow!
      You have a thousand Venuses in the sky of the *sema*!

The third *bend* uses verses taken from two *ghazals* in the *Divan-e Shams-e Tabrizi* (nos. 1302 and 1303). It is as though the entire mood of the *ayin* has changed. The identity of both speaker and addressee is undetermined and mysterious. Is Rumi addressing the soul of Shams? Or is a Divine Voice addressing him? In either case we are now transported into the *sema* in all its mystery, beauty, and ecstasy. 'Come for you are the flowing cypress in the garden of the *sema*!'

Ex. 8.10 Beyati Ayini, Bend III (A, A[1]+B+B[1]).

The musical strophe is constructed out of two musical lines (A and B) of only three cycles each. The melody is an ingenious combination of elements from the very beginning of Bend I together with a variant of the recurring melody (in Saba) of Bend II. But now the tonal centre has been moved downward from *d* (*neva*) to the *finalis* A (*dügah*). This alone imparts a feeling of peace and resolution. Prosodically, the two long vowels of the word '*Biya*' (come) allow the composer to fit them into a rhythmic grouping similar to the one at the very start of the first *bend* of the *ayin*, used for '*Şaha*' ('Oh King'). The melody here is virtually a transposition of melody A of the first *bend*, up until the last *devir*, which introduces the *miyan* or melody B. With a dramatic flourish, the old tonal centre of Beyati (*d*) now is part of a modulation to a totally new *makam* – Nişabur, with its characteristic *C#* and *B* natural. Nothing in either of the previous *bend*s had prepared us for this change, which could not be more appropriate to Rumi's text:

> 'Come, for the eye of the sun lies beneath your shadow!'
> 'You have a thousand Venuses in the sky of the *sema*!'

And they also lead the way for the exalted words at the end of the Second Selam:

> 'Raise a glass for the love of Shams-e Tabrizi
> So that you will enter the Kingdom of God!'

The unattributed Dügah Ayini and the Beyati Ayini of Köçek Mustafa Dede analysed in the first part of this chapter both represent the earlier phase of *ayin* composition. The First Selam expresses the fundamental vision of each Mevlevi composer, within each *ayin*. Despite the shortness of the *usul*, the compositional techniques allows for significant developments and complications. By comparing one of the early anonymous *ayin*s – Dügah – with the earliest of the *ayin*s by a known composer – the Beyati – we can see something of what they have in common and also stylistic features separating them. A comparison with the Saba Ayini by Ismail Dede Efendi (1823), included in the website for this book (figs 8.7–9; exs 8.11–8.17) demonstrates the very large stylistic development within this mystical genre over a period of one and a half centuries.[6]

---

[6] Further analysis of these *ayin*s is included in 'A Note on the Second Selam' (website).

Fig. 8.7 [website] *Seyir* of Makam Saba by Şefik Gürmeriç.

Ex. 8.11 [website] Bend I (all of the Saba Ayini from İrsoy, *Mevlevi Ayinleri*, vol. 11, pp. 565–8).

Ex. 8.12 [website] Saba, Bend II.

Fig. 8.8 [website] Makam Eviç.

Ex. 8.13 [website] Mükerrer I.

Fig. 8.9 [website] Makam Hicaz.

Ex. 8.14 [website] Saba Bend III.

Ex. 8.15 [website] Second Selam (Saba Ayini; Ismail Dede), first hemistich.

Ex. 8.16 [website] Second Selam (Dügah Ayini), first hemistich.

Ex. 8.17 [website] Second Selam (Beyati Ayini), first hemistich.

9

THE *SEMA'I* IN THE THIRD SELAM AND THE *SON YÜRÜK SEMA'I*: NUCLEUS OF THE ANTECEDENT *SAMĀ*'?

'Ey ki Hezar Aferin'

To introduce the *sema'i* in the Third Selam of the Mevlevi *ayin*, it is worth quoting two statements from the section on the instrumental *sema'i* in my 1996 monograph, *Music of the Ottoman Court:*

> The *sema'i* as a musical genre was deeply connected to both the ethnic and the religious identity of the Anatolian Turks. As a Sufi genre it was used primarily by the two *tarikat*s which had been most influential in pre-Ottoman Anatolia, i.e., the Mevleviye, and the conglomeration of early Anatolian Sufi movements which became known in Ottoman times as the Bektaşiye.

> The *sema'i* is unique among Turkish classical compositional forms in its lack of definition as either vocal or instrumental. This ambivalence probably stems from two sources – the traditions of both vocal and instrumentally accompanied vocal music in the Sufi *sema*, and the early history of Muslim art music, in which certain vocal forms could also be performed instrumentally (e.g., *tariqa* and *sawt*). (1996: 490–1)

Sema'i as both a term and a musical form has been adopted into the secular Ottoman musical repertoire, where its protean quality as both an instrumental and vocal form makes it anomalous. As this chapter demonstrates, vocal and instrumental pieces in the *sema'i usul* in the Third Selam display quite different structures, though an antecedent musical practice may have blurred this distinction at times.

Instrumental *sema'i*s are well-represented in both the Ali Ufuki and Cantemir musical collections. Cantemir's Collection shows a new development of the *sema'i usul* in 10/8, which would become very productive in the *fasıl* during the eighteenth century and beyond (Feldman 1996: 477–85). Within the *fasıl*, a form of the old *murabba* had come into existence in the seventeenth century that used the 6/8 *sema'i usul*, with the drumming pattern *düm tek tek düm tek*. And while to Es'ad Efendi and Ali Ufuki these vocal pieces were still '*murabba*', but in the *sema'i usul*, to Hafiz Post and to Cantemir they had become '*sema'is*' with a Turkish-language text. As for the *ayin*, recent research has uncovered evidence that, during the nineteenth century, in at least some Mevlevihanes – for example, Kasımpaşa – instrumental sections of the *ayin*s were strung together as a small suite (*takım*), including sections in either *sema'i* or *aksak sema'i usul*s (in 10/8) that were used as a pedagogic tool for younger dervishes or *muhibb*s to learn the music of the *ayin* (Değirmenci 2018). In the Mevlevi *ayin* this newer *sema'i* in 10/8 has only a small role, mainly as a transition between acknowledged sections of the *ayin*.[1] In other parts of the Sufi cultural sphere, many of the hymns (*nefes*) of the Bektashi Dervishes are set to the *sema'i usul*. Some may be almost indistinguishable from instrumental *sema'i*s that had been played in the seventeenth century in a largely secular context.

As the various '*sema'is*' developed in instrumental and vocal music, and within Mevlevi, Bektashi, and secular cultural contexts, a web of musical and cultural allusions began to take shape. At the same time, kindred practices of *sema'i*-like music outside of the Anatolian and Ottoman cultural realm preserved elements of antecedent ethnic and Sufistic traditions that, as I suggest in this chapter, may have provided a source for the development of the *sema'i* among Mevlevi composers. In an unpublished study 'Ali Ufki Bey and Turkish Religious Music', Gültekin Oransay transcribed and commented on a great many *ilahi* hymns and some other Sufi and mosque musical materials that Ali Ufuki (Bobowski) had written in Western

---

[1] There is no suggestion of an 'ovoid' transitional form between 6/8 and 10/8. On the concept of a transitional, 'ovoid' expression of the *sema'i usul*, see Ekinci in Harris and Stokes 2018: 42–67. My own earlier analysis of the *sema'i* is in *Music of the Ottoman Court*, 460–93.

staff notation in his *Mecmu'a-i Saz ü Söz* from c. 1650, now in the British Museum (Sloane Collection). By the time the *Mecmu'a-i Saz ü Söz* appeared, Ali Ufuki was 'inside' the Ottoman musical tradition, including its Sufi dimension. Indeed, he was attached to the Celveti Order, a branch of the Halvetis, which explains the origin of much of the Sufi materials in his Collection, though he seems to have notated only a single Mevlevi item, which he named *Devran-i Dervişan-i Zi-Şan*: 'The Whirling Cycle of the Illustrious Dervishes'. The poem is in Turkish, beginning '*Ey ki Hezar Aferin bu Nice Sultan Olur!*' or 'Oh, a thousand praises for such a sultan as this!' These are the opening words of a poem by Eflaki (d. 1353), whom we have seen before as the dervish and companion of Mevlana's grandson Ulu Arif Çelebi. It was Eflaki, in his *Menakib-ül Arifin*, who wrote up Ulu Arif Çelebi's remarkable journeys as well as material on the earlier generations of saints. Here is my own translation of the first stanza of Eflaki's poem:

> *Ey [her] ki hezar aferin bu nice sultan olur*
> *Kulu olan kişiler Hüsrev ü Hakan olur*
> *Her ki bugün Veled'e inanuben yüz süre*
> *Yoksul ise bay olur bay ise sultan olur*

> Oh, a thousand praises for such a sultan as this!
> Those who are his slaves become the Khusrev and the Khaqan
> Today, whoever humbles himself trustingly before Veled,
> If he is poor, he'll become rich, and if he is rich, he'll become a Sultan.

In the second line, the poet uses Khusrev as a general title for the pre-Islamic Iranian Shah, and the term Khaqan – later pronounced 'Khan' – that had been the title of the pre-Islamic Türk Emperor. The same poem, set to a different tune and rhythm, had also been notated in 1654, around the same time as Ali Ufuki's *Mecmu'a-i Saz ü Söz*, by the French traveller Antoine Sieur du Loir, whose description of the *mukabele* from 1639 was quoted in chapter 7.[2] Sieur du Loir, however, does not provide a clear context for the piece.

---

[2] See the notation in Feldman 2001: p. 56. As I observed there 'the extract is not from the third selam but rather represents another usage of the text, perhaps as an *ilahi* (p. 49: note 16)'.

Oransay identified both the poem and its music as coming from the Mevlevi Selam-i Salis (Third Selam). In his study he provides an interlinear transcription of Ali Ufuki's notation along with a version of the same piece from an undated, but apparently late nineteenth-century, manuscript in Western notation in the collection of the Mevlana Müzesi in Konya, included here as examples 9.1a and 9.1b, respectively (Oransay n.d.: 22–3). While identifying the *makam* of both items as Muhayyer, Oransay does not claim that the nineteenth-century item reproduced in example 9.1b is a direct descendant of Ali Ufuki's piece, but rather, that it belongs to a series of variants composed for different *ayin*s. One such variant is a melody in the Third Selam of Dügah Ayini, published in 1923 by the Darülelhan (vol. 1: 286), and included here as example 9.1c.

The three transcriptions in Example 9.1 demonstrate that Ali Ufuki's notated piece displays a musical structure that remains both tonally and rhythmically within the Mevlevi tradition as it was transmitted orally from at least the mid-seventeenth century until the early twentieth century. Indeed, the basic structure of Ali Ufuki's transcription appears in various melodic transformations in virtually every Mevlevi *ayin* composed since the mid-seventeenth century.

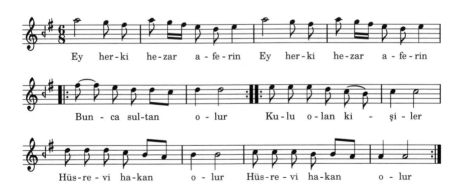

Ex. 9.1a "Ey Ki Hezar Aferin' Ali Ufuki London Sloane MS. P. 42, *Devran-i Dervişan-i Zi-Şan* (The Whirling of the Illustrious Dervishes).

Ex. 9.1b [website] Konya Mevlana Müzesi MS. No. 2198.

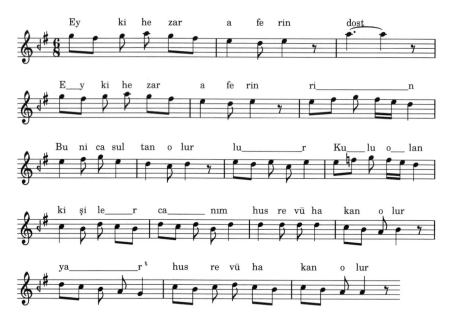

Ex. 9.1c 'Ey Ki Hezar Aferin', Dügah Ayini Selam III.

The most obvious point of similarity among the three items in ex. 9.1 is that their rhythmic structure is identical, despite the passage of almost three centuries (c. 1650 to 1923). The basic *usul* is indeed the *sema'i* in six beats, as it was transcribed both by Ali Ufuki and by Cantemir half a century later. Beyond that, the rhythmic idiom in opening and cadential formulas is virtually identical. Even where we might expect greater note-density, as is the case in several *son sema'i* melodies, greater note-density does not appear in the internal sections of 'Ey Ki Hezar Aferin'.

Ali Ufuki's mid-seventeenth-century notation of the piece reveals a quite sophisticated handling of secondary tonal centres within a general descending motion, as would be expected in *makam* Muhayyer. The piece is created out of two large melodic sections, both of them ending textually with the word *olur*. Tonally the first section concludes on the note *d*, and the second section on the finalis *A*. Internally, the first section is composed of three units of 12/8 (6/8+6/8) while the second section contains four such units.

Characteristically, both the nineteenth-century version (ex. 9.1b) and the 1923 version (ex. 9.1c) create asymmetry by introducing verbal exclamations

and repetitions that add measures to each section. For example, the third measure is taken up by the exclamation '*dost!*' in the upper octave of the *makam*,
on *a* (*muhayyer*), complicating a simple repetition of the opening two measures, ending on *e* (*hüseyni*). The nineteenth-century and 1923 versions may be
understood as variants of one and the same underlying melody. Compared with
the seventeenth century version, they display melodic elaboration, but without
any sign of 'rhythmic retardation', to use Wright's terminology. Moreover, it
is not difficult to see clear signs of the seventeenth century 'original' beneath
both later versions. It is very likely that similar types of melodic elaboration
using a short *usul* cycle also occurred among the extant versions of the First
Selam melodies in the pre-eighteenth-century *ayin*s as they have come down
to us. These would include the Dügah and Beyati *ayin*s that were discussed in
the preceding chapter. Without other seventeenth-century notated versions of
these *ayin*s, any conclusions must of course be limited in scope. Nevertheless,
these three examples of the 'Ey ki hezar aferin' *sema'i* – all within the same
makam Muhayyer – can provide some idea of the nature of the melodic transmission and transformations from the seventeenth to the late nineteenth and
early twentieth centuries.

Another major point about the transmission of the Third Selam is that
the canonical status of Eflaki's 'Ey Ki Hezar Aferin' meant that it could
not be replaced by any other poem. Moreover, it is usually the only, or
one of the only, Turkish-language poems in the entire *ayin-i şerif* corpus.
Not only must its melody bear strong resemblance to an evidently older
prototype, but it is always succeeded by a long section in the Third Selam
featuring only hymns in *usul sema'i* in 6/8. This connection between the
Turkish language and the *sema'i usul* cannot be accidental. Rather, it would
suggest a cultural memory that was given an aesthetic shape. This cultural
memory was continued in the *son yürük sema'i* section at the very close of
the *ayin*. As I have written elsewhere, it is likely that the retention of the
ancient form of the *sema'i* along with the most archaic form of their melodies – always performed to an early poetic text in the Turkish language – is
a gesture to the basic ecstaticism of the culminating section of the *ayin* as a
whole (Feldman 2001: 49).

My 1996 monograph *Music of the Ottoman Court* includes a comparison of the rhythmic structure of several instrumental *sema'i* melodies in the

Ali Ufuki/Bobowski London Manuscript with the Turkish Sufi hymn '*Şol cennetin ırmakları*' (those rivers of Paradise) set to a text by the thirteenth-century Sufi poet Yunus Emre. This hymn was evidently old and universal enough among Anatolian Turks to transcend the deep cultural and religious divisions between the Bektashi *nefes* and the Sunni *ilahi* genres (Feldman 1996: 462–3). I also compared Yunus's hymn with a Tuvan ritual song for wrestling (*khuresh*). Among Turkic peoples, wrestling had a highly ritualistic significance. Evidently it maintained this cultural role in some form among both non-Islamic and some Islamic Turkic peoples. From the Altai to the Balkans, an identical word is employed (Tuvan *khuresh* = Turkish *güreş*), and the contest is always preceded by a dance of the wrestlers themselves. In Turkey, *güreş* is often regarded as the '*ana sporu*', the 'mother of all sports'. And wrestling was surely not unrelated to the warrior ethos that had been a defining feature of the more politicised Turkic peoples. While wrestling was not among the skills specifically linked to shamans, music and dance surrounding the *güreş* event may well have lent themselves to ritualisation. And in their ritualised form, they may have made the cultural transference to a Sufi context in the process of Islamisation.[3]

Another pair of musical examples, which illustrate both the geographic and temporal spread of a *sema'i* antecedent, reinforce the notion of the *sema'i* as an import to pre-Ottoman Anatolia from Inner Asia.

Irak Sema'i, Sultan Veled 'Kadim'

Toward the end of Cantemir's Collection, a *sema'i* in *makam* Irak appears, written in Cantemir's own handwriting. However, another early Ottoman hand has written there 'Sultan Veled. *Kadim*' ('Sultan Veled. Ancient'). The identical *sema'i* appears in Ali Ufuki's London manuscript, but without the ascription to Sultan Veled (Wright 1992 b: 517–18). Although a number of *sema'i*s in both of these early notated collections have a place in the nineteenth- and twentieth-century Mevlevi *ayin* repertoire, this item is not among them. It is an elaborate composition, with three *hane*s and a *mülazime* (ritornello).

---

[3] The role of shamanist and Sufi figures in the Islamisation process is treated by Devin De Weese, in *Islamization and Native Religion in the Golden Horde*, University Park, Pennsylvania: Penn State University Press, 1994, and in more general terms by Fuad Köprülü, *Influences du shamanism turco-mongol sur les ordres mystiques musulmans*, Istanbul: University of Istanbul, 1929.

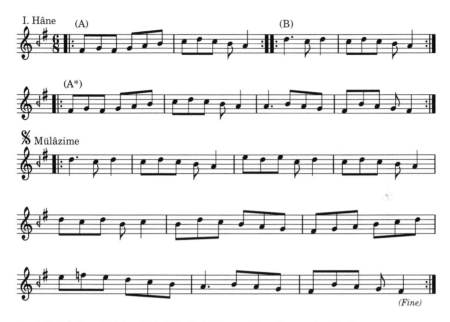

Ex. 9.2 Irak Sema'i 'Sultan Veled; Kadim' (Cantemir): *serhane* and *mülazime*.

Compared to most of the other *sema'i*s in both the Ali Ufuki and Cantemir Collections (Feldman 1996: 465–77), this *sema'i* appears melodically developed. The mention of 'Sultan Veled' does suggest that in late seventeenth- or early eighteenth-century Mevlevi usage, this item may well have played a role, and may perhaps form a link, with an earlier form of the Mevlevi *sema*. While this is only a hypothesis, it is instructive to view a somewhat similar musical item. As in introducing the Tuvan ritual song in connection with the ancient *ilahi sema'i* of Yunus Emre, the present example comes from far to the east of the Anatolian musical zone.

'Ali Qambar' was recorded in Urgench, the capital of the Khorezm region of northwest Uzbekistan. The population speaks Uzbek, but in the Oghuz dialect, which has many phonological similarities to Anatolian Turkish. This territory, as well as the region to the north of the Aral Sea, in present-day Kazakhstan, had been part of an Oghuz homeland, and it was from these territories that the Oghuz Turks entered Anatolia in the eleventh century. The shrine of Qorqyt Ata, the 'Father of Music', is located near the city of Qyzylorda, Kazakhstan, east of the Aral Sea. This is the same figure who

Ex. 9.3 Khorezm Dutar Maqom: 'Ali Qambar', performed by Rustam Baltaev, *tanbur*. Batir Matyakubov, *dutar* (rec. Urgench, 1990).

appears as Dede Korkut in the eponymous Anatolian Turkish epic cycle. Thus the old cultural links between the Oghuz homeland and Turkish Anatolia are clear. Janos Sipos's ethnomusicological research with the Kazakh population further to the west, in Mangystau, bordering the Caspian Sea, demonstrated the dissimilarity of this region's music to Kazakh music in the east of the country, as well as to Mongolian, Tuvan, Bashkir, Tatar, and other musics of Inner Asia. At the same time, musical connections between Mangystau and Turkish Anatolia are rather close (Sipos 2001: 107–8). While Sipos did not conduct fieldwork in Khorezm, many of the same results could be obtained there across a range of expressive culture.

The *usul* of 'Ali Qambar', the Khorezmian piece in ex. 3, is the 6/8 metro-rhythmic cycle *ufor*, which is exactly equivalent to the Ottoman *sema'i*, down to the pattern of the drum beats:

Ufor: bum bak bak bum bak —	*Sema'i: düm tek tek düm tek —*
1 2 3 4 5 6	1 2 3 4 5 6

The name *ufor* (Ar. *awfar*) means 'most abundant', 'numerous', and this may refer to the ubiquitousness of the rhythmic pattern in Oghuz Turkic music (Feldman 1996: 462). As observed by Jung (1989: 132), the name does not appear in any early Arabic or Persian treatise, but is mentioned first in the sixteenth-century Bukharan treatise of Kawkabi.

'Ali Qambar' is part of a repertoire of instrumental melodies known as *dutar maqom* ('cycles for the *dutar*'), and has a quasi-ritualistic function at the beginning of one of these cycles. It is named after the legendary groom of the magical horse of Hazreti Ali. While Khorezmian Uzbeks are Sunni Muslims, the link with Ali carries a Sufistic association, and hence is permitted within this Sunni society. While it is obvious that 'Ali Qambar' and the 'Irak Sema'i' – the Ottoman piece in ex. 9.2 – originate in different cultural zones and represent different melodic modes, their fundamental morphological similarity is striking. Their rhythmic patterns are almost identical and the tonal relationships that undergird their melodies are comparable. This general morphological similarity could be shown with many other early Ottoman *sema'i* melodies, but the particular example of a *sema'i* that Ottoman musicians of the seventeenth century regarded as both 'ancient' and linked with the founder of the Mevlevi Order suggests that both the 'Irak Sema'i' and 'Ali Qambar' retain something of the musical character, as well as the general cultural aura, of a form of Sufistic *sema* that had been practised by Oghuz Turkish speakers of the pre-Ottoman era. Hence they must have been part of a foundational level of *sema* practices inherited by the Mevleviye.

Bektashi *Nefes* and Instrumental *Sema'i*

The musical structure of the *sema'i* also formed part of the basis for the ceremonial hymns (*nefes*) of the other early Anatolian Sufi order, the Bektaşiye. An example is a *nefes* in the *sema'i usul*, in *makam* Neva, published by the Mevlevi scholar Gölpınarlı (1963). We can compare it with an unattributed instrumental *sema'i* in *makam* Neva transcribed by Ali Ufuki Bey in the London Manuscript.

The rhythmic patterns and general melodic shape of the *nefes* and the old *sema'i* are almost identical. Both melodies conform to a basic usage of *makam* Neva that emphasises the pitch *neva* (*re*) and adjacent pitches. Ali Ufuki's melody displays a descending third (from *d* to *B*) in its opening measure and sequential stepwise melodic movement in its first section. The Bektashi vocal *nefes* maintains greater symmetry in its opening two lines. The range expands upward in its *meyan* (middle) section with the words '*aşıkı çok imiş aradım*', bringing it yet closer to Ali Ufuki's instrumental piece. While the Bektashi *nefes* melody is unattributed, it was collected in the twentieth century, though it may have been joined to its poetic text some generations earlier. It is unlikely, however, to have been created contemporaneously with the *sema'i* tune recorded by Ali Ufuki Bey. But whatever its provenance, the Bektashi

Ex. 9.4a Neva Bektashi *Nefes*.

Ex. 9.4b Neva Sema'i, *Mülazıme* sections A and B (from Ali Ufuki Bey London Manuscript).

nefes suggests that a corpus of old Anatolian Sufi hymns provided a substrate of melodic material that Mevlevi composers would at times preserve and at other times rework into new instrumental and vocal *sema'ı* melodies.

Other than the single Irak Sema'i provided in ex. 9.2 as 'Sultan Veled', none of the other *sema'i*s notated by Ali Ufuki and Cantemir bear an overt connection with the Mevlevi *ayin* or any other Sufistic context. Cantemir never suggests any specifically Mevlevi context for the *saz sema'i* as a genre. Rather, he specified that these *sema'i*s came at the close of the vocal *fasıl* and also formed the finale of the instrumental *fasıl-i sazende*. It is striking, then, that later Mevlevi musicians felt no qualms about reusing older *saz sema'i* melodies within the *ayin* itself, appropriately modified to reflect general trends of stylistic modernisation.

In my 1996 monograph *Music of the Ottoman Court*, I provided several examples of such reuse, including a *sema'i* in Neva that appears first in Ali Ufuki's Collection and later, in the Mevlevi Ayinleri, as a Mevlevi *son yürük sema'i*, but only after being appropriately modernised.[4] As I mention in *Music of the Ottoman Court*, in some cases the Mevlevi version accepted only the initial section (*serhane*) of the old *sema'i*, and then added an entirely new piece.[5] Here let me present only one *sema'i – son yürük semai* pair (**website**).

Ex. 9.5a [**website**] *Uzzal Sema'i* (Ali Ufuki Bey, ca 1650).
Ex. 9.5b [**website**] *Hicaz son yürük sema'i* (Heper 1979:115), *hane* 1 and *mülazime* (H and M).

The underlying similarity of these two *sema'i* melodies is clear. The peculiar five-measure period of the *serhane* of the older *sema'i* (ex. 9.5a) is retained throughout the Mevlevi piece. The major change is the addition of a dense sixteenth-note fourth measure that replaces the much simpler descending phrase of the original fourth measure. Moreover, this dense phrasing has become almost a 'signature' for the *son yürük sema'i* in the Mevlevi *ayin* repertoire.

In this brief account, I have suggested a hypothetical pre-history of the Mevlevi *sema'i* based on genetic similarities with kindred musical forms in a broad geographic range of Turkic cultures. But in addition to this pre-history, a very lively musical history is contained in the surviving Mevlevi vocal composi-tions and their instrumental transitions for the latter part of the Third Selam. With their unrelenting quick rhythmic expression and rapid modulations, these compositions constitute the emotional climax of the entire ceremony.[6]

---

[4] See Feldman, *Music of the Ottoman Court*, 472–3.
[5] Ibid, 486.
[6] Signell (1977: 118–19) presented a general scheme of the modulatory pattern within the Beyati Ayini, including one example of the sung *sema'i*. Hatipoğlu's more recent book in Turkish (2011) presents the modulatory scheme with the notations of this and other *ayin* compositions.

A Brief Musicological Conclusion

A consideration of musical form in the four Selams of the Mevlevi *ayin* leads to some general observations about the *ayin* as a forum for mystical expression that draws on musical creativity, poetry, and kinetic movement. These observations are offered with full awareness that they are tentative, since, to apply them to the full corpus of *ayin*s spanning almost four centuries would require a much larger study.

In terms of sheer volume in the existing corpus of Mevlevi *ayin*s, two *usul*s stand out as the most ubiquitous: *devr-i revan* in 14/8, which is the usual rhythm of the First Selam, and *sema'i* in 6/8, which enters toward the middle of the Third Selam, and persists through a long cycle of compact melodies linked by contour and tonal structure. *Sema'i* is featured again as the *usul* of the instrumental *son yürük sema'i*. If we ignore, for the moment, the various forms of *devr-i kebir* as well as *usul evfer* in 9/4, which make much more discrete appearances, then these two rapid rhythmic cycles – *devr-i revan* in 14/8 and *sema'i* in 6/8 – dominate the initial and final sections of the entire *mukabele*. Before launching into any discussion of the aesthetic qualities of these *usul*s, I want to recall their ethno-historical background.

In this chapter, I outlined the broad distribution of *usul*s of the *ufor* and *sema'i* family from Bukhara and Khorezm in the east to Anatolia in the west. This distribution makes a case for a musical connection between southern Central Asia and Turkic-speaking Anatolia and Istanbul. The culturally more purely Iranian territory, including virtually all of the modern Iranian state and adjacent regions of Azerbaijan, also favours a great many 6/8 and 3/4 rhythms, but not generally with the same musical and percussive structure as the Central Asian-Anatolian *ufor* and *sema'i* complex. Within Ottoman music the *sema'i usul* has been extremely productive, bridging instrumental and vocal music, as exemplified by the modern Bektashi vocal *nefes* and the seventeenth-century instrumental *sema'i*. The Third Selam shows a sharper differentiation between vocal hymns and the instrumental *son sema'i*. Yet it is somehow emblematic that even in the seventeenth century, Mevlevis had preserved both the melodic nucleus of an ancient Turkish hymn about Sultan Veled ('Ey ki hezar aferin') and an archetypal instrumental *sema'i* attributed to Sultan Veled himself. My comparative analysis suggests at least a possible prototype for the instrumental *sema'i* from the genre of quasi-ritualistic instrumental *ufor* melodies preserved in modern Khorezm. By contrast, *usul devr-i revan* suggests an Iranian and

Sufi cultural lineage. As noted in the previous chapter, for the Safavid writer Mir Sadr al Din Muhammad (d. 1599) *devr-i revan* already had a Sufi association in the *sama'i-ye revan*. It is impossible to determine how far back in time the cultural antecedents of *sema'i* and *devr-i revani* might lead us. *Ufor/sema'i* may have come to Anatolia as part of the original eleventh-century migration of the Oghuz Turks. Contextual evidence for *revani* certainly suggests an Iranian Sufi usage in the sixteenth century, and possibly even a Khorasanian connection going back to Mevlana's time, although it is undocumented. At the very least these early connections of both *revani /devr-i revan* and *sema'i* demonstrate that the rhythmic basis for the most central sections of the Mevlevi *ayin* were known before the Mevlevi Order became well-established in Istanbul. The antiquity of these rhythmic structures also lends credence to the tradition of the presumed older provenance of the three anonymous *ayins*, which could well have originated between the sixteenth and early seventeenth centuries. What is certain is that their musical structures were not viewed by the later Mevlevis as quaint archaisms. Rather, they continued to provide the basis for more than half of the music in the *ayin*.

From the preceding analysis, a fundamental difference emerges between the compositional techniques of the *sema'i* section of the Third Selam and the compositional techniques of the First Selam sections of Dügah, Beyati, and Saba Ayins discussed in chapter 8. While both of these *ayin* sections use frequent modulations and rhythmic variations, the potential for musical sophistication in the First Selam, set in *usul devr-i revan*, is much greater. Especially in the generations following the composition of the Dügah Ayini, Mevlevi composers developed increasingly sophisticated ways to extend a musical 'sentence' well beyond a single unit of the rhythmic cycle. Such a sentence might reach its tone of repose somewhere after the start of the next unit (*devir*) of the *usul*. Meanwhile, the discrete sections (*terkib*) of each part of the A melodic unit (*zemin*) and the B melodic unit (*miyan*) might become longer, often spreading over six units instead of four. In addition, irregular transitional phrases might be inserted between sections of the Selam. By Ismail Dede Efendi's time, in the early nineteenth century, a separate transitional type of *terennüm* known as *mükerrer* had also developed.

By contrast, the short 6/8 structure of the *sema'i usul* could not permit this degree of lengthening of the melodic sentence and its irregular starting and ending point without risking the loss of the insistent and percussive rhythmic dynamism that rendered it appropriate for the climax of the entire *ayin*. Thus, both the reputedly archaic *devr-i revan* and *sema'i* became the bases for very different kinds of musical development. I suggest that the divergent musical techniques for setting melody over these two *usuls*, together with the different strategies for setting melody over *usul evfer* in the much shorter Second and Fourth Selams and over older and newer forms of *devr-i kebir* in the opening of the Third Selam, collectively became the medium for a mystical musical praxis.

The combination of the incessant and repetitive physical movement of the *sema* with the irregular and constantly changing rhythmic-melodic relationships, and finally, with an insistent but still modally mobile musical structure, evidently helped to produce a musical affect (*te'sir*) and spiritual state (*hal*) that could lift the dervish out of the physical realm. Within this musical and kinetic environment, a combination of the stirring poetry of Mevlana Jalaluddin Rumi, some spiritual 'slogans' in the *terennüm* sections, and a modicum of simple quasi-folkloric verse in both Persian and Turkish added to the overall effect. Techniques for manipulating the relationship of melody, mode, rhythm, and text became the object of continual experimentation and development by Mevlevi composers from the seventeenth to the nineteenth century and beyond. In a sense, the Mevlevi *ayin* constitutes a paradigm for how a musical tradition – and, in this case, a tradition with a particular spiritual aim – was able to innovate broadly while still alluding to its earliest stages. The evidence for this musical tradition, although far from complete, is sufficient to illuminate how composers over a period of perhaps three centuries maintained much older musical principles while integrating them into a contemporary musical language.

POSTLUDE: MUSIC, POETRY, AND MYSTICISM IN THE OTTOMAN EMPIRE

Love is the Way and the Path of our Prophet.
We are Love's children, and Love is our Mother.

– Rumi

These words echo down through the ages from when Mevlana Jalaluddin Rumi first wrote them, in the thirteenth century, to the Dügah Ayin ceremony in the sixteenth century, through to our own day. But how can one build a community whose life is based on love? And how can individual members of that community be transformed so that they can maintain this love in all of life's situations? Among many other practices, the *sema*, with its music, movement and poetry, is one important technique that the Mevlevis developed with this transformative aim. The dervish who has 'found' himself within the *sema* will be strengthened in his confrontation with life's challenges. And this must happen not only once, but repeatedly. As Celaleddin Dede, the last sheikh of the Galata Mevlevihane, told a French visitor, 'In the kitchen we cook food; in the *semahane* we cook people' (Ziya 1913: 29).

Rumi has been much treasured as a Sufi poet throughout the Persian-speaking and Persian-reading world, from Bukhara and Khorasan, to India and Iran itself. But today it is less widely appreciated that Rumi's spiritual and cultural legacy had no institutional basis in any of these countries. It had such a basis only within Anatolia under the Seljuqs and Karamanids, and then in the territories of the former Ottoman Empire. It is a challenging but extremely rewarding task to attempt to penetrate the development and inner workings of the Mevlevi *tarikat* in several historical and political eras.

In order to follow the history of the Mevlevi *tarikat*, one needs a degree of knowledge of three major historical eras: that of the Seljuqs, the Karamanids, and the Ottoman Empire. Even among specialists on Islam, such a broad famil-iarity is rare. The subtitle of the present book – *Music, Poetry, and Mysticism in the Ottoman Empire* – reveals my particular focus among these three. While the Ottoman era is the most crucial for a study of the surviving musical legacy of the Mevleviye, the institutional and social history of this musical legacy is considerably older.

The focus of the present work is to a large extent musicological, but we can-not lose sight of the purpose to which this music was put. The *sema* itself was primarily meant to be practised rather than observed. But even its observation held spiritual value, which was why the larger urban Mevlevihanes also had space for a non-participant audience. The Mevlevis created a unique musical structure. No doubt it was a contributing factor that many other Sufi groups within Muslim Anatolia as well as Iran had also created mystical musics for their own ceremonies. But only the Mevlevis evolved a largely pre-composed concert that functioned as the music for the kinetic movement of the mystical *sema* ritual. Everywhere else in the Muslim world, as the Sufi *sema* was being purged from society, in the Ottoman realm the *sema* could coexist with the more widespread and communal Sufi *zikr* rituals (Binbaş 2001: 79).

Apparently starting already in the Karamanid period during the fifteenth century, steps were taken to formalise a specific musical and choreographic structure for the Mevlevi *sema*. The circling around a point of truth (*noqta*) became the basis for a rapid kinetic movement, as suggested by Divane Mehmed Çelebi:

> For that pure essence is defined in a point
> From its swift movement all potentialities emerge.

While earlier forms of *sema* among the Mevlevis were more spontaneous and less virtuosic, by the beginning of the seventeenth century a highly disciplined whirling movement became the norm. As I have shown in chapter 2, the later Mevlevi tradition held that the *sema* practices attributed to Shams-e Tabrizi had emphasised ecstasy, joy, spiritual state (*hal*), Divine attraction, and love. By the time of Pir Adil Çelebi, in the fifteenth century, these were supplemented by 'control of the breath' and 'consciousness of the gait'. While these principles had many applications for the dervish, surely the *sema* was one of them. The Mevlevi training aimed at creating conscious, and, as far as possible, selfless, individuals capable of moral behaviour with the same effortlessness that they exhibited in the appreciation and creation of beauty.

The Mevlevis were able to accomplish this evolution over six centuries through a unique combination of factors. Other Sufi thinkers created literary monuments, but there is no real analogue to the conjunction of literature, specific mystical practice, hierarchical Sufi organisation, sacred lineage, and well-known quasi-historical hierography represented by Jalaluddin Rumi and the later Mevlevi *tarikat*. Within this whole complex, human artistic creation held a highly significant role.[1]

There is no way to follow the history of music in either pre-Ottoman or Ottoman Anatolia without understanding the role of the Mevlevis. The talents of the leading Mevlevi musicians were not confined to the ritual music of the *sema* ceremony alone. These musicians were able to distinguish a mystical use and structure of music from the secular styles that had developed in a courtly environment, and they were active in both of them. As explained in chapter 6, the *ilm al-musiqah* (Turkish: *ilmül-musiki*) – 'science of music' – also implied a repertoire that used the rhythmic cycles and compositional genres of art music. In each era these were codified and highly specific, differing from popular and folkloric genres. In an earlier publication, I noted the importance of the science of music to the Mevlevis: 'Evidently the Mevlevis seized on the practical, not just the theoretical application of the *ilm al-musiqah* as a way of granting autonomy to musical art, similar in this respect to the autonomy long granted in Islamic societies to poetry, while at the same time enrolling it within an ostensibly spiritual discipline, with the whole complex built upon an orthodox, Sunni Muslim foundation' (Feldman 2001: 58). It is evident from the career of the seventeenth-century Mevlevi musician Çengi Yusuf Dede, who was both a *neyzen* and a harpist, that specialisations in the music of the *mukabele* and in secular art music often coexisted within the same

---

[1] This paragraph is based on Feldman 2001: 59.

individual. Nevertheless, these involved differentiated musical practices. The music of the Mevlevi *mukabele* had its own history and lineage, quite distinct from what later became Ottoman court music. Thus, it is certainly not accurate to view Mevlevi music as a branch or repertoire within Ottoman court music. And it was in large degree thanks to these very same Mevlevi musicians that an artistic music was re-established some generations after the Ottomans had based themselves in Istanbul.

Prior to the Ottoman conquest of Constantinople in 1453, several Anatolian cities, including Konya, were the local centres of a transnational Persianate art music. A number of Mevlevi musicians, along with other Anatolian Turkish musicians, became actively involved in this transnational art music, whose centre then was far to the east, in Timurid Khorasan. Outstanding figures such as the theorist Kırşehirli, in the fifteenth century; the secular musician, *zakir*, and teacher Tokatlı Derviş Ömer, in the early seventeenth century; and the Konya-trained Çengi Yusuf Dede, in the mid-seventeenth century, exemplified this pattern. Moreover, the Mevleviye constituted a strong cultural institution that integrated the highest level of culture, including but not confined to music, between Anatolia and Istanbul. They were also able to fill a similar role with centres as distant as Aleppo, Tripoli, and, at one time, Baghdad, in the east, and Salonika, Plovdiv, and Sarajevo in the west.

In the early Mevlevi centuries there was also a geographical complexity. Prior to the Shiite takeover of Iran under the Safavids early in the sixteenth century, several Mevlevi sheikhs and dervishes maintained contact with Iran, especially with the province of Azerbaijan, as well as with several areas of eastern Anatolia. On one level this contact involved the penetration of esoteric (*batini*) ideas and practices characteristic of several heterodox groups among both urbanites and Turkish- and Kurdish-speaking tribal Sufis. In a sense the assimilation of such esoteric ideas and practices was almost like a return to the original synthesis of the thinking of Jalaluddin and his mentor, Shams-e Tabrizi. Several Mevlevi leaders, including Divane Mehmed Çelebi (d. 1529), in Karahisar, saw these esoteric ideas and practices as a legitimate part of their heritage.

It was in the early decades of the seventeenth century that the Mevlevis became firmly established – or, in the case of Galata, re-established – within

Istanbul. From this point on we can trace their multifaceted cultural influence in the Ottoman capitals of Istanbul and Edirne. Particularly in these cities, the Mevlevi *neyzen*s became teachers and, in general, interlocutors with musicians and cantors of the Greek, Armenian, and Jewish communities. Given the strong Mevlevi presence in secular art music as well, this musical communication came to transform much of the music of the Ottoman court as well as several important genres of Greek church music. Only by examining the musical results of this multidirectional communication does it become possible to understand the transformations that overtook many genres of secular and religious music of both Muslims and non-Muslims during the long eighteenth century, i.e., the period from roughly 1680 to 1810.

Some evidence survives for the emergence of this pattern throughout the long eighteenth century and continuing until the end of the Ottoman Empire. The influence of the Mevlevis was very much facilitated by the political and cultural crises of much of the seventeenth century, when the Ottoman court was no longer in a position to lead the way in either music or poetry. What Ahmed Hamdi Tanpınar had termed the 'Sufi Era' of Ottoman culture during the mid-seventeenth century characterised the most creative movements in poetry, which looked to Mughal India as its cultural centre. These creative poets generally received only minimal support from the Ottoman court. The major figures – Cevri, Neşati, and Mezaki – were Mevlevis. Na'ili was connected with the Halvetiye, and only Fehim seems to have been unaffiliated. During the seventeenth century a great deal of creative interaction occurred between the Mevleviye and other *tarikat*s concerning both music and poetry. Derviş Ömer was both a Gülşeni and a Mevlevi. The musical circle surrounding the composer Koca Osman – who was apparently not a dervish – included both the Halveti Hafiz Post and the Mevlevi follower Mustafa Itri as well as a large number of ulema musicians.

At this point Mevlevi musicians achieved great prominence in every sphere, from performance to composition in all musical genres, and in music theory. All these aspects are evident in the careers of musicians such as Itri, Nazim, and Kutb-i Nayi Osman Dede, and later, in the 'family' of Yenikapı sheikhs, Abdurrahman Künhi, Ali Nutki, and Abdülbaki Nasır Dede. Osman Dede's grandson, Nasır Dede, was also a major music theorist, and was directly patronised by Sultan Selim III (1789–1808).

Selim III represents what may be termed the apotheosis of Mevlevi influence on the Ottoman court. For the first time in Ottoman history, a reigning sultan combined in his person the role of a Mevlevi, a major Ottoman musician-composer, a patron of music theory and notation, and the patron of the major literary figure of his generation, Sheikh Galib Dede of Galata. The latter's *mesnevi Hüsn ü Aşk* (Beauty and Love) remains the great Ottoman classic of the genre. But the fact that Selim was assassinated in yet another Janissary-led rebellion highlights the inherent fragility of this situation. Nevertheless, even under the reign of his nephew Mahmud II (1808–39), the great composer Ismail Dede Efendi, continued to be patronised. And, in fact, it was under Sultan Mahmud that Dede created all of his *ayin* compositions. It is related that the dying sultan had his bed carried to the Yenikapı Mevlevihane so that he could hear Dede's new Ferahfeza Ayini.

The role of Mevlevi musicians underwent yet further transformations during the nineteenth century, first under the Tanzimat Reforms after 1839, and then during the long reign of the musically indifferent Abdülhamid II (1876–1908). The creation of the new Muzika-yi Hümayun Orchestra in 1838 involved several Mevlevi musicians, the most illustrious of whom was Salih Dede, the brother of Sheikh Said Dede of Beşiktaş. His nephew, Osman Paşa, likewise had a prominent role in the official Orchestra and went on to become the most influential composer of *peşrev*s and *saz sema'i*s in the mid to late nineteenth century. Although Ismail Dede had left the Court in 1846, his prominent student Zekai Dede (d. 1896) remained a major composer of both Mevlevi *ayin*s and the courtly *fasıl* genres. But he too left Istanbul for some years to become a court musician for an Egyptian prince.

The changes in musical life during the reign of Sultan Abdülhamid II included a bifurcation of musical expertise into the public and professionalised sphere of the new *gazino* nightclubs – generally run and often staffed by non-Muslims – and the more private sphere of the Mevlevi musicians and others with more aristocratic musical tastes. Thus, even before the abrupt closure of 1925, the era in which the Mevlevi *neyzen* could function as an 'ideal representative of Ottoman culture' was drawing to an end. As the mystical and the worldly drew further apart, there was less social and cultural space for a single individual who combined musical, poetic, and calligraphic skills within a framework that integrated several realities and worldviews. It would be a mistake to view this kind of cultural and spiritual integration as something that is only of historical interest. These are values that are essential to the survival of human civilisation. And indeed, toward the close of the Ottoman era, the Mevlevis furnished many examples of individuals who were able to adapt their traditional skills to modern needs.

At the turn of the twentieth century the Yenikapı *neyzen* Rauf Yekta Bey took it upon himself to modernise Ottoman music theory, and to use Western notation to document both the Mevlevi and the secular courtly repertoire. Using his knowledge of French and of Western musicology, he was able to publish the seminal article '*La Musique Turque*' in Albert Lavignac's Encyclo-pédie de la musique et dictionnaire du Conservatoire (Part I, vol. 5, 1922). Rauf Yekta helped to found the new Darülelhan conservatory, where he col-laborated with Zekai Dede's son, Ahmed Irsoy. Their contemporary, Tanburi Cemil Bey (d. 1916), was a secular aristocrat who represented a brilliant syn-thesis of the courtly with the new nightclub musical style. After the closing of the Turkish music section of the conservatory, Yekta then worked with Irsoy and Cemil Bey's son, the European-trained cellist and *tanburi* Mesut Cemil, on the Classification and Stabilisation Committee that still represented Ottoman music within the conservatory. This phase was a prelude to an even more drastic cultural marginalisation, when Ottoman music was banned from Turkish radio shortly after Rauf Yekta's death in 1935.

In his own, more scholarly way, Rauf Yekta Bey was one of those *neyzen*s who acted as an ideal representative of Ottoman culture in the drastically changed conditions of the early Republic. And in his case, as in the case of his contemporary Emin Dede Yazıcı (d. 1945), the latter part of his life played out in a cultural space in which the Mevlevi spiritual and musical practice was no longer possible. Several contemporary or somewhat younger *neyzen*s worked to ensure that the art of the Mevlevi *ney* would survive in Turkish society, even without its full role in Mevlevi spiritual practice. Rauf Yekta and Zekaizade Ahmed were aware that in the absence of regular *mukabele* per-formances in Mevlevi architectural spaces, oral transmission alone would no longer be effective. It is thanks to them that we have an extraordinary notated repertoire that reaches back at least in part to an early stage in the genesis of the *ayin-i şerif*, in the sixteenth century, and extends from then until the turn of the twentieth century.

Partial though it is, even this corpus demonstrates that the Mevlevis had created the most demanding musical forms in the entire Turkish musical culture. Among the many unique and striking features of the Mevlevi *ayin* is the degree of individuality each composer could demonstrate. Even with some technical modernisation in the course of oral transmission, these individual differences are still evident. Thus, the study of each and every Mevlevi *ayin* is, in some sense, a new exploration. Moreover, Mevlevi composers felt free to allude to much earlier compositional models while situating such allusions to the past in a musical language of the present. As the Mevlevi musical tradition developed between the sixteenth and the early twentieth centuries, we can see complex uses of modality in the creation of melodies in which the connection with the rhythmic cycles becomes increasingly subtle. At the same time, poetic lyrics issue spiritually profound statements coupled with moments of mental 'relaxation' in the *terennüm* sections – all designed as part of a kinetic movement that symbolises humanity's role in the cosmos. The full musical depth of the multifaceted *mukabele* ceremony still remains to be explored and appreciated.

Thanks to the great efforts of the current generations of *neyzen*s – themselves usually the products of earlier Mevlevi musical lineages – the *ney taksim* and many subtle aspects of the articulation of the Mevlevi performance are still alive as an oral tradition. And the composition of the *ayin-i şerif* has not ceased. It reached a high musical level with the oud virtuoso Cinuçen Tanrıkorur (1938–2000) but it still has talented representatives today – among them, Ahmet Çalışır (b. 1966), in Konya. There are appreciative musicians and audiences in Turkey, in neighbouring countries, and further abroad. Of course, this appreciation in itself cannot be a substitute for a full living Mevlevi spiritual practice. Nevertheless, one can only hope that making available material that integrates an analysis of music and poetry with a deeper understanding of the full scope of Mevlevi history can bring the many rich strands of this culture to a wider and more discerning public.

GLOSSARY

(Pers.= Persian; Ar.=Arabic; T=Turkish)

ayin (Pers.) 'ceremony', used broadly for the Mevlevi *sema*. More specifically it refers to the vocal compositions within the four *selam* sections, created by a single composer.

ayin-cem 'Ceremony of unity'; Sufi ritual dance of the Alevis.

ayin-i şerif 'The noble ceremony'; designates in particular the Mevlevi *sema*.

Alevi Tribally-based Sufi groups among Turkish- and some Kurdish-speakers in Anatolia.

amal (Ar.) courtly genre of Persian music consisting, from the fourteenth to seventeenth centuries, of four sections, and using the middle range of rhythmic cycles (*usul*).

aruz (Ar.) metrical pattern in poetry.

asitane (Pers.) 'threshold'; a large and central Mevlevi convent or lodge, where the training of dervishes as well as *sema* performances could take place.

ayinhan Singer of the *ayin* during the *mukabele* ceremony.

batini (Ar.) 'internal'; movements within Sufism emphasising the esoteric aspects of reality.

241

Bektashi   Sufi order named after Haci Bektaş Veli (1209–71) but largely originating among the Alevi. It became the Sufi order of the Janissary (Yeniçeri) Corps of the Ottoman army.

bend   (Pers.) musical 'strophe' in the Mevlevi *ayin*.

beste   (Pers.) 'composition'; development of the quasi-folkloric *murabba* in early 17th-century Ottoman vocal music; after the later seventeenth century, the dominant vocal form of the Ottoman *fasıl*.

beyt   (Ar.) 'house'; the couplet within Persian and Ottoman poetry.

Çelebi   (T.) Based on much earlier Turkic usage as 'holy man' (through Nestorian Aram. *saliba*: 'the cross'), in Ottoman it came to mean: (1) descendant of a sacred Sufi lineage, hence (2) in Mevlevi usage the hereditary leader of the Mevlevi Order, who was resident in the Mevlevi Asitane in Konya; (3) an educated Ottoman who did not become part of the judiciary (*kadı*) or the professorship (*müderris*); (4) a refined gentleman.

çile   (T.) period of withdrawal and learning, lasting for 1001 days among the Mevleviye, after which an aspirant was declared a dervish (*dede*).

dede   (T.) 'grandfather', dervish of the Mevleviye.

dergah   (Pers.) 'court'; any dervish convent.

dervish   (Pers.) 'poor man'; follower of one of the Sufi *tarikat* orders.

devir   (Ar. *dawr*) 'cycle' or revolution; (1) in music: one complete unit of a rhythmic cycle (*usul*); (2) in the Mevlevi *mukabele*: one complete cycle of the ceremony and its music; later replaced by *selam*.

devran   (Ar.) 'circling', hence (1) epoch; (2) circling motion during the *zikr*.

devşirme   Levy of male children from Christian families in the Balkans, for service in the Imperial Palace and in the Janissary Corps. Apparently instituted by Sultan Murat I (1360–89), it remained in force until the seventeenth century.

divan   Book of collected poems.

durak   Pre-composed rubato genre of the Sufi *tarikat*s, especially the Halvetiye and Kadiriye, employing Turkish texts. Stylistically and in performance practice, *durak* displays similarities to the *na'at* genre.

fasıl   (Ar.) 'season', hence 1. group of musical compositions in the same *makam*; 2. Ottoman concert suite with fixed order of genres in the same *makam*.

ghazal   (T. *gazel*) dominant form of Persian and Turkish lyric poetry, based on couplets (*beyt*).

gnosis   Hellenistic Greek term for a spiritual movement seeking esoteric knowledge; became Arabic and Persian *'irfan*.

halife   (Ar.) 'successor', hence a leading assistant to a Sufi sheikh, and one who would become his successor.

Halveti   Turkish Sufi order originating in fifteenth-century Azerbaijan. By the following century, it became one of the dominant orders of the Ottoman Empire.

hane   (Pers. *khāna*) 'house'. Used for a section of the instrumental *peşrev*.

hanende   (Pers. *khananda*) 'singer' in an urban or courtly context.

ilahi   (Ar.) 'divine', hence Sufi hymns of the Turkish orders.

ilmül musiki   (Ar. *'ilm al-Musiqah*) the science of music, i.e., the theory and practice of 'artistic' music, or *musique savante*.

kafiye   (Ar.) rhyme at the end of a poetic line (*mısra*).

Kalender   See Qalandar.

kar   (Pers.) leading genre of courtly Persian music from the fifteenth century, composed also by Ottoman musicians since the seventeenth century and thereafter, using Persian texts.

Karamanid   Leading Anatolian political dynasty based in Konya. They gradually came to replace the Seljuqs from the mid-thirteenth century. Their territory was finally annexed by the Ottomans in 1486.

khanegah   (T. *hanegah*) Sufi lodge or convent.

Khorasan   North-eastern province of Greater Iran. In the Timurid era, its capital was Herat.

kudüm   Small kettledrums used in the Mevlevi *mukabele* and in the courtly *fasıl*.

makam   (Ar. *maqam*: 'place') used since the fifteenth century for 'melodic mode', including both scale and codified melodic progression.

meclis   (Ar. *majlis*) 'assembly', hence formal social gathering.

mecmu'a   (Ar.) 'collection'. In Ottoman usage a book with song-texts, grouped
              according to *makam*, and including the name of the genre, its *usul*, the
              name of the composer of the music, and sometimes also of the poetry.
              Ali Ufuki Bey's *Mecmu'a-i Saz ü Söz* in the British Museum Library
              (London) is a unique *mecmu'a* collection written in Western notation
              circa 1650.

mehter, mehterhane

              (Pers.) 'greater'. Military and ceremonial ensemble of the Ottoman State.

melami   (Ar.) Sufi follower of the 'Path of Blame', i.e., avoiding apparently
              pious behaviour and dress in order to cultivate a deeper, inner piety.

mesnevi   (Pers. *masnavi*, Ar. *mathnawi*) long, narrative or 'thematic' poem in
              rhythmed couplets. In the Mevlevi context refers to the *Masnavi-yi
              Ma'navi* of Jalaluddin Rumi.

mesnevihan   (Pers.) 'singer of the Mesnevi'. Refers to a *dede* or sheikh who was
              competent to recite and interpret Rumi's *Masnavi*.

Mevlevihane   'House of the Mevlevis'; a Mevlevi dervish lodge of any size and capacity.

meydan   (Ar.) 'public square'; Among Sufis the space where either the *zikr* or for
              Mevlevis, the *sema* was performed.

mısra   (Ar.) hemistich; the first line of a *beyt* (couplet).

miyan   (Pers.) 'middle'; hence the variant B section of a vocal composition,
              sometimes modulating from the melodic mode of the A section.

müezzin   (Ar.) mosque singer who sang the formal Call to Prayer (*ezan*).

muhibb   (Ar.) 'affectionate'; a non-initiated 'follower' of the Mevleviye.

mukabele   (Ar.) 'facing one another', term used since the fifteenth century for the
              entire Mevlevi *sema* ceremony. In the twentieth century it is used to
              refer to the entire ceremony, including the *Na'at-i Peygamberi* and the
              instrumental *peşrev*.

mülazime   (Ar.) *hane* (section) functioning as a ritornello in a *peşrev* (sixteenth to
              late eighteenth century).

murabba	(Ar.) Ottoman vocal composition based on four poetic lines, generally with AABA musical structure. Developed out of a quasi-folkloric form by the later seventeenth century as the courtly *murabba beste*.
mutrıp	(Ar.) musical ensemble for the *mukabele*.
na'at	(Ar.) 'poetic eulogy', hence *Na'at-i Peygamberi*: 'Hymn to the Prophet Muhammad'. In Mevlevi music, refers to the composition in *makam* Rast by Buhurizade Itri (d. 1712). These relate to the *durak* genre of other Sufi Orders.
naqsh	(T. *nakş*) one of the lighter genres of Persian art music from Timurid times. In Turkey it might use either Turkish or Persian lyrics.
Naqshibandi	Sufi order originating in fourteenth-century Transoxiana. It takes its name from Bahauddin Naqshiband (d. 1389). It maintained a Sunni basis and became influential during the seventeenth century in the Ottoman Empire.
ney	From Pers. (Ar. *nai*) 'reed', hence 'reed-flute'. A dominant instrument among medieval Sufis, and the leading instrument among Mevlevis.
neyzen	Performer on the *ney*.
neyzenbaşı	('Head *neyzen*') was an official title in the Mevlevi lodges.
peşrev	(Pers.) 'goes before'. The leading genre of Ottoman instrumental music, based on Timurid antecedents. During the sixteenth century it was developed by *mehter* musicians, and by the mid-seventeenth century, it became the opening part of the Ottoman *fasıl* concert.
post	(Pers.) 'sheepskin'; in Sufi orders, it became a symbol of the authority of the sheikh.
postnişin	(Pers.) 'one who sits on the *post*' (sheepskin), hence a sheikh.
Qalandar	(T. *Kalender*) of obscure origin. A movement that encompassed usually individual, wandering Sufis originating in Greater Iran.
rabab	Short-necked Iranian lute with a skin face, favoured in the Seljuq era. By the later seventeenth century, it went out of fashion in Turkey. The name was later re-used for a skin-faced Persian spike fiddle.
redif	(Ar.) 'monorhyme' ending each poetic couplet (*beyt*).

rind   (Pers.) Lit. 'thug'. A word for someone – including some Sufis – who seek the spiritual through idiosyncratic, or antinomian behaviour.

ruba'i   (Ar.) Dominant quatrain form of Persian poetry.

selam   (Ar.) 'Peace'. Through a semantic shift, by the early seventeenth century it came to replace *devir* as the term for the separate cycles of the Mevlevi *ayin*.

Seljuq   Major Eastern Islamic dynasty, originating among Oghuz Turks. By the mid-eleventh century featuring separate Iranian and Anatolian branches. The latter submitted to the Mongols in the mid-thirteenth century.

sema   (Ar. *samā'*: 'audition'). Form of mystical music and 'dance' favoured by medieval Sufis. In the Persian and Arabic context this book uses *samā'* and in the Turkish, *sema*. Throughout their history the Mevlevis continued to use this term to refer broadly to the entire *mukabele* ceremony, and to the whirling of the *semazen*s within that ceremony.

semahane   'House of the *sema*', large room within each *mevlevihane* where the *sema* was performed.

semazen   Among the Mevleviye, a dervish who practised the *sema*.

sema'i   (1) Musical genre of Ottoman music; (2) short *usul* in 6/8, which formed the basis for the *sema'i;* (3) instrumental and vocal sections of the Third Selam within the Mevlevi *sema*.

seyir   (Ar.) 'journey', hence melodic progression within a *makam*.

sheikh (*şeyh*) (Ar.) 'elder', 'leader of a tribe'. Hence the head of a branch of a Sufi Order. Among Mevlevis the head of a particular *mevlevihane*.

Sultan Veled Devri

              'The Cycle of Sultan Veled'. Custom of circumambulating the *semahane* at the beginning of the *mukabele*, to the music of a *peşrev* in the new *usul devr-i kebir* (28/4). The custom probably originated in the mid to later eighteenth century.

ta'ifa   (Ar.) 'clan'; refers to sub-divisions within a Sufi Order. Not in use among the Mevleviye, who remained more centralised.

taksim	(Ar.) 'division', term for improvisation in flowing rhythm that first appeared in later sixteenth century Ottoman music. It was also much developed by Mevlevi *neyzen*s. The opening *taksim* of the *mukabele* is termed *baş-taksim* ('head *taksim*').
tanbur	Long-necked Turkic lute whose antecedents were developed in the fifteenth century, but that came to dominate the Ottoman instrumentarium after the second half of the seventeenth century.
tarikat	(Ar. *tariqah*) A hierarchically organised Sufi order.
tasawwuf	(Ar.) The mystical movement within Islam known in English as Sufism.
tecvit	(Ar. *tajwid*) the chanting of the Qur'an according to flowing rhythm but using the *makam* system of art music.
tekke	(T.) Lodge or convent of any dervish order.
terennüm	(Ar.) Text of a musical line with either non-verbal syllables or conventional words and exclamations.
ulema	(Ar.) sing. *'alim*; the Islamic clergy.
usul	(Ar.) 'rule'; rhythmic cycle. *Usul*s can be short, medium or long. Within the Mevlevi *ayin*, the individual *selam*s were defined by separate *usul*s.
velvele	Lit. 'commotion'; percussive filling in of a basic *usul* pattern.
vezn	(Ar.) 'measure'; hence the long and short syllables of the poetic metrical system known as *aruz*. Cantemir (c. 1700), however, used it only as a term for relations of tempo and note-density in his notational system.
zaviye	(Ar.) 'place of retreat'; among Mevlevis, a smaller *mevlevihane* that could offer hospitality, but not full training, of dervishes.
zemin	(Pers.) 'ground'; in music the basic A section of a vocal composition.
zikr	(Ar. *dhikr*) the basic form of devotion among most Sufi orders. For some it involved quiet chanting of Divine Names and meditation. For others the singing of *ilahi* hymns and circular or other movements.

REFERENCES CITED

Abbasi, Mohammad, ed., *Kolliyat-e Saeb*, Tehran: Tulu, 1366/1946.

Abdülbaki Nasır Dede, *Tedkik ü Tahkik* (Examination and Confirmation), Istanbul: Topkapı Sarayı Kütüphanesi, Türkçe Yazmalar no. 2.069.

Abdülbaki Nasır Dede, *Tedlik ü Tahkik* (Examination and Confirmation), ed. Yalçin Tura, Istanbul: Pan, 2006.

Abdülbaki Nasır Dede, *Tahririye*, Istanbul: Süleymaniye Kütüphanesi, Nafiz Paşa, 1, 242.

Abdülbaki Nasır Dede, *Tahririye*, ed. Recep Uslu and Nilgün Doğrusöz Dişiaçik, Istanbul: Istanbul Technical University, 2009.

Abou-El-Haj, Rifa'at Ali, *The 1703 Rebellion and the Structure of Ottoman Politics*, Istanbul: Nederlands Historisch Institut, 1984.

Akdoğu, Onur, *Müzik Yönüyle Neyzen Tevfik* (The Musical Direction of Neyzen Tevfik), Izmir: Mey Ofset, 1991.

Aksel, Malik, *Religious Pictures in Turkish Art*, Istanbul: Elif Kitabevi, 1967.

Aksoy, Bülent, *Sermuezzin Rifat Bey'in* Ferahnak *Mevlevi Ayini* (Rifaat Bey's *Ferahnak* Mevlevi Ayin), Istanbul: Pan, 1992.

Aksoy, Bülent, *Avrupalı Gezginlerin Gözüyle Osmanlılarda Musiki* (Music Among the Ottomans in the Eyes of European Travellers), Istanbul: Pan, 1994.

Aksoy, Bülent, *Geçmişin Musiki Mirasına Bakışlar* (Views of the Musical Heritage of the Past), Istanbul: Pan, 2008.

Ambrosio, Alberto Fabio, Eve Feuillebois, and Thierry Zarcone, *Les derviches tourneurs: doctrine, histoire et pratiques,* Paris: Cerf, 2006.

Andrews, Walter, *Poetry's Voice, Society's Song: Ottoman Lyric Poetry*, Seattle: University of Washington Press, 1985.

Andrews, Walter, Najaat Black, and Mehmet Kalpaklı, *Ottoman Lyric Poetry: An Anthology*, Austin: University of Texas Press, 1997.

Andrews, Walter and Mehmet Kalpaklı, *The Age of Beloveds*, Durham, NC: Duke University Press, 2005.

Ankaravi, Ismail (Rusuhi Dede), *Er-Risaletüt Tenzihiyye fi Şe'nil Mevleviye*, in *Mevlevilik ve Musiki* (Mevlevism and Music), ed. Bayram Akdoğan, Istanbul: Rağbet, 2009.

Anvar, Iraj and Anne Twitty, *Say Nothing: Poems of Jalal al-Din Rumi in Persian and English*, Sandpoint, Idaho: Morning Light Press, 2008.

Apostolopoulos, Thomas, *Petros Peloponnesios* (CD notes), Thessalonika: Enchordais, 2005.

Asadi, Hooman, 'Toward the Formation of the Dastgah Concept: a Study on the History of Persian Music', unpublished paper, ICTM Study Group, Samarkand (2001).

Ayangil, Ruhi, 'Western Notation in Turkish Music', *Journal of the Royal Asiatic Society*, 18 (2008), pp. 403–47.

Ayvazoğlu, Beşir, *Neyin Sırrı* (The Secret of the Ney), Istanbul: Kapı, 2007.

Ayan, Hüseyin, *Cevri: Hayatı, Edebi Kişiliği, Eserleri ve Divanının Tenkidli Metni* (Cevri: his Life, his Literary Personality, his Works and the Critical Text of his Divan), Erzurum: Atatürk Üniversitesi, 1981.

Arı, Ahmet, *Sakıb Mustafa Dede'nin Hayatı, Eserleri ve Edebi Kişiliği* (The Life, Works and Literary Personality of Sakıb Mustafa Dede), Konya: Selcuk Universitesi, 1995.

Avery, Kenneth S., *A Psychology of Early Sufi Sama: Listening and Altered States*, London: Curzon, 2004.

Babar (Babur), Zahir al-Din, *The Bábar-Náma, being the Autobiography of the Emperor Bábar, the founder of the Moghul dynasty in India*, trans. and ed. Annette Susannah Beveridge, Leiden: Brill, 1905.

Babur, Zahir-ud-Din Muhammad, *The Bábur-nama in English* (*Memoirs of Bábur*), trans. Annette Susannah Beveridge, London: Luzac, 1922.

Baki, Edip Ali, *XV Yüzyıl Konya-Karaman Şairlerden Ayni* (Ayni: One of the Fifteenth-Century Poets of Konya-Karaman), Ankara: Ulus, 1949.

Behar, Cem, 'The Technical Modernization of Turkish Sufi Music: The Case of the Durak', in *Sufism, Music and Society in Turkey and the Middle East*, ed. Anders Hammarlund, Tord Olsson and Elizabeth Özdalga, Istanbul: Swedish Research Institute, 2001, pp. 97–110.

Behar, Cem, 'Traditional Teaching Methods of a Sacred Instrument: the Ney in Ottoman/Turkish Music', unpublished paper, 2003.

Behar, Cem, 'Hayrı Tümer ve Ney Metodu' (Hayrı Tümer and Ney Method), in *Musıkiden Müziğe* (From *Musiki* to Music), Istanbul: Yapı Kredi, 2004, pp. 117–35.

Behar, Cem, *Saklı Mecmua: Ali Ufki'nin Bibliothèque Nationale de France'taki [Turc 292] Yazmasi*. ("The Hidden Collection"), Istanbul: Yapı Kredi, 2008.

Behar, Cem, *Şeyhülislam'ın Müziği* (The Music of the Sheykh al-Islam), Istanbul: Yapı Kredi, 2010.

Behar, Cem, 'The Show and the Ritual: The Mevlevi Mukabele in Ottoman Times', in *Medieval and Early Modern Performances in the Eastern Mediterranean*, ed. Arzu Özturkmen and Evelyn Birge Witz, Turnhout: Brepols, 2014, pp. 515–33.

Beyatlı, Yahya Kemal, *Eski Şiirin Rüzgariyle* (With the Breeze of the Old Poetry), Istanbul: Yahya Kemal Enstitüsü, 1974.

Binbaş, Ilker Evrim, 'Music and Sama' of the Mavlaviyya in the Fifteenth and Sixteenth Centuries: Origins, Ritual and Formation,' in *Sufism, Music and Society in Turkey and the Middle East*, ed. Anders Hammarlund, Tord Olsson and Elizabeth Özdalga, Istanbul: Swedish Research Institute, 2001, pp. 67–80.

Bobowski, Wojciech (Ali Ufuki Bey), *Mecmua-i Saz ü Söz. c. 1650* (Collection of Instrumental and Vocal Music), British Museum Library, Sloane 3114.

Bobowski, Wojciech, *Saray-i Enderum Penetrale del Seraglio (1665)*, trans. Robert Martin, *Turkish Music Quarterly*, 3(4) (1990), pp. 1–3.

Cahen, Claude, *Pre-Ottoman Turkey*, London: Sidgwick & Jackson, 1968.

Can, Şefik, *Fundamentals of Rumi's Thought*, Clifton, NJ: Tughra, 2004.

Can, Halil, 'Emin Dede', *Türk Musikisi Dergisi* (The Journal of Turkish Music), 1 (1948), pp. 4–5.

Cantemir, Demetrius, *Kitab-i 'Ilmül Musiki 'ala Vech'il Hurufat* (The Book of the Science of Music According to the Alphabetic Notation), Istanbul: Istanbul Üniversitesi Kütüphanesi, Türkiyat Enstitüsü, No. 2768, c. 1700–1703.

Cantemir, Demetrius, *Kitab-i 'Ilmül Musiki 'ala Vech'il Hurufat*, Facsimile and Modern Turkish Translation, 3 vols, ed. Yalçın Tura, Istanbul: Tura Yayınları, 1976.

Cantemir, Demetrius, *History of the Growth and Decay of the Ottoman Empire*, trans. Nicholas Tindal, London: J. J. and P. Knapton (1714–16) 1734.

Çengi Yusuf Dede, *Risale-i Edvar* (1650?), ed. Recep Uslu, Ankara: Çengi Yayinevi, 2015.

Chittick, William, 'On the Cosmology of Dhikr', in *Paths to the Heart: Sufism and the Christian East*, ed. James Cutsinger, Louisville: Fons Vitae, 2002.

Chittick, William, *Me & Rumi: The Autobiography of Shams-i Tabrizi*, Louisville: Fons Vitae, 2004.

Çıpan, Mustafa, *Fasih Divanı: Inceleme – Tenkidli Metin* (The Divan of Fasih Dede: a Study and Critical Edition), Istanbul: Milli Eğitim, 2003.

Çıpan, Mustafa, *Divane Mehmed Çelebi*, Konya: Konya Valiliği, 2002.

Covel, John, *The Diaries of Dr. John Covel. Voyages and Travels in the Levant, no. 87*, London: The Hakluyt Society, 1670–79.

Dar-al-Masnavi. Website of the American Institute of Masnavi Studies (AIMS), http://dar-al-masnavi.org (accessed 3.03.2021).

Değirmenci, Tülin, 'Takım: Hamparsum Defterlerinde Unutulan Bir Geleneğin Izleri' (The Takım: Traces of a Forgotten Tradition in the Hamparsum Notebooks), *Darülelhan Mecmuası*, 10 (2018), pp. 8–11.

DeWeese, Devin, *Islamization and Native Religion in the Golden Horde*, University Park: Penn State University Press, 1994.

Dickie, James (Yaqub Zaki), 'The Mawlavi Dervishery in Cairo', *Art and Archaeology Research Papers*, 15 (1979), pp. 9–15.

Dikmen, Halil, 'Mevlevi Müziği', in Abdülbaki Gölpınarlı, *Mevlana'dan Sonra Mevlevilik* (Mevlevism after Mevlana), Ankara: Inkılap ve Aka (1953) 1983, pp. 455–65.

Doğrusöz, Nilgün, 'Nayi Osman Dede'nin Müzik Yazınsına Dair Birkaç Belge' (Some Documents of Osman Dede's Musical Writing), *Musikişinas*, 8 (2006), pp. 47–66.

Doğrusöz, Nilgün, *Yusuf Kırşehri'nin Müzik Teorisi* (The Music Theory of Yusuf Kırşehri), Kırşehir: Kırşehir Valiliği, 2012.

During, Jean. *Quelque chose se passe: le sens de la tradition dans l'Orient musical*, Paris: Lagrasse, 1995.

Duru, Necip Fazil, 'Mevlevi şairlerde ney metaforu' (The Ney Metaphor Among Mevlevi Poets), *Uluslararası Mevlana Sempozyumu Bilderileri 1*, Istanbul: Motto, 2007, pp. 359–84.

Eflaki (Aflaki), Shamsuddîn Ahmad, *Ariflerin Menkibleri* (The Feats of the Knowers of God or Tales of the Gnostics), trans. (into Turkish) Tahsin Yazici, Ankara: Milli Egitim, 1953.

Eflaki (Aflaki), *The Feats of the Knowers of God*, trans. (into English) John O'Kane, Leiden: Brill, 2002.

Ekinci, Mehmet Uğur, *Kevseri Mecmuası: 18. Yüzyıl Saz Müziği Külliyatı* (The Kevseri Mecmua: an Eighteenth Century Musical Collection), Istanbul: OMAR and Pan, 2016.

Elias, Jamal, 'Mevlevi Sufis and the Representation of Emotion in the Arts of the Ottoman World', in *Affect, Emotion and Subjectivity in Early Modern Muslim Empires*, Leiden: Brill, 2017, pp. 185–209.

Emre, Side, *Ibrahim-i Gulshani and the Khalwati-Gulshani Order: Power Brokers in Ottoman Egypt*, Leiden: Brill, 2017.

Ergun, Sadettin Nüzhet, *Türk Musikisi Antolojisi: Dini Eserler* (Anthology of Turkish Music: Religious Works), Istanbul: Rıza Koşkun, 1943.

Erguner, Kudsi, *Journeys of a Sufi Musician*, London: Saqi, 2005.

Ernst, Carl W, *Words of Ecstasy in Sufism*, Albany: State University of New York Press,1985.

Esrar Dede, '*Tezkire-i Şu'ara-yi Mevleviye* (Biographical Dictionary of the Mevlevi Poets), ed. Ilhan Genç, Ankara: Atatürk Kültür Merkezi, 2000.

Ezgi, Subhi, *Nazari Ameli Türk Musikisi* (Theory and Practice of Turkish Music), 5 vols, Istanbul: Hüsnütabiat, 1954.

Faroqui, Suraiya, 'Agricultural Crisis and the Art of Flute Playing: 1595–1652', *Turcica*, 20 (1988), pp. 43–70.

Faroqui, Suraiya, and Arzu Öztürkmen, *Celebration, Entertainment and Theatre in the Ottoman World*, London: Seagull, 2014.

Al-Faruqi, Lois Ibsen, 'Music, Musicians and Muslim Law', *Asian Music*, 17(1) (1985), pp. 3–36.

Feldman, Walter, 'Musical Genres and Zikir of the Sunni Tarikats of Istanbul', in *The Dervish Lodge: Art, Architecture, and Sufism in Ottoman Turkey*, ed. Raymond Lifchez, Berkeley: University of California Press, 1992, pp. 187–202.

Feldman, Walter, 'Mysticism, Didacticism and Authority in the Liturgical Poetry of the Halveti Dervishes of Istanbul', *Edebiyat*: N.S. vol. II (1) (1993), pp. 243–65.

Feldman, Walter, *Music of the Ottoman Court: Makam, Composition and the Early Ottoman Instrumental Repertoire*, Berlin: Verlag für Wissenschaft und Bildung, 1996.

Feldman, Walter, 'The Celestial Sphere, the Wheel of Fortune and Fate in the Gazels of Nâ'ilî and Bâkî', *International Journal of Middle East Studies*, 28(2) (May 1996), pp. 193–215.

Feldman, Walter, 'Imitatio in Ottoman Poetry: Three Ghazals of the Mid-Seventeenth Century', *The Turkish Studies Association Bulletin*, vol. 21, no. 2 (Fall 1997), pp. 41–58.

Feldman, Walter, 'The "Indian Style" in Seventeenth Century Ottoman Poetry: Imitation and Interpretation' (unpublished MS, 1999).

Feldman, Walter, 'Structure and Evolution of the Mevlevi Ayin: the Case of the Third Selam', in *Sufism, Music and Society in Turkey and the Middle East*, ed. Anders Hammarlund, Tord Olsson and Elizabeth Özdalga, Istanbul: Swedish Research Institute, 2001, pp. 49–66.

Feldman, Walter, 'Music in Performance: Who Are the Whirling Dervishes?', in *The Garland Encyclopedia of World Music*, vol. 6, ed. Virginia Danielson, Scott Marcus, and Dwight Reynolds, Abingdon and New York: Routledge, 2002, pp. 107–12.

Feldman, Walter, 'Manifestations of the Word: Poetry and Song in Turkish Sufism', in *The Garland Encyclopedia of World Music*, vol. 6, pp. 189–97.

Feldman, Walter, 'The Functioning Repertoire; Organization, Elements of Form: Ottoman Turkey', in Feldman and Guettat: *Music in the Mediterranean: Modal and Classical Traditions*. Volume I: History, Volume II: Theory and Practice. Thessaloniki: EnChordais (2005, unpublished).

Feldman, Walter, 'Buhurizade Mustafa Itri', *Arta* (Chişinau, Moldova), 2012, pp. 30–2.

Feldman, Walter, 'The Musical "Renaissance" of Late Seventeenth Century Ottoman Turkey: Reflections on the Musical Materials of Ali Ufki Bey (c. 1610–1675), Hafiz Post (d. 1694) and the "Maraghi" Repertoire', in *Writing the History of 'Ottoman Music'*, ed. Martin Greve, Würzber: Ergon, 2015, pp. 87–138.

Feldman, Walter, 'The Art of Melodic Extension Within and Beyond the Usul', in *Rhythmic Cycles and Structures in the Art Music of the Middle East*, ed. Zeynep Helvaci, Jacob Olley and Ralf Martin Jaeger, Würzburg: Ergon, 2017, pp. 154–76.

Feldman, Walter, 'The "Indian Style" and the Ottoman Literary Canon', in *Sabk: Essays on Form, Manner and Stylistics of Metaphor in Persian and Indo-Persian Literatures*, ed. S. R. Faruqi and A. Korangy, *International Journal of Persian Literature*, 3 (2018), pp. 3–38.

Feldman, Walter, "Kutb-i Nayi Osman Dede', in *The Encylopedia of Islam*, Third Edition, ed. Kate Fleet, et al., Leiden: Brill, 2021.

Ferriol, Charles, *Recueil de cents Estampes représentant différentes Nations du Levant*, Paris: (n.p.), 17.

Foltz, Richard C., trans., *Conversations with Emperor Jahangir by 'Mutribi' al-Asaman of Samarqand*. Washington, DC: Mazda, 1998.

Fonton, Charles, *Essai sur la musique orientale comparée à la musique européene* (Paris 1751), in *Zeitschrift für Geschichte der Arabischen-Islamischen Wissenschaften*, ed. Eckhard Neubauer, Frankfurt, 1986, pp. 324–77. English translation 1988–9 by Robert Martin in *Turkish Music Quarterly*, vol. 1(2) and vol. 2(1).

Gill, Denise, *Melancholic Modalities: Affect, Islam, and Turkish Classical Musicians*, Oxford: Oxford University Press, 2017.

Gölpınarlı, Abdülbaki, *Mevlana'dan Sonra Mevlevilik* (Mevlevism after Mevlana), Istanbul: Inkılap (1953) 1983.

Gölpınarlı, Abdülbaki, *Şeyh Galib: Seçmeler ve Hüsn-ü Aşk* (Sheikh Galib: Selections and Beauty and Love), Istanbul: Kapı, 1976.

Gölpınarlı, Abdülbaki, *Mevlevi Adab ve Erkanı* (Mevlevi Manners and Rules), Istanbul/Ankara: Inkılap, 1963.

Gölpınarlı, Abdülbaki, *Alevi-Bektaşi Nefesleri* (Alevi-Bektashi Hymns), Istanbul: Inkılap, 1963.

Gültaş, Ayhan, 'Cevri ve 17 Yüzyıl Türk Müzikisi Tarihine IşıkTutmuş Olan bir Manzümesi' (Cevri and a Poem Which Sheds Light on the History of Turkish Music of the 17th Century), *San'at ve Kültürde Kök*, vol. 13, pp. 30–2; vol. 14, pp. 34–6, Istanbul, 1982.

Halman, Talat, and Metin And, *Mevlana Celaleddin Rumi and The Whirling Dervishes*, Istanbul: Dost, 1992.

Harris, Rachel, and Martin Stokes, eds, *Theory and Practice in the Music of the Islamic World: Essays in Honour of Owen Wright*, London: Ashgate, 2018.

Hatipoğlu, Emrah, *Mevlevi Ayinleri Makamlar ve Geçkiler* (Makams and Modulations of the Mevlevi Ayins), Konya: Konya Valiliği İl Kültür ve Turizm Müdür, 2011.

Haug, Judith, *Ottoman and European Music in 'Ali Ufuki's Compendium, MS Turc 292: Analysis, Interpretation, Cultural Context: Monograph*, doctoral dissertation, University of Münster, 2019.

Haug, Judith, 'Representations of *Usul* in 'Ali Ufuki's Manuscripts', in *Rhythmic Cycles and Structures in the Art Music of the Middle East*, ed. Zeynep Helvacı, Jacob Olley and Ralf Martin Jaeger, Würzburg: Ergon, 2017, pp. 91–105.

Heper, Sadettin, *Mevlevi Ayinleri* (Mevlevi Ayins), Konya: Konya Turizm Derneği, 1979.

Hodgson, Marshall G. S., *The Venture of Islam: Conscience and History in a World Civilization*, vol. 2, Chicago: University of Chicago Press, 1974.

Inançer, Toğrul, 'Mevlevi Musikisi ve Sema' (Mevlevi Music and Sema), *Istanbul Ansiklopedisi*, 1994, pp. 420–2.

Ipekten, Haluk, *Na'ili-i Kadim Divanı* (Divan of Na'ili-Kadim), Istanbul: Milli Eğitim, 1968.

Işın, Ekrem, "Mevlevilik," *Istanbul Ansiklopedisi*, 1994, pp. 422–30.

Işın, Ekrem, "Istanbul'un Mistik Tarihinde Mevlevihaneler" (The Mevlevihanes in the Mystical History of Istanbul," in *Istanbul'da Gündelik Hayat* (Daily Life in Istanbul), Istanbul: Yapı Kredi, 1999, pp. 299–346.

Işın, Ekrem, 'A Social History of the Mevlevis', in *Candidature File of the Mevlevi Sema Ceremony known historically as the Mevlevi Ayin-i Şerif or Sema Mukabele-i Şerif*, unpublished document submitted to Turkish National Commission for UNESCO, Ankara, 2004, pp. 16–25.

Işın, Ekrem, *Saltanatın Dervişleri, Dervişlerin Saltanatı* (The Dervishes of the Sultanate; the Sultanate of the Dervishes), Istanbul: Istanbul Araştırma Enstitüsü, 2007.

Karamustafa, Ahmet T., *Vahidi's Menakib-i Hoca-i Cihan ve Netice-i Can* (Vahidi's 'The Deeds of the Master of the World and the Goal of the Spirit'), Cambridge, MA: Harvard University Printing Office, 1993.

Karamustafa, Ahmet T., *God's Unruly Friends: Dervish Groups in the Islamic Later Middle Period 1200–1550*, Salt Lake City: University of Utah Press, 1994.

Karamustafa, Ahmet T., *Sufism: The Formative Period*, Berkeley: University of California Press, 2007.

Karay, Refik Halit, *Bir İçim Su* (A Drink of Water), Istanbul: Semih Lutfi, 1939.

Köprülü, Fuad, *Influences du shamanism turco-mongol sur les ordres mystiques musulmans*, Istanbul: University of Istanbul, 1929.

Krstic, Tijana, *Contested Conversions to Islam: Narratives of Religious Change in the Early Modern Empire*, Palo Alto: Stanford University Press, 2011.

Küçük, Sezai, 'Ortak kader: Osmanlının son yılları ve Mevlevilik' (The Shared Fate: The Later Years of the Ottomans and Mevlevism), *Uluslararası Mevlana Sempozyumu Bildirileri 2*, Istanbul: Motto, 2007, pp. 715–32.

Küçük, Harun, 'Natural Philosophy and Politics in the Eighteenth Century: Esad of Ionina and Greek Aristotelianism at the Ottoman Court', *The Journal of Ottoman Studies*, 41 (2013), pp. 125–58.

Küçük, Harun, 'Leisure in the Ottoman Eighteenth Century', Lecture at the New York University Abu Dhabi Institute, 29 January 2019.

Levend, Agah Sırrı, *Divan Edebiyati: Kelimeler ve Remizler Mazmunlar ve Mefumlar* (Divan Poetry: Words and Allusions, Metaphors and Understandings), Istanbul: Inkılap, 1943.

Levin, Theodore, with Valentina Süzükei, *Where Rivers and Mountains Sing: Sound, Music, and Nomadism in Tuva and Beyond*, Bloomington: Indiana University Press, 2006.

Lewis, Franklin, *Rumi: Past and Present, East and West*, Oxford: Oxford University Press, 2000.

Lifchez, Raymond, ed., *The Dervish Lodge: Art, Architecture, and Sufism in Ottoman Turkey*, Berkeley: University of California Press, 1992.

Lucas, Ann. E., *Music of a Thousand Years: A New History of Persian Musical Traditions*, Berkeley: University of California Press, 2019.

Manz, Beatrice Forbes, "The Development and Meaning of Chaghatay Identity," in *Muslims in Central Asia: Expressions of Identity and Change*, ed. Jo-Ann Gross. Durham, NC: Duke University Press, 1992.

Mecmua, Konya Mevlana Müzesi no. 1295, 1114/1704.

Mesara, Gülbün, and Özen Mine Esiner, eds, *Süheyl Ünver'in Konya Defterleri* (Süheyl Ünver's Konya Notebooks), Istanbul: Kubbealtı, 2006.

Milstein, Rachel, *Miniature Painting in Ottoman Baghdad*, Washington, DC: Mazda, 1990.

Molé, Marijan, 'La danse extatique en Islam', *Les Danses Sacrées* (Sources Orientales 6), Paris: Seuil, 1963, pp. 147–280.

Moyne, John, *Rumi and the Sufi Tradition*, Binghamton: State University of New York Press, 1998.

Müstakimzade Süleyman Sa'deddin Efendi, *Şerh-i Ibarat: Mevlevilik, Musiki ve Sema* (Music and Dance in Mevlevism) (1202/1788); Arabic text, Abdülgani b. Ismail en-Nablusi; trans. Ensar Karagöz, Istanbul: Türkiye Yazma eserler Kurumu Başkanlığı, 2019.

Na'ini, Baqiya, *Zemzeme-ye Vahdat* (The Murmur of Unity), trans. Amir Hosein Pourjavady, unpublished.

Nicholson, Reynold A., *The Mathnawi of Jalalu'ddin Rumi*, London: Luzac, 1977.

Ocak, Ahmet Yaşar, 'Remarques sur le role des derviches kalenderis dans la formation de l'ordre bektachi', in *Bektachiya: Etudes sur l'ordre mystique des Bektachis et les groupes relevant de Hadji Bektach*, ed. Alexandre Popovic and Gilles Veinstein, Istanbul: Isis, 1995, pp. 55–63.

Olley, Jacob, 'Rhythmic Augmentation and the Transformation of the Ottoman Peşrev', in *Rhythmic Cycles and Structures in the Art Music of the Middle East*, ed. Zeynep Helvacı, Jacob Olley and Ralf Martin Jaeger, Würzburg: Ergon, 2017, pp. 177–88.

Olley, Jacob, 'Towards a New Theory of Historical Change in the Ottoman Instrumental Repertoire', in *Theory and Practice in the Music of the Islamic World: Essays in Honour of Owen Wright*, ed. Rachel Harris and Martin Stokes, Aldershot: Ashgate, 2018, pp. 22–40.

Oransay, Gültekin, 'Ali Ufki ve Dini Türk Musikisi' (Ali Ufki and Religious Turkish Music), Ankara: Ilahiyat Fakültesi, 1972, unpublished.

Osman Dede, Nayi, *Rabt-i Tabirat-i Musiki* (Organization of the Terminology of Music), ed. Onur Akdoğu and Fares Hariri (Istanbul Üniversitesi Kütüphanesi, Türkiyat Enstitüsü), Izmir: Sevdi, 1991.

Özemre, Ahmet Yüksel, *Üsküdar'da bir Attar Dükkanı* (A Perfume Shop in Üsküdar), Istanbul: Kubbealtı, 1996.

Özergin, Kemal, 'Evliya Çelebi'ye Göre: Osmanlı Ülkesinde Çalgilar' (Instruments of the Ottoman Land According to Evliya Çelebi), *Türk Folklor Araştırmaları* 13 (1972), pp. 5955–6055.

Öztuna Yılmaz, *Türk Musikisi Ansiklopedisi*, vols 1 and 2, Istanbul: M. E. B. Devlet Kitapları, 1969 and 1974.

Öztuna Yılmaz, *Dede Efendi*, Ankara: Kültür Bakanlığı, 1996.

Pacholczyk, Josef, 'A Model for the Comparative Study of the Maqam as a Cyclic Format: Kashmir and Morocco', paper delivered to the International Maqam

Study Group of the International Council for Traditional Music, Berlin, 1992, unpublished.

Pakalin, Mehmet Zeki, *Osmanlı Tarih Deyimleri ve Terimleri Sözlüğü* (Dictionary of Ottoman Historical Expressions and Terms), 3 vols, Istanbul: Milli Eğitim Basımevi, 1971.

Peacock, A. C. S., 'Sufis and the Seljuk Court in Mongol Anatolia: Politics and Patronage in the Works of Jalal al-Din Rumi and Sultan Walad', in *The Seljuks of Anatolia: Court and Society in the Medieval Middle East*, ed. A. C. S. Peacock and Sara Nur Yıldız, London: I. B. Tauris, 2013, pp. 206–26.

Peacock, A. C. S., and Sara Nur Yıldız, *Islamic Literature and Intellectual Life in Fourteenth and Fifteenth Century Anatolia*, Würzburg: Ergon, 2016.

Pehlivan, Gürol, Bülent Bayram, and Mehmed Vesi Dörtbudak, *Tevhide Hanım ve Divanı: Osmanlı Taşrasında Kadın, Şair, Mevlevi Olmak* (Tevhide Hanım and her Divan: A Provincial Woman, Poet and Mevlevi), Manisa: Manisa Belediyesi, 2007.

Pekin, Ersu, 'Theory, Instruments and Music', in *Ottoman Civilization*, vol. 2, ed. Halil Inalcık and Gunsel Renda, Istanbul: Kultur ve Turizm Bakanliği, 2003, pp. 1009–43.

Popescu-Judetz, Eugenia and Jacob Ciortea, *Dimitrie Cantemir: cartea ştinteii musicii* (Dimitrie Cantemir: The Book of the Science of Music), Bucharest: Editura Musicala, 1973.

Popescu-Judetz, Eugenia, *Tanburi Küçük Artin: A Musical Treatise of the Eighteenth Century*, Istanbul: Pan, 2002.

Popescu-Judetz, Eugenia, and Adriana Adabi Sirli, *Sources of 18th Century Music: Panayiotes Chalathzoglou and Kyrillos Marmarinos*, Istanbul: Pan, 2000.

Pourjavady, Amir Hosein, *The Musical Codex of Amir Khan Gorji (1108/1697)*, Ph.D. dissertation, UCLA, 2005.

Pourjavady, Amir Hosein, *Music Making in Iran: Developments between the Sixteenth and Late Nineteenth Centuries*, Ph.D. dissertation, The Graduate Center, City University of New York, 2019. https://academicworks.cuny.edu/gc_etds/3455/ (accessed 23.11.2021).

Qureshi, Regula, *Sufi Music of India and Pakistan*, Cambridge: Cambridge University Press, 1986.

Ritter, Helmut, 'Die Mevlanafaier in Konya 11–17 December, 1960', *Oriens* 18–19 (1967), pp. 5–32.

Rumi Jalaluddin, *Rumi: The Masnavi*, trans. with an introduction and notes by Jawid Mojaddedi, Oxford: Oxford University Press, 2004.

Rumi Jalaluddin, *Kolliyat-e Shams-e Tabriz*, ed. Bediuzzaman Furuzanfar (8 vols), Teheran: Tehran University, 1957–66.

Sakıb Dede, Mustafa, *Sefine-i Nefise-i Mevleviyan* (The Elegant Ship of the Mevlevis), Cairo: Matbaa-i Vehbiye, 1866–7.

Schimmel, Annemarie, *The Triumphal Sun: A Study of the Works of Jalaloddin Rumi*, Albany: State University of New York Press, 1978.

Şehsuvaroğlu, Bedi, *Eczaci Yarbay Nayzen Halil Can (1905–1973)* (Pharmacist, Lieutenant Colonel and Neyzen Halil Can), Istanbul: Hüsnütabiat, 1974.

Şenay, Banu, 'Artists, Antagonisms and the Ney in the Popularization of "Sufi Music" in Turkey', *European Journal of Cultural Studies* (2014), pp. 1–18.

Şenay, Banu, 'Rethinking Spirituality Through Music Education in Istanbul', *European Journal of Turkish Studies* 25 (2017), pp. 1–20.

Şenay, Banu, *Musical Ethics and Islam: The Art of Playing the Ney*, Urbana-Champaign: University of Illinois Press, 2020.

Şenel, Süleyman, 'Ottoman Türkü', in *Writing the History of Ottoman Music*, ed. Martin Greve, Würzburg: Ergon, 2015, pp. 195–209.

Şengel, Ali Riza, *Türk Musikisi Klasikleri: Ilahiler* (Classics of Turkish Music: Ilahis), ed. Yusuf Ömürlü, Istanbul: Kubbealtı, 1979.

Seroussi, Edwin, 'From the Court and Tarikat to the Synagogue: Ottoman Art Music and Hebrew Sacred Songs', in *Sufism, Music and Society in Turkey and the Middle East*, ed. Anders Hammarlund, Tord Olsson and Elizabeth Özdalga, Istanbul: Swedish Research Institute, 2001, pp. 81–93.

Seydi, *Seydi's Book on Music: A 15th-Century Turkish Discourse*, trans. Eugenia Popescu-Judetz and Eckhard Neubauer, Frankfurt: Institute for the History of Arabic-Islamic Science, 2004.

Shaw, Stanford, *History of the Ottoman Empire and Modern Turkey*, vol. 1, *Empire of the Gazis: The Rise and Decline of the Ottoman Empire, 1280–1808*, Cambridge: Cambridge University Press, 1976.

Shimosako, Mari, 'Japan: Philosophy and Aesthetics', in *Garland Encyclopedia of World Music*, vol. 7, *East Asia: China, Japan, Korea*, ed. Robert C. Provine, Yosihiko Tokumaru, and J. Lawrence Witzleben, Abingdon and New York: Routledge, 2002, pp. 545–55.

Sieur du Loir, Jean Antoine. *Les Voyages du Sieur du Loir*, Paris: Francois Clovzier, 1654.

Signell, Karl, *Makam: Modal Practice in Turkish Art Music*, Seattle: University of Washington Press, 1976.

Sipos, Janos, *Kazakh Folksongs from the Two Ends of the Steppe*, Budapest: Akademia, 2001.

Sipos, Janos, *Comparative Research on the Folk Music of the Turkic and Hungarian People*, Ankara: Publications of the Embassy of the Hungarian Republic in Ankara, 2005.

Sipos, Janos, and Eva Csaki, *The Psalms and Folk Songs of a Mystic Order*, Budapest: Akademia, 2009.

Subtelny, Maria, 'Ali Shir Navai: Bakhshi and Beg', in *Eucharisterion: Essays Presented to Omeljan Pritsak on his Sixtieth Birthday*, ed. I. Sevcenko and F. Sysyn. *Harvard Ukrainian Studies*, vol. 3/4 (1979–80), Part 2, pp. 797–807.

Summits, Will and Theodore Levin, 'Maqom Traditions of the Tadjiks and Uzbeks', in *The Music of Central Asia*, ed. Theodore Levin, Saida Daukeyeva, and Elmira Köchümkulova, Bloomington: Indiana University Press, 2016, pp. 320–43.

Tabbaa, Yasser, *The Transformation of Islamic Art During the Sunni Revival*, London: I. B. Tauris, 2001.

Tanman, Baha, 'Settings for the Veneration of Saints', in *The Dervish Lodge: Art, Architecture, and Sufism in Ottoman Turkey*, ed. Raymond Lifchez, Berkeley: University of California Press, 1992, pp. 130–71.

Tanman, Baha, 'Musiki Tarihimizde Önemli Yeri olan Bahariye Mevlevihanesi'nin Tarihçesi ve Sosyokültürel Çevresi' (A Short History and the Sociocultural Context of the Bahariye Mevlevihane; an Important Place in Our Musical History), *Darülelhan* no. 8 (2017), pp. 13–22.

Tanpınar, Ahmet Hamdi, *Huzur* (Peace of Mind), Istanbul: Dergah, 1949.

Tanrıkorur, Barihüda, 'Mevlevi Training and 'Adab ve Erkan', in *Candidature File of the Mevlevi Sema Ceremony known historically as the Mevlevi Ayin-i Şerif or Sema Mukabele-i Şerif*, unpublished document submitted to the Turkish Commission for UNESCO, Ankara, 2004, 27–8.

Tanrıkorur, Barihüda, 'Karahisar Mevlevihanesi', *Islam Ansiklopedisi* (2001), pp. 418–21.

Tanrıkorur, Barihüda, 'Mısır Mevlevihanesi', *Islam Ansiklopedisi* (2004), pp. 586–8.

Tanrıkorur, Barihüda, 'Ikinci Manisa Mevlevihanesi', *Sufi Araştırmaları* no. 6 (2011), pp. 31–50.

Tanrıkorur, Cinuçen, 'Osmanlı Musikisinde Mevlevi Ayini Besteciliği' (The Art of Composing the Mevlevi Ayin in Ottoman Music), *Osmanlı Kültür ve Sanat*, vol. 10, Ankara, 1999, pp. 707–21.

Tanrıkorur, Cinuçen, *Saz ü Söz Arasında* (Among Music and Words), Istanbul: Dergah, 2003.

Tezcan, Baki, *The Second Ottoman Empire: Political and Social Transformation in the Early Modern World*, Cambridge: Cambridge University Press, 2010.

Thibaut, P. J., 'La musique des Mevlevis ou derviches tourneurs' 1, *La Revue Musicale*, 2(8) (1902), Paris.

Thibaut, P. J., 'La musique des Mevlevis ou derviches tourneurs' 2, *La Revue Musicale*, 2(9) (1902), Paris.

Türk Musikisi Ansiklopedisi, vols 1 and 2, Istanbul: M. E. B. Devlet Kitapları, 1969 and 1974 (see Öztuna, Yılmaz, 1969).

Toderini, Giambattista, *De la Littératures des Turcs*, Paris: Poincot (1787) 1789.

Top, H. Hüseyin, *Mevlevi Usul ve Adabı* (The Fundamental Procedures and Rules of Good Manners and Behaviour of the Mevlevi), Istanbul: Otüken, 2001.

Töre, Abdülkadir, *Türk Musikisi Klasikleri: Ilahiler* (Classics of Turkish Music: Ilahis), ed. Yusuf Ömürlü, Istanbul: Kubbealtı, 1984.

Trimingham, J Spencer, *The Sufi Orders in Islam*, Oxford: Oxford University Press, 1971.

Truschke, Audrey, *Culture of Encounters: Sanskrit at the Mughal Court*, New York: Columbia University Press, 2016.

Tsuge, Genichi, 'Rhythmic Aspects of the Avaz in Persian Music', *Ethnomusicology*, 14(2) (1970), pp. 205–27.

Ünver, Ismail, *Neşati*, Ankara: Kültür ve Türizm Bakanliği, 1986.

Uslu, Recep, *Fatih Sultan Mehmed Döneminde Musiki ve Şems-i Rumi'nin Mecmua-i Güftesi* (Music in the Period of Mehmed the Conqueror and the Collection of Şems-i Rumi, Istanbul: Istanbul Fetih Cemiyeti, 2007.

Uzluk, Şahabeddin, *Mevlevilikte Resim, Resimde Mevleviler* (Painting Within Mevlevism and Mevlevis within Painting), Ankara: Iş Bankası, 1957.

Uzunçarşılı, Ismail Hakkı, 'Osmanlılar Zamanında Saraylarda Musiki Hayatı' (Musical Life in the Palace during the Time of the Ottomans), *Belleten* (Türk Tarih Kurumu), 41(161) (1977), pp. 79–114.

Van Bruinessen, Martin, 'When Haji Bektash Still Bore the name of Sultan Sahak', in *Bektachiya: Etudes sur l'ordre mystique des Bektachis et les groupes relevant de Hadji Bektach*, ed. Alexandre Popovic and Gilles Veinstein, Istanbul: Isis, 1995, pp. 117–38.

Vett, Carl, *Dervish Diary: Two Weeks in a Sufi Monastery in Istanbul*, trans. Elbridge W. Hathaway, Brentwood, CA: Knud Mogensen Publishing, 1953.

Wright, Owen, 'Aspects of Historical Change in the Turkish Classical Repertoire', *Musica Asiatica* 5, ed. Richard Widdess, Cambridge: Cambridge University Press, 1988, pp. 1–108.

Wright, Owen, 'The Ottoman Usul System and its Precursors', in *Rhythmic Cycles and Structures in the Art Music of the Middle East*, ed. Zeynep Helvacı, Jacob Olley and Ralf Martin Jaeger, Würzburg: Ergon, 2017, pp. 31–48.

Wright, Owen, 'Amir Han Gurji and Safavid-Ottoman Usul Parallels', in *Rhythmic Cycles and Structures in the Art Music of the Middle East*, ed. Zeynep Helvacı, Jacob Olley and Ralf Martin Jaeger, Würzburg: Ergon, 2017, pp. 49–68.

Wright, Owen, *Music Theory in the Safavid Era, The Taqsīm al-Nagamāt* (SOAS Musicology Series), Abingdon and New York: Routledge, 2019.

Yavaşça, Alaettin, *Türk Musikisinde Komposisyon ve Beste Biçimleri* (Composition and Compositional Forms in Turkish Music), Istanbul: Türk Kültürüne Vakfı, 2002.

Yazıcı, Tahsin, 'Mevlana Döneminde Sema' (The Sema in the Period of Mevlana), *Şarkiyat Mecmuasi*, 5 (1964), pp. 135–50.

Yekta Bey, Rauf, 'La Musique Turque', in *Encyclopédie de la Musique et Dictionnaire du Conservatoire*, ed. Albert Lavignac, vol. 5, Paris: Librairie Delagrave, 1922, pp. 2945–3064.

Yekta Bey, Rauf, and Ahmet Irsoy, eds, *Mevlevi Ayinleri*, Istanbul: Darülelhan, 1923–1939.

Yekta Bey, Rauf, *Dede Efendi*, *Esatizül-Elhan* (Masters of Music), vol. 3, Istanbul: Darülelhan, 1925.

Zarcone, Thierry, 'L'Habit de Symbols des Derviches Tourneurs', *Journal of the History of Sufism* 6 (2015), pp. 47–76.

Ziya, Mehmet, *Yenikapı Mevlevihanesi* (The Yenikapı Mevlevihane), Istanbul: Araks Matbaası, 1913 (Ataç, 2005).

INDEX

Note: *italic* indicates images